Illustrator
Agi Palinay

Editor
Mary Kaye Taggart

Editorial Project Manager
Karen J. Goldfluss, M.S. Ed.

Editor-in-Chief
Sharon Coan, M.S. Ed.

Art Director
Elayne Roberts

Associate Designer
Denise Bauer

Cover Artist
Denise Bauer

Imaging
James Edward Grace

Product Manager
Phil Garcia

Publishers
Rachelle Cracchiolo, M.S. Ed.
Mary Dupuy Smith, M.S. Ed.

D1302860

Celebrate ABC's

A Learning Center Approach

Author

Tamara Nunn, M. Ed.

Teacher Created Materials, Inc.
6421 Industry Way
Westminster, CA 92683
www.teachercreated.com
ISBN-1-57690-034-7
©1998 Teacher Created Materials, Inc.
Reprinted, 2003
Made in U.S.A.

Table of Contents

Introduction

The activities in *Celebrate ABC's* are a welcome addition to any primary classroom! Use them as a culmination to a larger unit or for themes on which you just do not have the time to spend several weeks. The units are ideal if you team teach since the activities in this book are designed for two classrooms working together. Six to eight students work at each station. Each "day" consists of eight activity centers/learning stations. Each center activity is to be completed in a 15–20-minute time period.

Sample Theme Day Schedule

8:30–8:50 Rotation #1

8:50–9:10 Rotation #2

9:10–9:30 Rotation #3

9:30–9:50 Rotation #4

9:50–10:00 RECESS (It is recommended that you use this recess time to provide a break for both the children and parent helpers.)

10:00 — 10:20 Rotation #5

10:20 — 10:40 Rotation #6

10:40 — 11:00 Rotation #7

11:00 — 11:20 Rotation #8

11:20 — 11:30 Classroom Cleanup

Thematic Day Activities

Activities

Most centers have extra activities should the children finish early. The format for each thematic day is basically the same and includes activities spanning the curriculum:

- **Story**—Quality children's literature is suggested. The literature is based on the theme. A list of suggested theme books is provided at the beginning of each unit.
- **Shape book**—This writing activity is based on the story or theme. (Shape book patterns are provided for each theme letter. Use the patterns for cutting the shapes of the covers and the interior pages.)
- **Art activity**
- **Color page or game activity**—This page may be provided for use during clean-up times or restroom breaks.
- **Cooking activity**
- **Math or science activity**
- **Extra activity**— Additional activities may be presented in the areas of art, story or video retelling, drama, etc. They have been provided to support and round out each unit. These activities include the following:
  - ✔ Coloring/handwriting page
  - ✔ Short story that can be used as a programmed writing assignment for younger students or dictation for older students
  - ✔ Vocabulary lists that can be used as spelling lists, creative writing word banks, or with the shape book writing station
  - ✔ Thematic flash cards
  - ✔ Matching picture cards
  - ✔ Incentive page that includes a thematic name tag pattern, a thematic bookmark, and a thematic motivational chart

Introduction (cont.)

Asking for Help

You will need at least eight parents, aides, and/or teachers to cover the stations. (If more than one helper is needed at a station, it is noted in the instructions.) The helpers will be needed for three hours. Write letters asking for parent help, donations, and/or supplies. You may wish to use the thematic stationery in each unit for writing your letters. Parents will probably look forward to these days almost as much as the children.

Send the parent letters out at least a week and a half before the scheduled theme day. Ask the parents to send items no later than a day or two before the actual theme day so that you can get any last-minute items needed. Never assume they will come in the day of the activity. As you receive the responses, make a master list of who is bringing what and which parents have offered to help. If you have more of one item coming in than you will need, send the note back and ask for something else. It is a good idea to confirm the attendance of the parents who offer to help out. Write a note of thanks to all of the parents who participate in one way or another.

When shape books, patterns, or other pieces need to be cut, add that to your list of needed materials. Parents who cannot be present in the classroom on theme day are often willing to cut out things at home. Provide all of the paper, patterns, and instructions needed in a manila envelope.

Preparation

Getting Organized

Organization is important in preparing for these theme days. At the beginning of each unit you will find a bibliography. (For foreign distributor information, refer to page 6.) A materials checklist is also provided. This page will help you compile the things that you will need for the unit without looking through the entire section. It is designed to be a timesaver. Decide which of the activities or versions of activities you are going to use. Divide the physical space in your classroom(s) to best accommodate the specific activities. The stations do not have to be completed in the order listed. Just remember to allow time for cleanup, hand-washing, and a bathroom break before the cooking station. If you have a source of water in the room, place the cooking station close to it.

Getting the Stations Ready

Your next step is to make sure everything is ready for each station. Several days ahead, prepare a manila envelope for each station. In the envelopes include the following:

1. **Station Title Name Plate.** Prepare the name plate by folding a 9" x 12" (23 cm x 30 cm) sheet of colored construction paper in half lengthwise. Then glue a thematic name tag from the incentives page onto it. Write "Station # " on it with a black permanent marker.

2. **Activity Card.** This provides the instructions to your helper for running the center.

3. **Group Folder.** Fold a 9" x 12" (23 cm x 30 cm) sheet of construction paper in half. This can hold all of a group's papers, books, and motivational charts as the students rotate. It will move with them from center to center.

4. **Samples.** Include any samples that you wish to make the activity more simple.

Introduction *(cont.)*

By the Day Before:

1. Make sure that all of the copies, patterns, etc., have been made. Place them in the corresponding station envelopes.

2. If scratch paper is needed, add it to the station envelopes.

3. Sharpen the needed pencils and place them in the proper envelopes.

4. Put any needed crayons, colored pencils, scissors, glue, tape, staplers, staples, etc., in containers and store these with the proper envelopes. (Shoeboxes work well.) If you have to borrow extra staplers, etc., do so. It is important to have what you need at each station.

5. Gather all of the cooking materials. Check twice! Do not wait until the morning of the theme day to get the hot plate from the resource room or to bring a spatula from home.

6. Put all of the books and manipulatives in the appropriate station boxes.

7. Make a note of any items you still need and get them as soon as possible.

8. Match your parent volunteers to the stations. This will be hard the first time, especially if you do not yet know your parents well. The person at the literature station needs to read well. The person at the writing station needs to be able to read and write well. The math station generally has word problems to read, so keep that in mind as well. Non-English speaking parents can be great helpers too. Pair them with another parent who can speak English. It is wise to decide where you want each parent ahead of time. Sometimes you will have to revise your plan, for instance, if someone does not show up, but in the long run you will save time.

The Morning of the Theme Day

The following suggestions and reminders will help you make the transition smoothly into the theme day:

1. Get to school early!

2. Set out the materials at the stations where the students will not be sitting when they enter the room.

3. Check everything again!

4. Before school starts, explain the stations and direct the parent volunteers to their stations. Have them briefly look over their activity cards and materials. As they do this, go to each station and give brief directions and answer any questions they may have.

5. Have your students enter the classroom and complete the morning routine activities quickly. Divide the class into groups. The groups should each have a mix of genders, abilities, etc. (If you are teaming with a bilingual class, or if you have a multi-age classroom for which you will need to modify the activities, it is usually best to group students according to their language or grade levels.)

6. Invite the children, one group at a time, to go to their assigned stations.

7. Let the fun begin!

Introduction *(cont.)*

A bibliography of suggested reading is provided at the beginning of each theme unit. It references American publishers only. For distributors in Canada, the United Kingdom, and Australia, refer to the following listings:

Chronicle Books
Canada - Raincoast Book Distrubutors

Dorling Kindersley (Knopf Books for Young Readers)
Canada - Penguin Books Canada
UK - Dorling Kindersley
Australia - Harper Collins

Franklin Watts (Orchard Books)
Canada - Gage Distributors
UK - Baker and Taylor
Australia - Franklin Watts Australia

HarperCollins (HarperCollins Children's Books)
Canada, UK and Australia - Harper Collins Publishers, Limited

Harcourt Brace Jovanovich
Canada - Harcourt Brace Jovanovich
UK - Harcourt Brace Jovanovich
Australia - Harcourt Brace Jovanovich Australia

Henry Holt and Company
Canada - Fitzhenry and Whiteside
UK - Pan Demic Limited
Australia - C.I.S. Publishers

H.J. Kramer
Canada - Publishers' Group West
UK - Airlift
Australia - Gemcrest

Holiday House
Canada - Thomas Allen and Son
UK and Australia - Baker and Taylor

Houghton Mifflin (Clarion Books, Ticknor and Fields)
Canada - Thomas Allen and Son
UK - Cassell
Australia - Jackaranda Wiley

John Gile Communications
Canada - Scholastic Canada
UK and Australia - Baker and Taylor

Lerner Publications (Carolrhoda)
Canada - Riverwood Publications
UK - Turnaround
Australia - Stafford Books

Little, Brown and Company
Canada - Little, Brown, and Company
UK - Little, Brown Limited
Australia - Penguin

Penguin Putnam (Dial Books for Young Readers, Doubleday, Dutton, Philomel Books, Viking)
Canada - Penguin Books Canada
UK - Penguin UK
Australia - Penguin Books Australia

Philomel Books
Canada - BeJo Sales
UK and Australia - Warner International

Random House
Canada - Random House
UK - Random Century House
Australia - Prentice Hall

Scholastic (Cartwheel Books)
Canada - Scholastic
UK - Scholastic Limited
Australia - Ashton Scholastic Party Limited

Simon & Schuster (Atheneum Children's Books, Prentice Hall, Silver Burdette Press)
Canada - Distican
UK - Simon & Schuster
Australia - Prentice Hall

Thames and Hudson
Contact the publisher at (212) 354-3763.

Troll Books
Canada - Vanwell Publishing
UK and Australia - Penguin

Usborne Publishing
Contact the publisher at 800-475-4522.

Western Publishing Company
Canada and UK - Western Publishers
Australia - Golden Press Party Limited

William Morrow (Greenwillow Books; Lothrop, Lee, and Shepard; Morrow Jr.; Mulberry Books)
Canada - Gage Distributors
UK - H.I. Marketing
Australia - Grolier Australia

Final Notes to the Teacher

Consider these helpful reminders as you proceed through your thematic day:

1. Do not assign yourself to one particular station. You are the problem solver, timekeeper, and overseer. You go where you are needed. If the cooking station needs more help, you help there. If the art station needs more help, that is where you need to be. If a child is behaving inappropriately, you need to attend to it. If a parent is getting tired of reading the same book over and over or does not seem to understand his or her assignment, you can handle it without stopping the whole process.

2. Let everyone know when they have only five minutes left in the rotation. This gives them time to finish the project and clean up before the next rotation.

3. Ask another teacher if he or she would be willing to take a child if there are any behavior problems, should the need arise. Have materials ready for this possibility. Other teachers will be much more cooperative if you have something ready for these students to work on in their classrooms.

4. If you cannot get another teacher to team with you on a thematic day, or if you just want to try thematic teaching, spread the center activities out over several days. The literature, writing, and estimating activities can be done as whole group activities, as can many of the math, science, and art activities. Then you will only need extra help for an hour or so for the cooking and art activities. Older students can help here too.

5. On occasion you may wish to expand the thematic day to include several classrooms at one grade level (including bilingual classes). Consider using a large room, such as a cafeteria or multipurpose room, to accommodate more children and parent helpers per group. The ideas in each unit could easily be modified to include a whole school. If you are in a K–6 school, the older students can be your helpers.

6. There are many cooking lessons in this book. Before proceeding, write a letter to the parents, asking them to inform you of any food restrictions for the children. Allergies, diabetes, religious beliefs, etc., are important factors to consider when serving children food. Also, make sure that you understand your district's regulations for food in the classroom.

As you move through the alphabet, you will observe that your students and parents are having a wonderful time with the thematic learning centers.

Apples

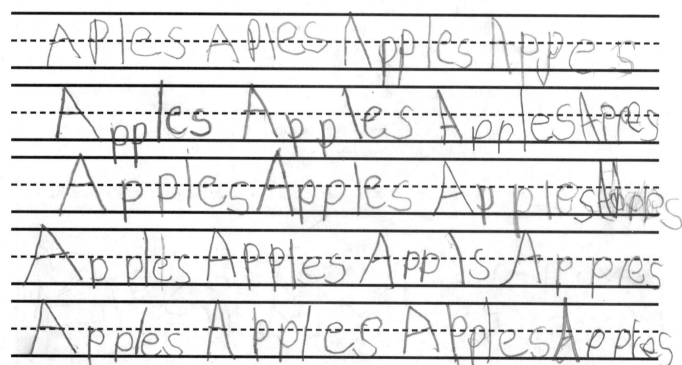

Teacher Note: Use this page as an introduction to the Apples theme. Have your students color the picture. Lines are provided for writing activities of your choice.

Unit Materials

Bibliography

Aliki. *The Story of Johnny Appleseed.* Prentice-Hall, 1963.

Hutchings, Amy and Richard. *Picking Apples and Pumpkins.* Scholastic, 1994.

Kellogg, Steven. *Johnny Appleseed.* Morrow, 1988.

Lember, Barbara Hirsch. *A Book of Fruit.* Ticknor & Fields, 1994.

Prelutsky, Jack. *The Random House Book of Poetry for Children.* Random House, 1983. (For the following poems: "McIntosh Apple" by Steven Kroll, "Pie Problem" by Shel Silverstein)

Materials Checklist

Station 1—Literature
_____ literature selections
_____ activity card

Station 2—Writing
_____ shape books
_____ crayons
_____ vocabulary list
_____ pencils
_____ activity card

Station 3—Patterns
_____ patterns
_____ crayons
_____ pencils
_____ activity card

Station 4—Cooking
_____ sugar cookie dough
_____ sliced apples
_____ activity card
_____ brown sugar
_____ white sugar
_____ butter
_____ teaspoon
_____ cinnamon
_____ baking cups
_____ nutmeg
_____ resealable plastic bags
_____ paring knife
_____ 2 spatulas
_____ paper towels
_____ cookie sheets
_____ 2 butter knives
_____ measuring spoons

Station 5—Graphing
_____ graph
_____ pencils or markers
_____ yellow apples
_____ self-stick notes
_____ green apples
_____ napkins
_____ paring knife
_____ red apples
_____ scratch paper/coloring page
_____ activity card
_____ resealable plastic bags
_____ crayons

Station 6—Word Problems
_____ word problems
_____ scratch paper
_____ pencils and crayons
_____ activity card

Station 7—Apple Man
_____ 1 apple per child
_____ cloves
_____ candy-coated chocolate pieces
_____ toothpicks
_____ frozen peas/carrots/corn
_____ chocolate chips
_____ cauliflower and broccoli
_____ tube icing
_____ marshmallows
_____ popcorn
_____ construction paper
_____ markers
_____ hot cinnamon drops
_____ activity card

Station 8—Stages of the Apple Tree
_____ 12" x 18" (30 cm x 46 cm) white construction paper
_____ dirt
_____ popcorn
_____ 1 apple seed per child
_____ markers
_____ glue
_____ red paint or ink pad
_____ activity card
_____ colored construction paper

Alternate Activities:

1. Apple Sequence Cards
_____ sequence cards
_____ pencils
_____ glue
_____ scissors
_____ crayons
_____ white paper
_____ activity card

2. Apple Shape Books Short "a"
_____ apple shape books
_____ pencils
_____ crayons
_____ activity cards

Station 1 Activity Card—Literature

Read and discuss a combination of the following books or poems:

- *Johnny Appleseed* by Steven Kellogg and *The Story of Johnny Appleseed* by Aliki. These tell the story for your students. Choose one or both.

- *A Book of Fruit* by Barbara Hirsch Lember. This book has wonderful illustrations and a very simple text that show where different fruits come from.

- *Picking Apples and Pumpkins* by Amy and Richard Hutchings. This shows how the two fruits are grown and how they are picked.

- One of these poems from *The Random House Book of Poetry for Children*, edited by Jack Prelutsky:

    "McIntosh Apple" by Steven Kroll

    "Pie Problem" by Shel Silverstein

- If time permits, have students illustrate their favorite stories.

Station 2 Activity Card—Writing

Materials: shape books, pencils, crayons, vocabulary list

Directions: Using the apple shape book pattern provided on page 11, make a shape book for each child. On theme day, you can use the following samples or let children write their own. Write a sentence on each page and illustrate it. Guide students, using the suggested samples and allowing the students to think their sentences through. Ask the following questions: What do we put at the beginning of a sentence? What goes at the end? What does the word start with? What letter makes that sound? Note where phonics rules are not followed, special punctuation, etc.

Kinds of Apples

Some apples are red.

Some apples are green.

Some apples are yellow.

Some apples are in between.

I like_____ apples best.

Things Made from Apples

I like apples. . .

Apple pie,

Apple juice,

Applesauce,

Candied apples,

And just plain apples.

Shape Book Pattern

Apples

Vocabulary List

Thematic	Short "a" Sound	Begins with "a"
1. apples	1. has	1. apple *
2. red	2. pan *	2. ant *
3. yellow	3. man	3. and
4. green	4. ran	4. at
5. seed	5. can	5. an
6. core	6. land	6. ask
7. peel	7. cat *	7. as
8. tree *	8. bat *	8. add
9. pie *	9. mat	9. after
10. juice	10. fat	10. am
11. blossom	11. sat	11. acrobat *
12. sauce	12. cap	12. antler
13. slice	13. can't	13. ax *
14. bake	14. pants *	14. astronaut *
15. cut	15. jam	15. ankle *
16. fruit	16. ham	16. aquarium *
17. orchard	17. map	17. arm *

Note: The asterisk denotes words that have corresponding flash cards and picture cards. (See pages 13 and 14. You may wish to make several sets of cards and laminate them.)

Word Flash Cards

apple	pie
acrobat	aquarium
astronaut	arm
bat	tree
ankle	cat
pants	ax
pan	ant

Picture Flash Cards

Station 3 Activity Card—Patterns

1. Have the students trace the patterns and then color their tracings at this station. See page 16 for the patterns of leaves, apples, trees, and baskets. Students can trace around the outside edges of these patterns.

2. Allow them 10–15 minutes at this activity and then, if needed, take them on a restroom break. This provides an opportunity for the students to wash their hands and get a drink of water before they start cooking at the next station.

3. Come back prepared for Station 4—Cooking activity.

Station 4 Activity Card—Cooking

Apple Tarts

Ingredients (for 60 tarts):
- 3–4 rolls of sugar cookie dough
- 4 cups presliced apples, in resealable plastic bag
- 1 cup (250 mL) brown sugar
- 1 cup (250 mL) white sugar
- 1 T (15 mL) cinnamon
- nutmeg to taste
- 3-4 sticks of butter or margarine

Materials:
- 2–3 cookie sheets
- 2 spatulas
- 1 paring knife
- 2 butter knives
- paper towels
- baking cups
- measuring spoons
- teaspoon

Directions: Give each child a ¹/₂" (1.3 cm) slice of cookie dough. Have them work the dough into a small bowl shape. Place the cookie bowl into a baking cup. Place 1 heaping teaspoon (5 mL) of finely sliced apples into the cookie bowl. Sprinkle with sugars, cinnamon, and nutmeg and dot with butter. Bake in a 350° Fahrenheit (180° Celsius) oven for 8–10 minutes. Watch carefully!

Patterns

Station 5 Activity Card—Graphing

Materials:

- graph
- pencils or markers
- self-stick notes
- red, yellow, and green apples
- napkins
- resealable plastic bags
- crayons and extra coloring page or scratch paper
- paring knife

Prepare the following ahead of time: Slice the red, yellow, and green apples and store each type separately in a plastic bag. For each student you will need one slice of each type of apple. Make a three-columned graph on butcher paper or poster board. On the bottom, add labels for the three types of apples.

On Apple Day:

1. Let students in your group taste a slice of each kind of apple and choose which apple slices they like the best.
2. Give each student a self-stick note. Have students write their names on the notes and place them in a column to indicate their favorite apple.
3. Have students discuss the graph results. When finished, estimate how many seeds an apple has. Open one up and count.
4. Allow the members of a group that finishes early to color apple trees.

Station 6 Activity Card—Word Problems

Materials:

- math word problems (page 18)
- pencils
- scratch paper
- crayons

Directions:

1. Provide students with paper, pencils, and crayons.
2. Have students work a problem together before trying them on their own. The helper can do this by using the minichalkboard to illustrate. Ask students to illustrate the problem first and then find the solution.
3. If students are still having problems, ask them questions such as the following:
   –What facts are given?
   –How can we use those facts to find the answer?
4. If necessary, do the problem with the students on the chalkboard, but do not do it for them.

Page 18 Answers:

1. 5	3. 3	5. 6	7. 10	9. 1	11. a. 200	12. 6
2. 17	4. 11	6. 18	8. 8	10. 36	b. 100	

Rishaan

Math Word Problems

Directions: Choose the problems that will work the best for your group.

1. Tom had 3 red apples and 2 green apples. How many apples did he have in all?

    5 apples

2. Joe had 8 green apples and 9 red apples. How many apples did he have in all?

    17 apples

3. Betty picked 6 apples. She gave 3 away. How many did she have left?

    23 apples

4. Lucy picked 23 apples. She sold one dozen to Mrs. Jones. How many did she have left?

    $-\dfrac{23}{12}$ 11

5. Maria has 2 red apples, 2 green apples, and 2 yellow apples. How many does she have in all?

    6 apples

6. Amy has 7 red apples, 5 green apples, and 6 yellow apples. How many does she have in all?

    18 apples

7. John picked 5 green apples, 1 yellow apple, and 4 red apples. How many did he pick in all?

8. Juan picked 17 apples yesterday. He ate 2 and gave 7 to Mrs. Lewis for a pie. How many does he have left?

9. Susan had 4 apples. She gave 1 to her mom, 1 to her dad, and 1 to her brother. How many does she get to keep?

10. Sally has 3 baskets of apples. Each basket has 12 apples. How many apples does she have in all?

11. a. David has 4 boxes of apples. Each box holds 50 apples. How many apples does he have in all?

    b. If David gives $\frac{1}{2}$ of his apples to his grandmother, how many will he keep?

12. Mandy is making pies for a bake sale. For each pie, she needs 4 apples. She has 2 dozen apples. How many pies can she make?

Station 7 Activity Card—Apple Man

Materials:

- 1 medium apple per child

- cloves

- frozen peas, carrots, corn

- broccoli florets

- icing in tubes

- marshmallows

- popcorn

- candy-coated chocolate pieces

- construction paper

- markers

- chocolate chips

- cauliflower florets

- hot cinnamon drops

Directions:

Using the apple like a Mr. Potato Head, have the students make a person by gluing on items with tube icing. You can decide on a pattern you want them to follow or let them create on their own.

Station 8 Activity Card—Stages of the Apple Tree

Materials:
- white construction paper
- 1 apple seed per child
- glue
- popcorn
- dirt
- markers
- colored construction paper
- red paint or ink pad

Directions:

Prepare a 12" x 18" (30 cm x 46 cm) sheet of construction paper by folding it in half and then in half again. Open it to reveal four boxes. Have the students "plant" their seeds by gluing on a little dirt and then gluing the real apple seeds to the dirt. Students will show how the seedling grows by making a little tree with markers, crayons, or construction paper in the second box. In the third box, have them demonstrate how flowers blossom by making the tree larger and by adding more leaves. To show the blossoms, have them glue popcorn "blossoms" onto their trees. Finally, ask the students to show the apples ready to be picked. Have them make another tree with leaves and add apples by using thumbprints of red paint or ink.

Alternate Activity 1—Apple Sequence Cards

Materials:

- sequence cards (pages 21-23)
- glue
- scissors
- pencils
- crayons
- white paper

Directions:

1. Choose either set of sequence cards on pages 21-23. Ask the students to color and cut them out.

2. Challenge the students to arrange them in order on another piece of paper.

3. Younger children can cut out the word cards and match them to the pictures, gluing them on the paper. Older children can write the sentences themselves.

Alternate Activity 2—Apple Shape Books, Short "a"

Materials:

- apple shape books
- pencils
- crayons

Directions:

1. Talk about the short "a" sound, as in apple. Say "apple". What sound does it begin with? Can you think of any other words that might begin with that sound? What about words that have the short "a" sound in them, like hat?"

2. Write words in the apple shape book that either begin with short "a" or have the short "a" sound in them. Do not mix these in the same book for younger students. (For examples, see the provided vocabulary lists on page 12.) Older students should try writing whole sentences.

3. Illustrate the words.

Sentence Sequence Cards

Set 1

Watch it grow.	**Give it lots of water and sunshine.**
Plant an apple seed.	**Pick the apples and put them in your basket.**
Now you are ready to make a pie.	**See the pretty blossoms.**

Set 2

Pick them.	**Slice them.**
Eat them.	**Peel them.**
Wash them.	**Bake them.**

Picture Sequence Cards for Set 1

Picture Sequence Cards for Set 2

Stationery

Incentives

Use the following cards for positive reinforcement during your rotations. When a student successfully demonstrates positive behavior and completion of his or her tasks, cut an apple square and paste it on his or her basket. If you do not have time to cut and paste, a small apple sticker or stamp would work well. Distribute awards/name tags and bookmarks where appropriate.

Pick the apples and put them in your basket.

Award/Name Tag

Bookmark

Hooray for Apple Day!

Read Every Day!

25

Bears

Teacher Note: Use this page as an introduction to the Bears theme. Have the students color the picture. Lines are provided for writing activities of your choice.

Unit Materials

Bibliography

Turtle, Brinton. *Deep in the Forest.* Dutton, 1976.

At least two versions of *Goldilocks and the Three Bears.*

Nonfiction books, such as Zoobooks, are excellent.

Materials Checklist

Station 1—Literature
_____ literature selections
_____ lunch-sized paper bags
_____ puppet character faces
_____ glue
_____ scissors
_____ crayons
_____ activity card

Station 2—Writing
_____ bear shape books
_____ pencils and crayons
_____ *Deep in the Forest*
_____ activity card

Station 3—Cooking
_____ rolled sugar cookie dough
_____ chocolate pieces with candy shells
_____ toaster oven (or school kitchen)
_____ knife
_____ spatula
_____ icing in tubes
_____ cookie sheets
_____ paper towels
_____ activity card

Station 4—Word Problems
_____ bear cutouts for manipulatives
_____ word problems
_____ activity card
_____ crayons
_____ scissors

Station 5—Bear Information Flip Book
_____ nonfiction bear books
_____ 12" x 18" (30 cm x 46 cm) white construction paper
_____ pencils
_____ crayons
_____ scissors
_____ stapler
_____ activity card

Station 6—Button Bears
_____ fuzzy or stiff fabric
_____ scissors
_____ puff paint
_____ pencils
_____ paper
_____ markers
_____ activity card

Station 7—Stuffed Bears
_____ colored butcher paper (construction paper tears too easily)
_____ markers
_____ wiggle eyes
_____ small, fuzzy pompons
_____ glue
_____ ribbon
_____ bear pattern
_____ stapler
_____ scissors
_____ old newspaper
_____ sample
_____ activity card

Station 8—Bear Bingo
_____ Bingo number cards
_____ picture cards
_____ beans (or other markers)
_____ activity card

Alternate Activity:
The Three Bears Sequence Cards

_____ sequencing picture cards
_____ sequencing word cards
_____ pencils
_____ scissors
_____ crayons
_____ paper
_____ activity card

Station 1 Activity Card—Literature

Materials:

- puppet faces on pages 30 and 31
- crayons
- scissors
- glue
- lunch-sized paper bags
- *Goldilocks and the Three Bears* (at least two versions)

Directions: Read and compare at least two versions of *Goldilocks and the Three Bears*. Allow students to retell the story, using paper sack puppets. To make the puppets, give each child a character's face to color and then cut out. Glue the faces onto the bottoms of the paper lunch bags. Have the students decorate their bags to look like the bodies of the characters. If there is enough time, allow the students a couple of minutes of practice before performing their interpretations of *Goldilocks and the Three Bears*.

Station 2 Activity Card—Writing

Materials: bear shape books, pencils, crayons, *Deep in the Forest*

Directions for Option 1:

1. Using the pattern on page 29, make a bear shape book for each student ahead of time.

2. Look through *Deep in the Forest* and talk about how it differs from *Goldilocks and the Three Bears*.

3. Ask the students to write their own versions of *Deep in the Forest* in their shape books.

4. Illustrate the books if time permits. (This can always be done later.)

Directions for Option 2:

1. Discuss words that start with the letter "b."

2. Direct the students to draw a picture of a "b" thing on each page of their bear shape books.

3. Finally, have the students label each item or write a sentence about each picture.

Shape Book Pattern

Sack Puppet Faces

Goldilocks

Baby Bear

30

Sack Puppet Faces (cont.)

Papa Bear

Mama Bear

Station 3 Activity Card—Cooking

Cookie Bears

Ingredients:

- rolled sugar cookie dough from the refrigerated section of the market
- candy coated chocolate pieces
- icing in tubes (Small tubes with thin tips would be the best for this activity.)

- knife
- cookie sheets
- toaster oven
- spatula
- paper towels

Directions: Before you begin this activity, be sure each child has washed his or her hands. Give each child in the group one and a half slices of dough. Demonstrate how to make a bear cookie by dividing a half slice into two parts and rolling each part into a ball. Place the balls on a cookie sheet and then flatten them for ears. Overlap the remaining slice of cookie dough over the ears as a face. Allow the children to add candies for the eyes and noses of their bears. Bake the cookies at 350° F (176° C) for 8–10 minutes. Read a favorite bear book to the groups that finish early. After the cookies have finished baking and they have cooled, let the children add icing mouths.

Station 3 Activity Card—Cooking *(cont.)*

The directions on the previous card are given assuming that you have access to the school's kitchen oven to bake the cookies. The children will not be able to eat their cookies until later. It is also hard to keep track of which cookie belongs to which child. If you have access to a toaster oven for your classroom, try to do the following:

- Give each child a small square piece of foil.
- With a pencil, put the child's name or initials on a corner of the foil. Let the students make their cookie bears directly on the foil.
- Cook the bears on the foil in the toaster oven.
- Take the cookies out of the oven carefully and put them on small paper plates or napkins to cool a bit.

If time runs out before the cookies have cooled, leave the cookies on the foil and finish later. Placing the names on the foil will keep you from getting the cookies confused later on.

Station 4 Activity Card—Word Problems

Materials:

- crayons
- several copies of page 34 (for use as manipulatives)
- scissors

Directions: Cut the copies of bear illustrations into single bears. Hand out several bears to each child to color. Then collect the bears and use them as manipulatives to demonstrate the word problems. Choose some of the problems below and on the next card that are at the appropriate level for the group. Do the problems orally with the students.

1. 5 little bears went out to play,
   Then 7 little bears came their way.
   How many bears were there in all that day?

2. 15 little bears met in the park one day.
   4 little bears could not stay.
   How many bears were left to play?

3. 3 little bears each ate 3 little pears.
   How many pears did they eat in all?

4. 27 bears were on the bus.
   3 bears sat in each seat.
   How many seats did the bus have?

Station 4 Activity Card—Word Problems *(cont.)*

5. 26 bears sat in pairs.
   How many pairs were there?

6. I have 4 teddy bears.
   Mandy has 6 teddy bears.
   Chris has one less than Mandy.
   How many do we have altogether?

7. If Tom has 12 bears and Mary has half
   as many, how many do they have in all?

8. If Hector has 8 bears and Linda has half
   as many bears as Hector, how many
   bears do they have together?

9. 10 bears live in a house.
   4 bears take a walk.
   How many bears are left at home?

10. If I have 5 little girls and I need 3 bears
    for each girl, how many bears do I need
    in all?

11. A zoo has 3 polar bears, 2 black bears,
    1 grizzly bear, and 3 brown bears.
    How many bears does it have in all?

Answers:

1. 12	3. 9	5. 13	7. 18	9. 6	11. 9
2. 11	4. 9	6. 15	8. 12	10. 15	

Word Problem Manipulatives

Station 5 Activity Card—Bear Information Flip Book

Materials: nonfiction bear books, 12" x 18" (30 cm x 46 cm) white construction paper, pencils, crayons, scissors, stapler

Directions: Read to the students about several types of bears (for example, grizzly, brown, polar, black). After reading, discuss what they learned about the bears. Explain that they will be writing about what they learned in flip books. To prepare the flip books, have the students do the following:

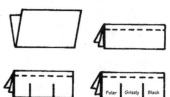

1. Fold a 12" x 18" (30 cm x 46 cm) piece of construction paper lengthwise. Fold the paper lengthwise a second time.

2. Staple the folded edges together. This will result in a long, thin book with three pages.

3. Cut the book in two places as shown.

After the flip books have been made, tell the students what to write on each page. "Write the name of a bear that we talked about on each top page. On the second set of pages, draw pictures of the bears that you named on the first set of pages. On the last set of pages, write one interesting thing that you learned about each bear."

Station 6 Activity Card—Button Bears

Materials: precut button bears (see below), pencils, paper, markers

Prepare the Following Ahead of Time: Enlarge the bear pattern on this card and cut out enough bears so that each child may have one. Use a fuzzy material or other stiff fabric. When you are finished cutting around the pattern outline, be sure to make a slit in the center of the face as shown. If you have enough time, add two dots of puff paint for the eyes.

Directions: When the students arrive at your station, hand out a button bear to each child. Demonstrate how to wear a button bear by slipping a button on your shirt through the slit in the face of a bear. The button will become the nose of the bear.

Before the children put on their button bears, have them name their new bears. Allow them to write their bears' names on the backs of the fabric cutouts in black marker. After the marker dries, let them try on their bears. (**Note:** If a student is not wearing any buttons, attach the bear to a shoelace, earring, etc.) Now, ask each child to write the name of his or her bear on the top of a piece of paper. Have them imagine that their bears are real, living creatures. Ask students to write below the bear names words that describe their bears as they imagine them (e.g., kind, soft, friendly, warm). Explain that these words are called adjectives.

Station 7 Activity Card—Stuffed Bears

Materials:

- colored butcher paper (construction paper tears too easily)
- markers
- wiggle eyes
- small, fuzzy pompons
- glue
- ribbon
- bear pattern
- stapler
- scissors
- old newspaper

Directions:

1. Enlarge the pattern below to the size of your choice by using a copy machine or overhead projector. Let the children trace the bear pattern onto folded butcher paper and cut out two bear shapes each. (For younger children, this can be done ahead of time.)

2. Staple the bears together around the edges. Leave an opening at the side for stuffing.

3. Tell the children to fully stuff the bears with crumpled pieces of newspaper.

4. Staple shut the openings in the bear sides.

5. Tie ribbons into bows around the necks.

6. Let the children glue the eyes onto their bears' faces and use markers to draw mouths and noses.

Let the bear dry fully on a paper towel with the child's name written on it. When dry (usually after school) turn the bear over and add a pompon tail. Let it dry overnight.

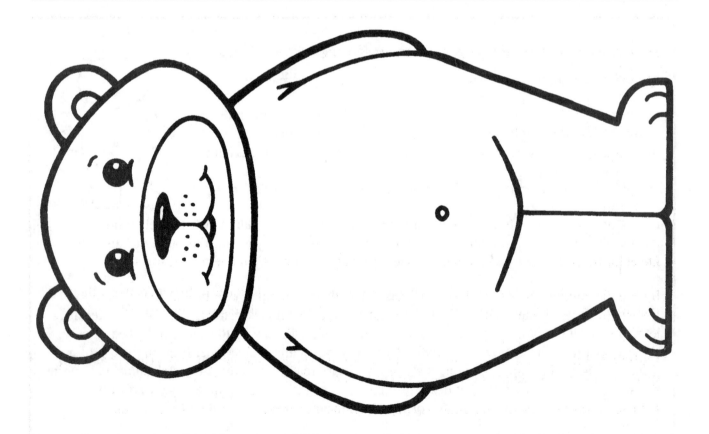

36

Station 8 Activity Card—Bear Bingo

Materials:

- Bingo number cards (page 38)

- Bingo picture cards (page 39)

- beans (or other markers)

Directions: Laminate the Bear Bingo Number Cards and Bear Bingo Picture Cards, if possible. Give each student a card with numbers on it and a handful of beans. Allow each child to cover three free spaces with his or her beans. (Since there are only four Bingo cards and there may be more than four students in a group, covering three spaces will make the cards all different.) Shuffle the Bingo cards and then flip one card at a time and show it to the students. Give the students time to cover the appropriate number if they have it. Continue playing until someone has filled the whole card.

Alternate Activity—The Three Bears Sequence Cards

Materials:

- sequence word cards (page 40)
- sequence picture cards (page 41)
- scissors
- crayons
- paper
- pencils

Directions: To provide sequencing practice, use pages 40 and 41 in one of two ways.

Option 1: Tell the students to put the picture cards in the correct sequence first. Then ask them to match the word cards to the correct pictures. (**Note:** Depending on the reading level of each group, you may need to read the word cards out loud to them.)

Option 2: Tell the students to put the picture cards in the correct sequence first. Then challenge them to write stories, using the sequenced cards as models.

If there is any extra time after either option, allow the students to color the picture cards.

Bear Bingo Number Cards

Make several copies of this page. Cut out the cards and laminate them.

Bear Bingo

5	8	2	9	3
4	6	7	9	1
4	6	2	8	6
6	5	9	2	1
7	8	4	3	6

Bear Bingo

8	7	3	9	4
5	6	8	1	9
1	2	3	9	5
5	9	3	2	8
7	5	8	6	3

Bear Bingo

1	5	7	3	2
4	8	2	4	3
3	1	5	9	6
3	6	7	2	9
8	4	5	6	2

Bear Bingo

5	8	2	3	5
4	9	6	1	3
2	8	4	9	1
4	9	3	5	9
6	1	8	4	2

Bear Bingo Picture Cards

Make six or seven copies of this page. Cut out the cards and laminate them.

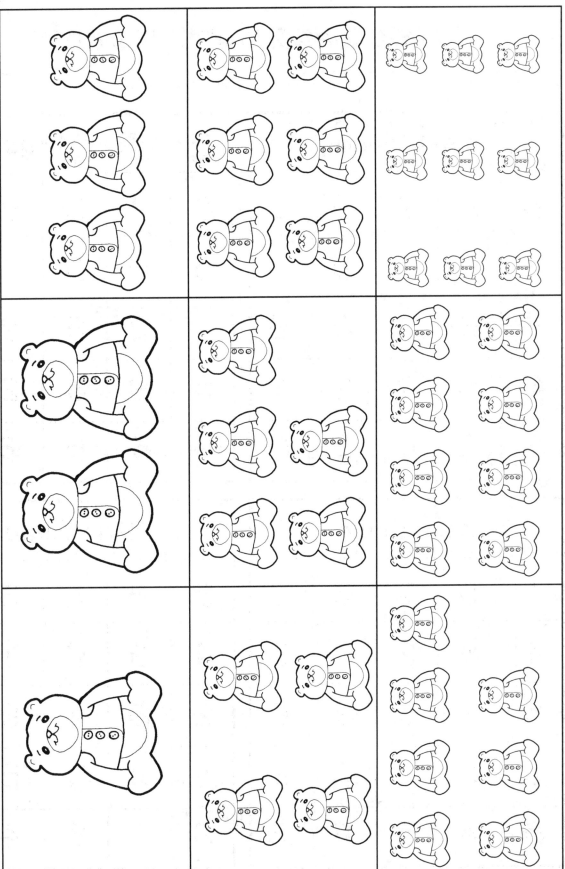

Sequence Word Cards

The three bears found the little girl asleep in Baby Bear's bed.	The bears noticed that Baby Bear's chair was broken.
The bears went for a walk in the forest.	She sat in Baby Bear's chair.
She fell asleep in Baby Bear's bed.	The three bears sat down to eat their porridge, but it was too hot.
She tasted their food and ate all of Baby Bear's food.	She woke up and ran away.
When they came home, Baby Bear's food was all gone.	A little girl came to their house while they were gone.

Sequence Picture Cards

Stationery

42

Incentives

Use the following cards for positive reinforcement during your rotations. When a student successfully demonstrates positive behavior and completion of his or her tasks, cut a honey pot square and paste it on his or her bear. If you do not have time to cut and paste, a small bear sticker or stamp would work well. Distribute awards/name tags and bookmarks where appropriate.

Fill the bear's tummy with honey!

Award/Name Tags

Bookmark

Beary Good Reader!

#2034 Celebrate ABC's

Cookies

Teacher Note: Use this page as an introduction to the Cookies theme. Have the students color the picture. Lines are provided for writing activities of your choice.

Unit Materials

Bibliography

Hutchins, Pat. *The Doorbell Rang.* William Morrow, 1986.

Numeroff, Laura. *If You Give a Mouse a Cookie.* HarperCollins, 1985.

Materials Checklist

Station 1—Literature
_____ *The Doorbell Rang*
_____ a variety of cookie recipes
_____ several cookies to use while retelling the story
_____ activity card

Station 2—Writing
_____ cookie shape books
_____ pencils
_____ crayons
_____ activity card

Station 3—Graphing
_____ butcher paper
_____ sugar wafers (vanilla, strawberry, and chocolate)
_____ napkins
_____ sticky notes
_____ activity card

Station 4—Cooking
_____ 2 small chocolate chip or oatmeal cookies per child
_____ vanilla or chocolate chip ice cream
_____ spoons or ice-cream scoop
_____ napkins
_____ activity card

Station 5—Cooking
_____ flour
_____ butter
_____ vanilla extract
_____ nuts (if desired)
_____ spatula
_____ paper towels
_____ baking soda
_____ brown sugar
_____ egg
_____ cookie sheets
_____ large bowl
_____ hand mixer
_____ salt
_____ sugar
_____ chocolate chips
_____ measuring cups
_____ stirring spoons
_____ teaspoons
_____ activity card

Station 6—Math
_____ one bag of chocolate chip cookies (mini or regular size)
_____ one bag of chocolate chips
_____ one large bakery-sized chocolate chip cookie per group
_____ estimation charts (page 50)
_____ pencils or markers
_____ "One Smart Cookie!" awards (see page 55)
_____ activity card

Station 7—Art
_____ 2 vanilla wafers per child
_____ 2 red cinnamon candies per child
_____ red string licorice (16 inches/40.6 cm per child)
_____ canned frosting
_____ icing in tubes
_____ scissors
_____ permanent black marker
_____ plastic bags
_____ plastic knives
_____ activity card

Station 8—Group Writing
_____ lined writing paper
_____ pencils
_____ crayons
_____ 12" x 18" (30 cm x 46 cm) construction paper
_____ *If You Give a Mouse a Cookie*
_____ activity card

Note: As with any activity involving food products, check for students who are allergic to chocolate, nuts, dairy products, etc., and adapt the lessons accordingly.

Station 1 Activity Card—Literature

Materials:

- *The Doorbell Rang*
- a small collection of cookie recipes
- several cookies

Directions:

1. Read *The Doorbell Rang.*

2. Retell the story, using real cookies to illustrate.

3. Look at the cookie recipes. Talk about your favorites. What are some of the common ingredients?

Station 2 Activity Card—Writing

Materials:

- cookie shape books
- pencils
- crayons

Directions: Use the cookie shape pattern on page 47 to create the covers and interior pages of the book. Have the students write and illustrate in their shape books about one of the following:

a. Kinds of cookies—chocolate chip, peanut butter, oatmeal, sandwich cookies, etc.

b. The "oo" sound as in cookie (compare with "oo" as in moon)

c. The "ch" sound as in chocolate chip

Shape Book Pattern

Station 3 Activity Card—Graphing

Which Cookie Do You Like Best?

Materials: sugar wafers in three different flavors—chocolate, vanilla, and strawberry; large graph made out of butcher paper; sticky notes; napkins

To Be Done in Advance: Before doing this activity, create a large empty graph. Draw three long columns. Label the columns, Chocolate, Vanilla, and Strawberry. Draw the rows far enough apart so that the sticky notes will fit in the boxes you create. Make the graph tall enough to include the answers of all of the students.

Directions:

1. Give each child samples of all three kinds of cookies to taste.

2. Let each child write his or her name on a sticky note and stick it on the graph in the appropriate spot.

3. Discuss the graph results. How did the group members vote? Compare the group's choices with the groups which have already come through. (Only the first group at this station will not be able to compare and contrast. However, ask these students to predict what will happen when the other groups come through.)

Station 4 Activity Card—Cooking

Mini Ice-Cream Sandwiches

Ingredients:

- two chocolate chip or oatmeal cookies per child

- vanilla or chocolate chip ice cream

- ice-cream scoop or spoon

- napkins

Directions:

1. Take the group to the restrooms to wash their hands in preparation for this activity and the next one.

2. Allow each child to scoop his or her own ice cream and put it between two cookies.

3. Tell them to press the cookies together to flatten the sandwiches slightly and enjoy their snacks!

Station 5 Activity Card—Cooking

Chocolate Chip Cookies

Ingredients (for 1 ½–2 dozen cookies):

- ¹/₂ cup (125 mL) butter, softened
- ¹/₂ cup (125 mL) brown sugar, firmly packed
- ¹/₂ (2.5 mL) teaspoon salt
- 1 cup (250 mL) flour
- ¹/₂ cup (125 mL) nuts, chopped (optional)

- ¹/₂ cup (125 mL) granulated sugar
- ¹/₂ teaspoon (2.5 mL) baking soda
- ¹/₂ teaspoon (2.5 mL) vanilla extract
- 6 ounce (180 mL) bag chocolate chips
- 1 egg

Additional Materials: teaspoons, mixing bowls, mixer, spatula, cookie sheets

Directions: Ask the students to help in the measuring as you make cookie dough. Cream the butter, granulated sugar, and brown sugar in a large bowl. Beat in the eggs and vanilla. Gradually add flour, baking soda, and salt to the mixture. Stir in the chocolate chips and nuts. Drop the dough onto a cookie sheet, using a teaspoon. Bake for about ten minutes, but check often after seven minutes. (If you are using the cafeteria oven, they may bake faster.) Remove the cookies from the oven, cool, and enjoy.

This recipe makes enough cookies for at least two groups. For additional groups, you will need to adjust your recipe quantities and the division of labor so there will be enough cookies and everyone can participate.

Station 6 Activity Card—Math

Estimations

Materials:

- one bag of chocolate chip cookies (mini or regular size)
- one bag of chocolate chips
- one large bakery-size chocolate chip cookie per group
- an estimation chart for each group (page 50)
- pencils or markers
- "One Smart Cookie" awards (see page 55)

Directions:

1. Set the bag of cookies, the bag of chocolate chips, and a bakery-sized chocolate chip cookie out on the table. Have each student estimate the answers to the three questions on the chart.
2. Tell the students to record their estimations on the chart under the appropriate headings.
3. With the group, count the items and compare the findings to the estimates.
4. The students with the closest guesses in each category get a "One Smart Cookie" award (see page 55).

Cookie Estimation Chart

How many chips are in a chocolate chip cookie?		How many chips are in a bag?		How many cookies are in a bag?	
Name	Estimate	Name	Estimate	Name	Estimate
Answer: _____		Answer: _____		Answer: _____	
Closest Guess: _____		Closest Guess: _____		Closest Guess: _____	

50

Station 7 Activity Card—Art

Spider Cookies

Materials:

- 2 vanilla wafer cookies per child
- plastic knives
- black permanent marker
- 2 red cinnamon candies per child
- plastic sandwich bags
- red string licorice
- icing in tubes
- canned frosting
- scissors

Directions: Have children wash their hands before making the spider cookies. Put a generous amount of frosting on one wafer. Give each child four licorice strings each about 4 inches (10 cm) long. Before the children make their spiders, demonstrate the following steps.

1. Lay the strings across the frosted wafer. Press them gently into the frosting. Add frosting over the strings.

2. Set the second wafer on top; squish the wafers to hold them in place. Secure the two red cinnamon candies to the top wafer with the tube icing. Once the students have replicated your demonstration, write their names on sandwich bags and store their spiders in these to take home. These can also be made with chocolate wafers for a more dramatic effect.

Station 8 Activity Card—Group Writing

Materials:

- *If You Give a Mouse a Cookie*
- pencils
- lined writing paper
- crayons
- construction paper

Directions:

1. Read *If You Give a Mouse a Cookie* to your students.

2. Discuss how each event brings about the next one.

3. Write a group story in the same manner, using the events in the book as a pattern. Add events until they lead back to the beginning. You may need to help the students until they get a story started. They should have at least five events.

4. If the group finishes early enough, have the students illustrate their story. Ask each student to transfer a line from the group story to a piece of paper. Then tell the students to illustrate their sentences. Put these pages together to make a group storybook.

Cookie-Making Sentence Cards

Use these sentence cards for sequencing, storytelling, writing activities, or for matching with the picture cards on page 53.

Bake for 10 minutes.	**Eat!**
Remove from oven and cool.	**Add chocolate chips and nuts if you wish.**
Preheat the oven.	**Mix the ingredients.**
Measure the ingredients into a bowl.	**Drop onto a cookie sheet.**

Cookie-Making Picture Cards

Use these picture cards for sequencing, storytelling, writing activities, or for matching with the sentence cards on page 52.

Stationery

Incentives

Use the following cards for positive reinforcement during your rotations. When a student successfully demonstrates positive behavior and completion of his or her tasks, cut a cookie square and paste it on his or her cookie jar. If you do not have time to cut and paste, a small cookie sticker or stamp would work well. Distribute awards/name tags and bookmarks where appropriate.

Fill the cookie jar with cookies!

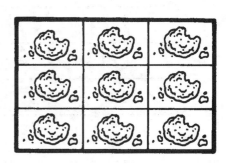

Award/Name Tag

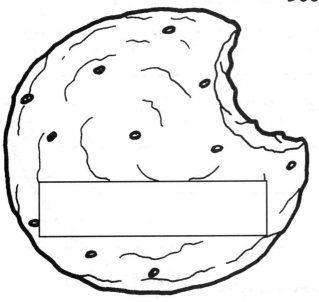

Bookmark

ONE SMART COOKIE!

Dinosaurs

- -

_____

- -

_____

- -

_____

- -

_____

- -

_____

Teacher Note: Use this page as an introduction to the Dinosaurs theme. Have students color the picture. Lines are provided for writing activities of your choice.

Unit Materials

Bibliography

Aliki. *Digging Up Dinosaurs.* HarperCollins Children's Books, 1988.

Carrick, Carole. *Patrick's Dinosaurs.* Clarion Books, 1986.

Carrick, Carole. *What Happened to Patrick's Dinosaurs?* Clarion Books, 1986.

Cooper, Don. *DinoSongs.* Random House, 1988. (an audio cassette)

In addition to these books, provide several extra nonfiction books or magazines about dinosaurs.

Materials Checklist

Station 1—Literature
_____ literature selections (fiction and nonfiction)
_____ activity card

Station 2—Writing
_____ dinosaur shape books
_____ information books
_____ pencils
_____ crayons
_____ activity card

Station 3—Pattern
_____ dinosaur patterns
_____ pencils
_____ crayons
_____ drawing paper
_____ activity card

Station 4—Cooking
_____ bread
_____ margarine
_____ cinnamon
_____ sugar
_____ dinosaur cookie cutters
_____ plastic knives
_____ napkins
_____ toaster oven
_____ activity card

Station 5—Word Problems
_____ pencils
_____ paper
_____ dinosaur counters
_____ activity card

Station 6—Art
_____ butcher paper
_____ crayons
_____ pencils
_____ markers
_____ scissors
_____ glue
_____ patterns
_____ construction paper
_____ paint
_____ activity card

Station 7—Dinosaur Bones
_____ literature
_____ white pipe cleaners
_____ scissors
_____ activity card
_____ *DinoSongs* cassette tape

Station 8—Dinosaur Bingo
_____ blank Bingo cards
_____ dinocards
_____ scissors
_____ glue
_____ beans or other Bingo markers

_____ laminated dinocards
_____ awards
_____ activity card

Alternative Activity:

Dino Toast
_____ bread
_____ plastic knives
_____ soft margarine
_____ napkins
_____ cinnamon and sugar shakers
_____ toothpicks
_____ tubes of icing or honey in a squeeze bottle
_____ activity card
_____ dinosaur patterns

Station 1 Activity Card—Literature

Materials:

- dinosaur literature selections

Directions:

1. Read and discuss *Patrick's Dinosaurs*.

2. Follow up with *What Happened to Patrick's Dinosaurs?*

3. Discuss both books. Then allow students to look through dinosaur information, books, and magazines. Give them time to share what they discover in the books with each other.

Station 2 Activity Card—Writing

Materials:

- dinosaur shape books
- pencils
- dinosaur information books
- crayons

Directions: Using the dinosaur shape book pattern on page 59 make a shape book for each student. Then choose one of the following ideas for the shape book:

Option 1: Dinosaur (can be done in a group or individually)

1. Read about a type of dinosaur to the students (or you may wish to let them read to each other, depending on their reading levels).

2. Ask the students to write about what they learned about the dinosaur on one page of their shape books.

3. Then, tell them to draw the dinosaur on the next page of their shape books.

4. Read about another dinosaur and repeat steps 2 and 3. Continue learning about types of dinosaurs until the time is up.

Option 2: "D" Sounds

1. Ask the students to write a word that begins with the letter D on each page.

2. Then ask them to illustrate each of their "D" words. (You may wish to ask older students to write a sentence for each word.)

Shape Book Pattern

Dinosaurs

Station 3 Activity Card—Patterns

Materials:

- several sets of patterns made from page 61
- pencils
- paper
- crayons
- drawing paper

Directions:

1. Allow the students about 15 minutes to trace dinosaur patterns and then color.
2. With the remaining time take the group to the restrooms to wash their hands in preparation for the cooking activity at the next station.

Station 4 Activity Card—Cooking

Dinosaur Cinnamon Toast

Materials:

- bread (one slice per child)
- cinnamon and sugar (in shakers)
- plastic knives
- toaster oven
- soft butter or margarine
- dinosaur cookie cutters
- napkins

Directions:

1. Let the students use cookie cutters to cut their bread into dinosaur shapes.
2. Butter the bread.
3. Sprinkle cinnamon and sugar on top of the bread.
4. Toast the bread until it is lightly browned.
5. Enjoy!

Dinosaur Patterns

Teacher Note: Enlarge and photocopy these patterns onto pieces of thick paper for tracing. If you are using these patterns for the alternate activity on page 64, do not enlarge the patterns.

Station 5 Activity Card—Word Problems

Materials:

- pencils
- paper
- counters to represent the dinosaurs (such as beans, pennies, or poker chips)

Directions:

Ask the students to find the answers to the word problems using one of three ways. Solutions may be found by . . .

> . . . using counters to illustrate the problem.

> . . . drawing the problem on scratch paper.

> . . . using the dinosaur cards from the game (pages 65 and 66) to illustrate the problem.

Start with problem number 1 on the card below. The problems become increasingly difficult so stop when you sense that you have gone beyond the ability level of the group you are working with. If the students finish early, have them make up their own problems for each other.

Station 5 Activity Card—Word Problems *(cont.)*

1. Patrick had 6 big dinosaurs and 7 little dinosaurs. How many did he have in all?

2. 4 of Patrick's dinosaurs were triceratops, 4 were oviraptors and 1 was a tyrannosaurus rex. The rest were pteranodons. How many were pteranodons?

3. 5 of Patrick's dinosaurs ran away. How many did he have left?

4. If those 5 came back and each one brought a friend, how many dinosaurs would Patrick have in all?

5. 2 of the new dinosaurs were mothers. They had 4 babies each. How many dinosaurs does Patrick have now?

6. If those babies grow up and each of them has 4 babies, how many dinosaurs will Patrick have?

7. If Patrick's original dinosaurs die, how many would he have left?

8. If ten of these remaining dinosaurs run away, how many does Patrick finally have?

Answers:

1. 13	3. 8	5. 26	7. 29
2. 4	4. 18	6. 42	8. 19

Station 6 Activity Card—Art

Dinosaur Mural

Materials:

- crayons
- patterns
- markers
- paint

- pencils
- scissors
- construction paper
- glue

- piece of butcher paper, 6-8 feet (1.8-2.4 m) long (one for each group)

Directions: Put the names of all of the students in the group in a corner of the backside of the butcher paper. Have half of the group work on making the background on the butcher paper (pictures of possible prehistoric habitats are helpful here). Let the children use crayons and markers for this. At the same time, have the other half of the students trace patterns of dinosaurs or sketch dinosaurs onto construction paper and then cut out the shapes. Glue the dinosaurs onto the backdrop. When the glue is dry, hang it and the other murals in the room, the hall, the library, or the cafeteria. Then, when it is time to take the murals down, roll them with the names to the outside and secure them with rubber bands. Have a drawing to see which student in each group will get to keep the murals.

Station 7 Activity Card—Dinosaur Bones

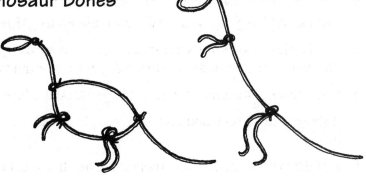

Materials:

- *Digging Up Dinosaurs*
- white pipe cleaners
- scissors
- *DinoSongs* cassette tape

Directions:

1. Read and discuss *Digging Up Dinosaurs* by Aliki.

2. Teach the children how to make pipe-cleaner dinosaur skeletons. Give each child two pipe cleaners and scissors. Let them design their own dinosaurs (real or imaginary; however, do make a few examples to start them off).

3. Let the children listen to the *DinoSongs* cassette as they work. When the dinosaurs are finished, have the students learn the words to the songs by singing along with the tape.

Station 8 Activity Card—Dinosaur Bingo

Materials:

- blank Bingo card for each student (page 65)
- 24 dinocards for each student (page 66)
- a set of laminated dinocards for the leader
- awards from page 68
- scissors
- glue
- beans or other Bingo markers

Directions:

1. Let each student randomly place and glue 24 dinocards on the blanks of his or her Bingo card.

2. Tell the students to leave one space on their cards blank and to label it "FREE."

3. Play the game as you would traditional Bingo. Shuffle the laminated dinocards and show them, one at a time, to the students. Tell the students to place a marker on the box that has the same dinosaur until someone has markers on five squares in a row either across, down, or diagonally.

4. The first player to do this gets a "Dinomite Reader!" award.

Alternate Activity—Dino Toast

If you do not have dinosaur cookie cutters for Activity 4, do this activity instead.

Materials:

- one slice of bread per child
- soft margarine
- cinnamon and sugar in shakers
- dinosaur patterns (page 61)
- plastic knives
- napkins
- toothpicks
- small tubes of icing or honey in a squeeze bottle

Directions:

1. Have students wash their hands before preparing Dino Toast. Spread butter on bread. Give the children the opportunity to sprinkle their toast with cinnamon and sugar. Toast lightly.

2. After the bread has toasted, give each child a dinosaur pattern (check to make sure that it fits on the bread first). Have the students set their patterns on their toast. Use toothpicks to hold these in place.

3. Let the students outline the dinosaur patterns with tubed icing or honey from a squeeze bottle.

4. Remove the toothpicks and patterns. The dinosaur outlines should remain on the pieces of toast.

Dinosaur Bingo Card

Dinosaur Bingo

Dinocards

66

Stationery

Incentives

Use the following cards for positive reinforcement during your rotations. When a student successfully demonstrates positive behavior and completion of his or her tasks, cut out a dinosaur square and paste it on his or her jungle card. If you do not have time to cut and paste, a small dinosaur sticker or stamp would work well. Distribute awards/name tags and bookmarks where appropriate.

Fill the jungle with dinosaurs!

Award/Name Tag

Bookmark

Dinomite

Reader!

Eggs

Teacher Note: Use this page as an introduction to the Eggs theme. Have the students color the picture. Lines are provided for writing activities of your choice.

Unit Materials

Bibliography

Heller, Ruth. *Chickens Aren't the Only Ones.* Grosset and Dunlop, 1981.

Seuss, Dr. *Green Eggs and Ham.* Random House, 1960.

Any version of *Humpty Dumpty* may also be used in this unit.

Materials Checklist

Station 1—Literature

_____ *Chickens Aren't the Only Ones*
_____ real eggs or pictures of eggs
_____ pencils
_____ crayons
_____ drawing paper
_____ activity card

Station 2—Writing

_____ shape books
_____ pencils
_____ crayons
_____ poem
_____ activity card

Station 3—Puppets

_____ plastic sandwich bags
_____ copies of puppet pieces
_____ scissors
_____ crayons
_____ tape
_____ book of nursery rhymes
_____ brass fasteners
_____ activity card

Station 4—Cooking

_____ *Green Eggs and Ham*
_____ eggs
_____ margarine
_____ green food coloring

_____ crackers
_____ salt and pepper
_____ small paper plates
_____ milk
_____ plastic knives
_____ hot plate
_____ ham, cut into small squares
_____ skillet
_____ mixing bowl
_____ spatula
_____ hand mixer
_____ activity card

Station 5—Word Problems

_____ plastic eggs
_____ pencils
_____ paper
_____ activity card

Station 6—Mosaics

_____ colored eggshells (prepared ahead)
_____ paper plates
_____ egg outline
_____ glue
_____ pencils
_____ activity card

Stations 7 and 8—Relays

_____ 2 plastic eggs
_____ 2 large wooden spoons
_____ activity card

Alternate Activities:

1. Cooking

_____ grapes
_____ Chinese noodles
_____ slivered almonds
_____ salad dressing
_____ lettuce
_____ lemon pepper (optional)
_____ paper plates
_____ teaspoon
_____ plastic forks and spoons
_____ activity card

2. Writing

_____ paper
_____ crayons
_____ pencils
_____ shape books
_____ activity card

Station 1 Activity Card—Literature

Materials:

- *Chickens Aren't the Only Ones*
- real eggs or pictures of eggs
- pencils
- crayons
- drawing paper

Directions:

1. Read and discuss *Chickens Aren't the Only Ones*.

2. Show real eggs or pictures of eggs to the children.

3. Ask the children to draw pictures of creatures which hatch from eggs and label the pictures.

Station 2 Activity Card—Writing

Materials:

- shape books
- pencils
- crayons
- poem

Directions:

Write the poem below on a large piece of paper. Give each student a shape book made from the pattern on page 72. Tell them to write one line of the poem on each page of their shape books. After children have written the poem, let them illustrate each page.

Eggs

I like eggs.	Dotted eggs,
White eggs,	Fried eggs,
Brown eggs,	And dyed eggs.
Spotted eggs,	Beating eggs
Cracked eggs,	And eating eggs.
Stacked eggs,	I like eggs.

Shape Book Pattern

Eggs

Station 3 Activity Card—Puppets

Materials:

- copies of pages 74 and 75
- scissors
- plastic sandwich bags
- book of nursery rhymes
- crayons
- brass fasteners
- tape

Directions: Read the nursery rhyme "Humpty Dumpty" to the children. Give each child copies of pages 74 and 75. Give them time to color and cut out the pieces. On the back of each egg, tape a plastic sandwich-sized bag. Point the mouth of the bag to the base of the egg. The children will place their hands in the bags to hold onto their puppets.

Fold the arms and legs accordion-style along the lines. Then, use the brass fasteners to attach these to the body by matching the letters.

Recite the nursery rhyme together, using the puppets as props. Take the students to wash their hands for cooking at the next station.

Station 4 Activity Card—Cooking

Green Eggs and Ham

Materials:

- *Green Eggs and Ham*
- eggs (one per every 2 to 3 students— they will only need a bite, not a whole serving)
- green food coloring
- salt and pepper
- milk
- ham, cut into small squares
- soft margarine or butter
- skillet
- crackers
- small paper plates
- plastic knives
- mixing bowl
- hand mixer
- hot plate
- spatula

Directions:

Read *Green Eggs and Ham* by Dr. Seuss to the students. Into a bowl, crack one egg for every two to three students. Let the students scramble the eggs with a hand mixer. Add a little milk and salt and pepper to taste. Color with a few drops of green food coloring. Stir in the ham squares. Cook the green eggs and ham in a little butter in a skillet on a hot plate. Serve with a cracker.

Humpty Dumpty Puppet Pattern

Humpty Dumpty Puppet Pattern *(cont.)*

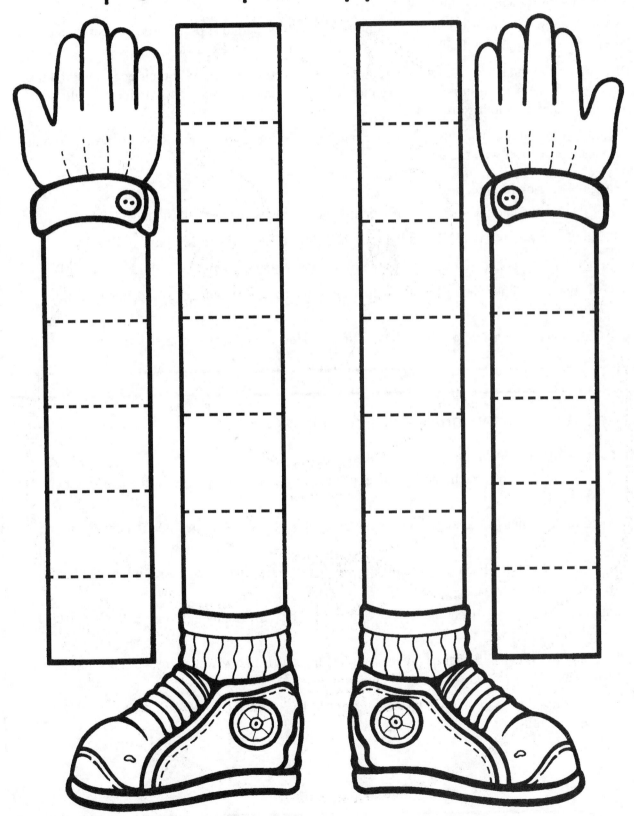

Station 5 Activity Card—Word Problems

Materials: plastic eggs, pencils, paper

To Be Done in Advance: Write each math problem on a separate slip of paper. (Answers are provided in parentheses.) Fold the papers and place each one in a plastic egg.

Directions: Let the students each choose an egg. Once they have opened their eggs and read the contents, tell them to illustrate and solve the problems. Have the students switch eggs with other students and solve another problem.

Note: For the younger students just choose one egg at a time as a group. Read the problem to the students and solve it with them.

Grades K–1 Word Problems

1. Ellen's hens laid 5 eggs today. Her family ate 3. How many does she have left? (2)

2. How many eggs would Ellen's hens lay in 2 days if they laid 5 each day? (10)

3. If Ellen's hens laid 10 eggs and her family ate 6 of them, how many would be left? (4)

4. If Ellen had 5 hens and they each laid 2 eggs one day, how many eggs did Ellen have that day? (10)

5. Ellen had 12 eggs. She sold 6 to Mrs. Smith. How many does she have left? (6)

Station 5 Activity Card—Word Problems *(cont.)*

Grades 2–3 Word Problems

1. Elmer has 3 hens. Each one lays an egg every day. How many eggs do the hens lay in one week? (21)

2. Edith has 5 hens. Each one lays an egg every day. How many eggs do the hens lay in one week? (35)

3. Elias has 4 hens. Each one lays an egg every day. How many days does it take the hens to lay 12 eggs? (3)

4. Esther has 6 hens. Each one lays an egg every day. How many eggs can Esther's hens lay in 5 days? (30)

5. Elmer has 6 hens. Esther has twice as many hens as Elmer. How many hens does Esther have? (12)

6. Elmer has 3 hens. Each one lays 2 eggs every day. How many eggs do the hens lay in one week? (42)

Station 6 Activity Card—Mosaics

Materials: colored eggshells (prepared ahead), paper plates, egg outline, glue, pencils

To Be Done in Advance: A month or so before this activity, ask the students to start saving eggshells. The shells must be washed thoroughly and dried, and it is best if the membranes are completely taken out. Collect as many shells as you can. Crush them carefully into small (but not too small) pieces. Divide the shell pieces into several piles. Color each pile a different color, using one of the following methods:

> a. Color the shells as you would Easter eggs, in cups with dye tablets.

> b. Place some of the pieces in a resealable plastic bag, and then add a few drops of food coloring and a little water, if needed. Zip the bag shut and knead it with your fingers to distribute the color evenly. Be careful not to crush the pieces any further. Repeat the process with another color.

After using either coloring process, allow the pieces to dry by spreading them out on paper towels. You might need to turn them once. Then put each color into a separate bag or jar. Make a copy of the egg mosaic pattern on page 78 for each student. Now you are ready for the activity.

Station 6 Activity Card—Mosaics *(cont.)*

Directions:

1. Give each student a copy of the egg outline. Ask the students to write their names at the bottom of their papers.

2. Set the egg shells on paper plates in the middle of the table for the students to share.

3. Demonstrate the following process for the students:

> a. Squirt glue on one section of the egg outline. (Do not use too much!)

> b. Spread the glue with your finger, if needed.

> c. Carefully sprinkle the eggshells onto the glue.

> d. Gently pat down the shells with your finger.

> e. Over a paper plate, lightly tap your paper so that any loose eggshells drop off.

4. Tell the students to repeat this process with different colors until they are finished.

5. Finally, let the mosaics dry completely.

Egg Mosaic Pattern

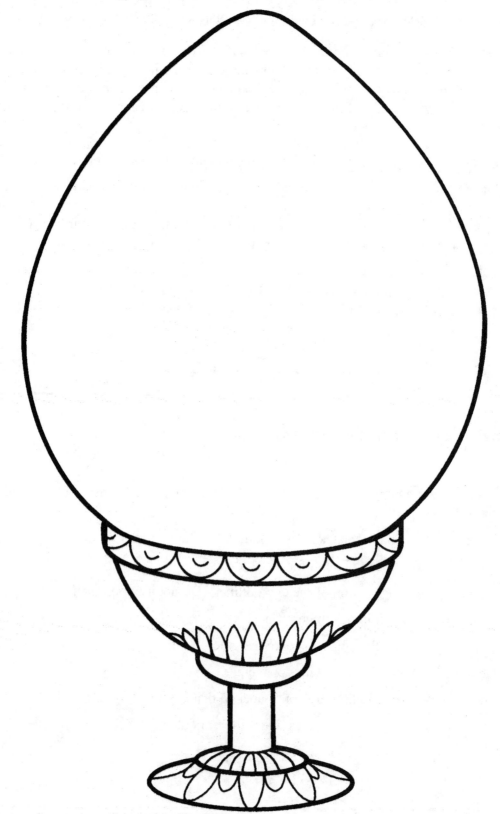

78

Stations 7 and 8 Activity Card—Relays

Materials: 2 plastic eggs, 2 large wooden spoons

Directions: You will have two groups at this station at one time. Do Relay #1 for the first rotation. After one group leaves and another one arrives, do Relay #2. Continue this pattern throughout the eight rotations.

Before the relays begin, mark off lines or use the lines on a basketball court.

Relay #1:

1. Line both groups up behind the starting line.

2. Give the first person in each group a spoon and a plastic egg.

3. When you yell, "Go!" the first competitors will carry the eggs on the spoons across the court and back. If an egg falls, the competitor must retrieve it and go on. (They cannot hold the eggs on the spoons, and they may only use one hand to carry the spoons.)

4. When the competitors return to their lines, they must pass the spoons and eggs to the next people in the lines.

5. The play will continue until all of the members of one group finish.

Stations 7 and 8 Activity Card—Relays *(cont.)*

Relay #2:

1. Line up both groups so the groups face each other and are several yards apart.

2. Give the first person in each line a plastic egg.

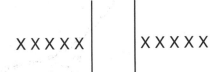

3. When you yell "Go!" the first people in the lines will pass the eggs over their heads to the students behind them.

4. The second students will then pass the eggs through their legs to the third people in the lines.

5. The play will continue in an over/under pattern until the last person in each line receives an egg. They will then run to the fronts of their lines and begin again.

6. When one of the original people who started the game returns to the head of his or her line, the relay is over and that team wins.

Alternate Activity 1—Cooking

Grape Eggs in Nests

Materials:

- grapes (3 or 4 per child)
- slivered almonds
- 1 lettuce leaf per child
- 2 small paper plates per child
- plastic forks or spoons
- Chinese noodles
- salad dressing (French works well)
- lemon pepper, if desired
- teaspoon

Directions: Give each child a small handful of Chinese noodles on a paper plate. Sprinkle 1 spoonful of almonds on top of the noodles. Pour enough salad dressing over the noodles to mix well and then let the children mold their mixtures into balls with their hands. Sprinkle the balls with lemon pepper if you wish. Lay a washed lettuce leaf on each child's second plate. Turn the noodle balls onto the lettuce leaves.

Tell the children to slightly flatten their noodle balls, and then they should each form a hole in the center to make a nest shape. Place several grapes in each nest.

Alternate Activity 2—Writing

Materials:

- paper
- crayons
- pencils
- egg shape books

Directions: Give each student a shape book. (Use the egg shape pattern on page 72 for a cover and add several pages in the same shape.) Write the rhyme on the right on a large piece of paper.

Ask the students to copy down the rhyme on a piece of paper. Tell them to fill in the blanks with words of their choice and then to illustrate their poems. This activity can also be done in shape books, or with younger children, you may wish to discuss the poem orally.

Eggs

Eggs and toast;
Eggs on a _____.
Egg in a cake.
Ready to _____.
Eggs on a wall;
Eggs down the _____.
Eggs in a pan;
Eggs on a _____.
Eggs in a dish;
Eggs on a _____.

Stationery

Incentives

Use the following cards for positive reinforcement during your rotations. When a student successfully demonstrates positive behavior and completion of his or her tasks, cut out an egg square and paste it on his or her chicken card. If you do not have time to cut and paste, a small egg or star sticker or stamp would work well. Distribute awards/name tags and bookmarks where appropriate.

Fill the hen's nest with eggs!

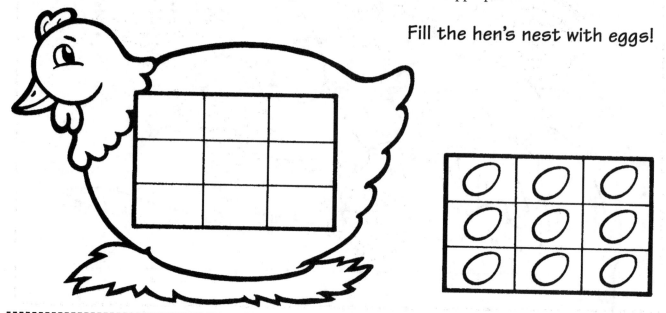

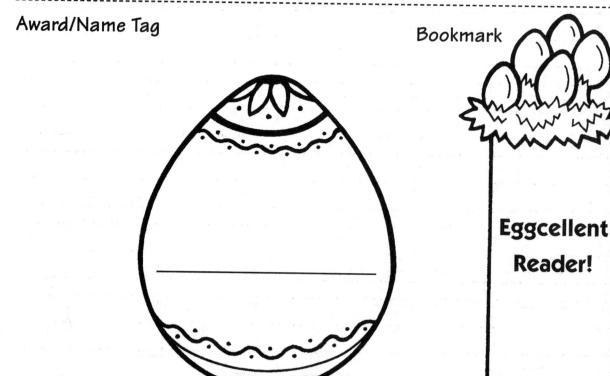

Award/Name Tag

Bookmark

Eggcellent Reader!

Five Senses

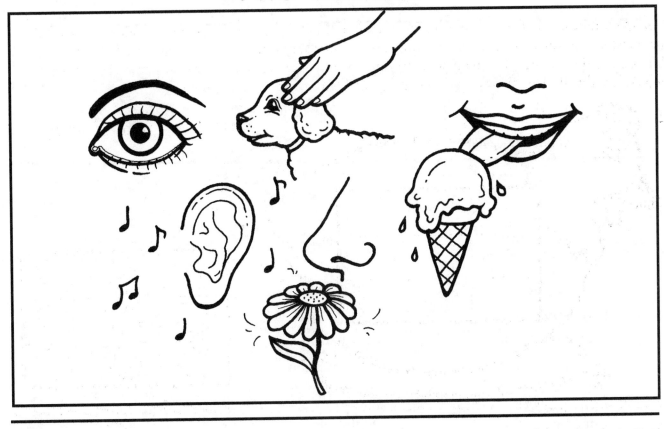

Teacher Note: Use this page as an introduction to the Five Senses theme. Have students color the picture. Lines are provided for writing activities of your choice.

Unit Materials

Bibliography

Aliki. *My Five Senses.* HarperCollins Children's Books, 1989.

Brown, Marc. *Arthur's Eyes.* Little, Brown, and Company, 1979.

Provide nonfiction books about smell, touch, taste, sight, and/or hearing.

Materials Checklist

Station 1—Literature

_____ literature selection
_____ pictures and/or real items as desired
_____ activity card

Station 2—Writing

_____ eye or hand shape books
_____ pencils
_____ crayons
_____ activity card
_____ sandpaper
_____ buttons
_____ foil
_____ cotton balls
_____ glue

Station 3—Finger Painting

_____ finger paint
_____ finger-paint paper
_____ black marker
_____ activity card

Station 4—Cooking

_____ large bowl
_____ paper cups
_____ juice

Any of the following:
_____ popcorn
_____ cereals
_____ banana chips
_____ candy coated chocolate pieces

_____ peanuts
_____ chocolate or carob chips
_____ raisins
_____ sunflower seeds
_____ coconut
_____ granola
_____ activity card

Station 5—Hearing Jars

_____ 14 film canisters with lids
_____ plastic tape
_____ marker
_____ dried beans
_____ dry rice
_____ nails or screws
_____ paper clips
_____ dry macaroni
_____ rocks or gravel
_____ pennies
_____ pencils
_____ answer key
_____ paper strips
_____ activity card

Station 6—Smelling Jars

_____ 14 film canisters
_____ blindfolds
_____ cotton balls
_____ perfume
_____ liquid soap
_____ toothpaste
_____ vinegar

_____ coconut
_____ cinnamon or cinnamon gum
_____ onion
_____ lemon juice
_____ grape gum
_____ watermelon gum
_____ peanut butter
_____ chocolate
_____ pickle juice
_____ activity card
_____ applesauce

Station 7—Venn Diagram

_____ two different flavors of jellybeans (enough that each student could try each flavor)
_____ blank Venn diagrams (one for each group)
_____ blindfolds
_____ marker
_____ activity card

Station 8—Trust Walk

_____ blindfolds
_____ activity card

Station 1 Activity Card—Literature

Materials:

- *My Five Senses*
- pictures and/or real items (see below)

Directions:

1. Read and discuss *My Five Senses.*

2. Have items such as the following available to continue the discussion:

   - a real flower
   - a plastic flower
   - a picture of a flower
   - real fruit
   - plastic fruit
   - a picture of a fruit

   Talk about how we use our senses to identify these items.

3. Show the students other items or pictures of items. Have them point to their eyes, noses, ears, tongues, or fingers, depending on which item or picture you show them.

Station 2 Activity Card—Writing

Materials:

- eye or hand shape books
- pencils
- crayons
- foil
- sandpaper
- cotton balls
- buttons
- glue

Option One

Directions: Give each student an eye shape book. (Use the pattern on page 86 for a cover and add several interior pages in the same shape.) At the bottom of each page tell them to write "I see _____." They may then go back and fill in the blanks with different items and illustrate the pages.

Option Two

Directions: Give each student a hand shape book. (Use the pattern on page 87 for a cover and add four interior pages in the same shape.) For the first page, tell students to glue a piece of foil and write "Smooth" at the bottom of the page. For the second page, tell them to glue a piece of sandpaper and label it "Rough." For the third page, give them cotton balls to glue on and label "Soft." For the last page, give the students buttons (or pebbles) to glue on and label "Hard."

Shape Book Patterns

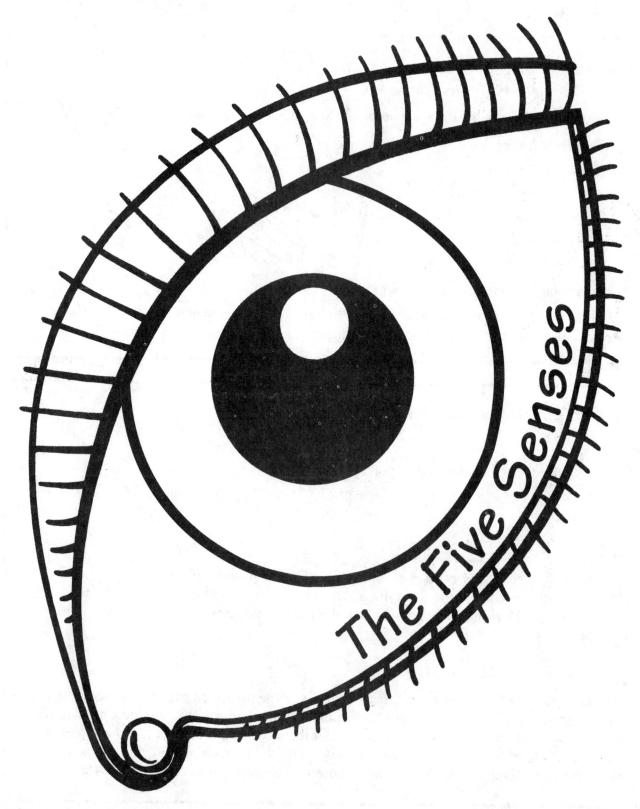

86

Shape Book Patterns (cont.)

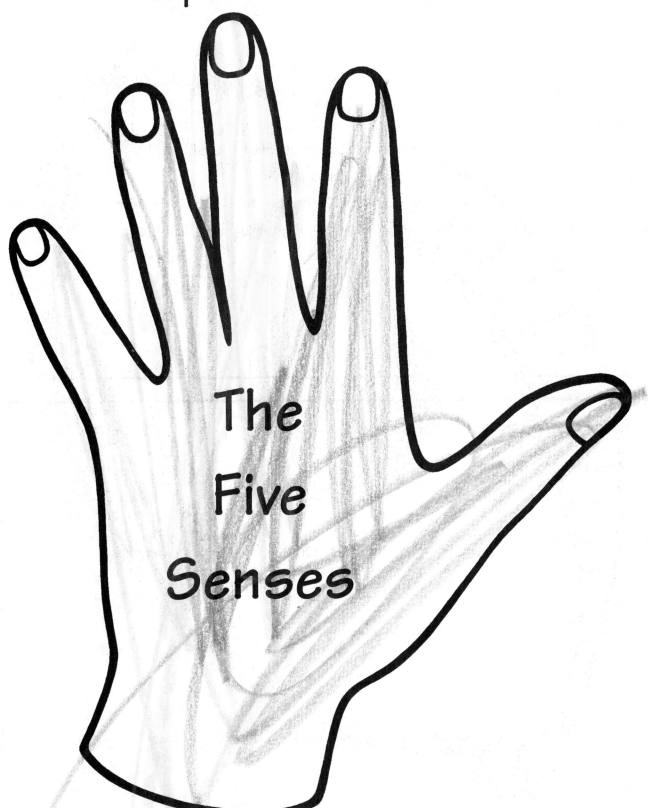

The
Five
Senses

Station 3 Activity Card—Finger Painting

Materials:

- finger paint
- finger-paint paper
- black marker

Directions:

1. Write each student's name on a piece of paper with black marker.

2. Let the students finger-paint for about 10 minutes.

3. Take them to the bathrooms to clean up in preparation for cooking, which is the next station.

4. If you still have extra time, discuss what it felt like to paint with their fingers.

Station 4 Activity Card—Cooking

Ingredients:

- popcorn
- cereal
- banana chips
- chocolate or carob chips
- peanuts
- candy-coated chocolate pieces
- raisins
- sunflower seeds
- coconut
- granola
- large bowl
- juice
- paper cups

Directions:

1. Begin with popcorn or cereal in a large bowl.

2. Add any of the other ingredients.

3. Pour the mixture into paper cups.

4. Serve with juice.

5. As the students eat their delicious snacks, discuss with them the taste, texture, sight, sound, and smell of what they are eating.

88

Station 5 Activity Card—Hearing Jars

Materials:

- dried beans
- 14 film canisters with lids
- nails or screws
- dry macaroni

- rocks or gravel
- pencils
- plastic tape
- dry rice

- paper clips
- pennies
- marker
- paper strips
- answer key (see next card)

To Be Done in Advance:

1. Label the canisters 1 through 14.
2. Put 5–6 dried beans into canisters #1 and #10. Put the lids on the cannisters and tape them shut.
3. Put a small spoonful of uncooked rice into canisters #2 and #7. Cover and tape.
4. Put three paper clips into canisters #3 and #12. Cover and tape.
5. Put three pennies into canisters #4 and #14. Cover and tape.
6. Put 3 or 4 small nails or screws into canisters #5 and #8. Cover and tape.
7. Put 4 or 5 pieces of uncooked macaroni into canisters #6 and #13. Cover and tape.
8. Put a small spoonful of gravel or three small rocks into canisters #9 and #11. Cover and tape.

Station 5 Activity Card—Hearing Jars *(cont.)*

Directions: Give the students pieces of paper and tell them to write their names down. Let the students rattle the canisters and try to match the ones with the same contents. When they think they have found matches, have them write the pair numbers. After all of the students in the group have matched the canisters, let them know the answers.

Answer Key

Match:

1 and 10	5 and 8
2 and 7	6 and 13
3 and 12	9 and 11
4 and 14	

Station 6 Activity Cards—Smelling Jars

Materials:

- blindfolds
- cotton balls
- liquid soap
- vinegar
- chocolate
- applesauce
- lemon juice

- onion
- coconut
- perfume
- toothpaste
- cinnamon or cinnamon gum

- pickle juice
- grape gum
- watermelon gum
- peanut butter
- film canisters (14)

To Be Done in Advance: Number the jars 1 through 14.

1. Spray or pour a liberal amount of perfume on a cotton ball. Place the cotton ball in canister #1.
2. Squirt a liberal amount of liquid soap on a cotton ball. Place the cotton ball in the bottom of canister #2.
3. Squeeze about 1 inch (2.54 cm) of toothpaste into the bottom of canister #3.
4. Chew a stick or two of cinnamon gum and place it in the bottom of canister #4.
5. Place a piece of onion in the bottom of canister #5.
6. Pour vinegar onto a cotton ball and place the cotton ball in the bottom of canister #6.

Station 6 Activity Cards—Smelling Jars (cont.)

7. Put a small spoonful of peanut butter into the bottom of canister #7.
8. Put several pieces of chocolate in the bottom of canister #8.
9. Pour pickle juice onto a cotton ball. Place the ball into the bottom of canister #9.
10. Put one small spoonful of applesauce into the bottom of canister #10.
11. Chew a stick of grape gum. Place it in the bottom of canister #11.
12. Pour lemon juice on a cotton ball. Place the ball in the bottom of canister #12.
13. Chew a stick or two of watermelon gum. Place it in the bottom of canister #13.
14. Place one small spoonful of flaked coconut into the bottom of canister #14.

Directions: Check all lids to be sure they are tightly closed. Divide the group into pairs. Blindfold one partner in each pair and let these students smell the first canister. When the first partner decides on the contents of the canister, have him or her tell partner number two who will then write it down. For example: #1—perfume. Then switch the blindfold to the second partner. Repeat the process with canister #2. Continue switching the blindfold back and forth until all of the pairs have had a chance to smell all of the canisters. Compare the partners' answers to the answer key.

Answer Key: 1. perfume, 2. liquid soap, 3. toothpaste, 4. cinnamon or cinnamon gum, 5. onion, 6. vinegar, 7. peanut butter, 8. chocolate, 9. pickle juice, 10. apples or applesauce, 11. grape gum, 12. lemon juice, 13. watermelon gum, 14. coconut.

Station 7 Activity Card—Venn Diagram

Materials:

- two different flavors of jellybeans (enough that each student could try each flavor)
- blank Venn diagrams (one for each group)
- blindfolds
- marker

To Be Done in Advance: For each group draw a large blank Venn diagram. Label the first circle "#1" and the second circle "#2." Label the overlapping section "Both."

Directions: Blindfold the students. Give them each a jelly bean of the same flavor and have them eat it. Then give them each a different flavor of jellybean to taste. Take off the blindfolds. Ask the students to guess what color the jellybeans were that they ate. Then ask them to identify the flavors they tasted. Show them the beans and ask if they tasted as the students imagined they would. Now, ask the students to consider which jellybeans they liked more. Explain how a Venn diagram works. Ask each student, one at a time, to write his or her name in the category they belongs in. If Marc likes jellybean number one, he would write his name in the first circle. Likewise, if Kelly enjoys jellybean number two, she would write her name in the second circle. However, if Anna likes both flavors just as much, she should write her name in the overlapping section.

Station 8 Activity Card—Trust Walk

Materials: blindfolds

Directions: Discuss with the students what it would be like to not be able to see. Emphasize the fact that people who lose their sight must learn to depend on their other senses more.

Take the group outside and divide them into partners (if there is an odd number of students, you can be someone's partner). Tell the sets of students to blindfold one partner. Explain that it will be the job of the other partner to gently guide and protect the blindfolded person; however, he or she should not interfere too much.

The students without sight should try to depend on their other senses as much as possible to get around. After awhile the partners should trade responsibilities. When everyone has had an opportunity to be blindfolded, discuss the experience. Be sensitive to the fact that some students may be very uncomfortable with this activity.

Stationery

Incentives

Use the following cards for positive reinforcement during your rotations. When a student successfully demonstrates positive behavior and completion of his or her tasks, cut out a candy square and paste it onto his or her mouth card. If you do not have time to cut and paste, a small candy or star sticker or stamp would work well. Distribute awards/name tags and bookmarks where appropriate.

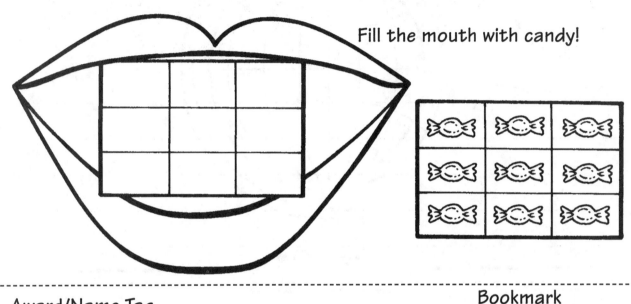

Fill the mouth with candy!

Award/Name Tag

Bookmark

See, Hear, and Feel Through Books!

Geography

Teacher Note: Use this page as an introduction to the Geography theme. Have the students color the picture. Lines are provided for writing activities of your choice.

Unit Materials

Bibliography

Dooley, Nora. *Everybody Cooks Rice.* Carolrhoda Books, 1992.

Provide children's maps, globes, and an atlas for use with this unit.

Materials Checklist

Station 1—Parts of a Map

_____ a children's atlas and maps
_____ white paper
_____ pencils
_____ markers
_____ crayons
_____ activity card

Station 2—United States Map

_____ United States map for each child
_____ crayons
_____ small star stickers
_____ activity card

Station 3—Cooking

_____ *Everybody Cooks Rice*
_____ globe or map
_____ instant white rice
_____ sugar
_____ butter
_____ milk
_____ raisins
_____ cinnamon
_____ bowls
_____ plastic spoons
_____ hot plate
_____ large spoon
_____ measuring cups
_____ saucepan with lid
_____ activity card

Station 4—Writing

_____ shape books
_____ pencils
_____ crayons
_____ activity card

Station 5—World Map

_____ world map
_____ small star stickers
_____ crayons
_____ pencils
_____ activity card

Station 6—Local Maps

_____ map of your city or state (one per group)
_____ markers
_____ activity card

Station 7—World Bingo

_____ group set of world Bingo cards
_____ place markers
_____ laminated cards for calling out
_____ activity card

Station 8—Make an Island

_____ crayons
_____ pencils
_____ island maps
_____ map keys
_____ activity card

Alternate Activities:

1. Locating Places on the Globe

_____ globe
_____ atlas
_____ activity card

2. Map Referencing

_____ blank map grids
_____ white paper
_____ pencils
_____ crayons
_____ activity card

Station 1 Activity Card—Parts of a Map

Materials:

- a children's atlas and maps
- white paper
- pencils
- markers
- crayons

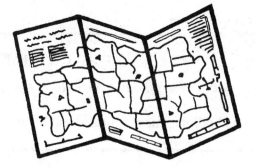

Directions:

1. With the students, examine the children's atlas and maps.

2. Discuss the parts of the maps, for example, the title, the key, symbols, and the compass rose.

3. Note geography terms such as land, water, rivers, mountains, lakes, cities, roads, airports, islands, countries, etc.

4. Allow each student to trace the map of his or her choice.

Station 2 Activity Card—United States Map

Materials:

- United States map for each child (page 97)
- crayons
- small star stickers

Directions: Tell the students to carefully listen to you read the following directions as they color their maps. With younger students, you may need to demonstrate each step on a map of your own as you go along.

1. Color the state you live in red.

2. Place a star sticker where your city is located on the map.

3. Color the states that border your state blue. Talk about these states with your group.

4. Color the rest of the United States green.

5. Label where Canada and Mexico would be located on the map.

After the students have followed all of your directions, take them to the restrooms to wash their hands to prepare for cooking at the next station.

Gg

United States Map

Station 3 Activity Card—Cooking

Sugared Rice

Materials:

- *Everybody Cooks Rice*
- sugar
- raisins
- plastic spoons
- measuring cups
- globe or map
- butter
- cinnamon
- hot plate
- saucepan with lid
- instant white rice
- milk
- bowls
- large spoon

Directions: Read *Everybody Cooks Rice* to the students. As you read, point out the places mentioned in the book on a map or a globe. Make sugared rice by following these directions.

1. Cook the rice according to directions on the package. Make about ½ cup (125 mL) of cooked rice per child.
2. Add your desired amount of butter or margarine.
3. Spoon into cups.
4. Add cinnamon and sugar to taste.
5. Add milk, as desired.
6. Sprinkle with raisins.
7. Enjoy!

Station 4 Activity Card—Writing

Materials: shape books, pencils, and crayons

Directions: Prepare a shape book for each student. Use the pattern on page 99 as a cover. Provide several sheets of paper cut in the same pattern shape. Then explain one of the three activities below to the students.

1. Ask the students to write a geography term on each page and then to illustrate the pages. Tell the older students to write a definition for each word also. Some possible entries are rivers, lakes, islands, mountains, deserts, continents, peninsulas, and forests.

2. Tell the students to write a word that starts with the letter "g" on each page. Then tell them to illustrate the pages.

3. Challenge the students to write words that begin with the letters "gl" and then illustrate the pages. Choose from the following examples, or use your own:

globe	glacier	glitter
glue	glad	glove
glow	glass	glide

Shape Book Pattern

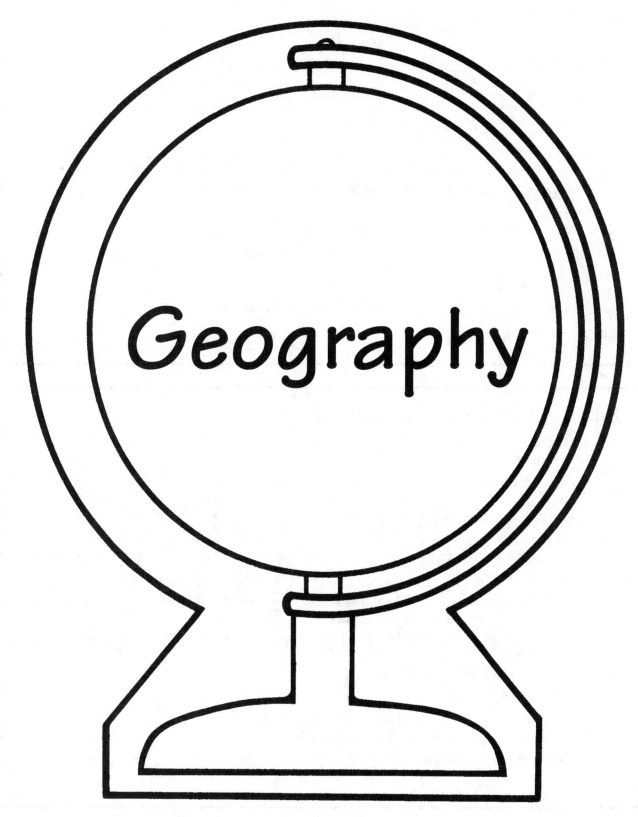

Geography

Station 5 Activity Card—World Map

The Continents

Materials:

- world map (page 101)
- crayons
- small star stickers
- pencils

Directions: Help the students find the following places on a map or globe. Then ask them to mark the locations on their individual maps according to your oral instructions.

1. Color North America blue.
2. Color South America red.
3. Color Africa green.
4. Color Europe yellow.
5. Color Asia purple.

6. Color Australia orange.
7. Write Antarctica where it belongs on the map.
8. Label the Atlantic Ocean.
9. Label the Pacific Ocean.
10. Put a star where you live.

Station 6 Activity Card—Local Maps

States or Cities

Materials:

- map of your city or state (one per group)
- markers

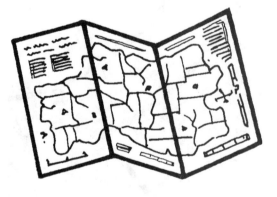

Directions:

1. Have the students find important landmarks or geographical regions, etc., on a city or state map. (If you have trouble finding a good city map, check with your local Chamber of Commerce. They often have simple, inexpensive ones.)

2. Look for airports, schools, hospitals, police and fire stations, shopping areas, tourist attractions, and the students' neighborhoods.

World Map

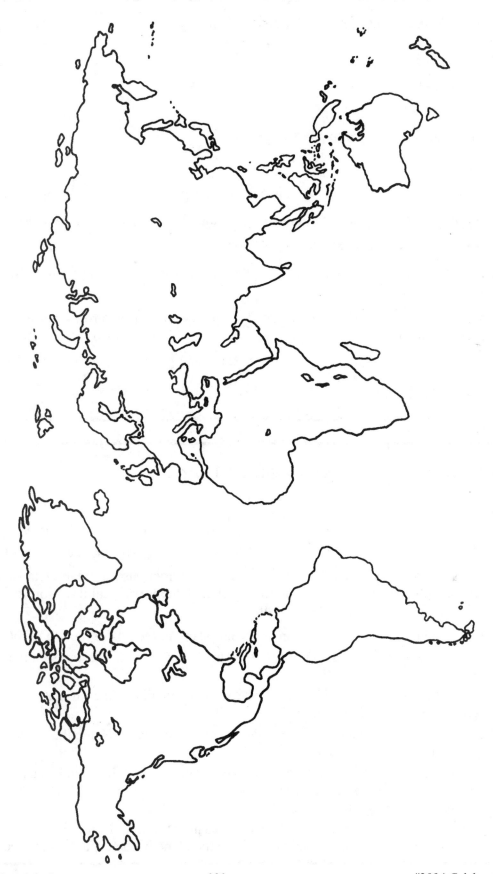

Station 7 Activity Card—World Bingo

Materials:

- group set of world Bingo cards (pages 104 and 105)
- place markers
- laminated cards for calling out (page 105)

Directions:

1. Make several copies of the continent cards (page 105) ahead of time and laminate them.
2. To play, give each student in the group a Bingo card and 20–25 place markers.
3. Shuffle the continent cards.
4. Call the cards out one at a time. Tell the students to place markers on the squares that show the continent they hear called.
5. Continue playing until someone has five squares covered in a row—vertically, horizontally, or diagonally.

Station 8 Activity Card—Make an Island

Materials:

- crayons
- pencils
- island maps (page 106)
- map key, one per student (page 107)

Directions: Slowly read to the students the following directions for creating an island. With younger students, you may need to carefully pick and choose several directions that may be at the appropriate level instead of doing all of them.

1. Name your island. Write the name of your island in the box at the top of the page.
2. In the small box, make a compass rose. This will show the directions on the map. North is up.
3. Name the water surrounding the island. Write the name on the lines at the left side of the island and again to the right.
4. A bay is a body of water that is partially enclosed by land. Name the island's bay. Write the name on the lines in the bay.
5. A peninsula is a long projection of land into water. Name the island's peninsula. Mark it with a black dot. On the key, place a black dot in the first box. Write "peninsula" (or give it a name) on the first line.
6. North of the bay, place a black star for the island's capital. Name the capital. On the key, place a black star in the second box. Write the name of the capital on the second line.

Station 8 Activity Card—Make an Island *(cont.)*

7. Just west of the peninsula, along the coast, make a yellow dot. This is another city. On the key, place a yellow dot in box 3. Name the city and write its name on the third line.

8. Down the center of the island, from north to south, make a blue wavy line. This represents a river. On the key, make a blue line in box 4. Name the river and write the name on line 4.

9. In the northeast corner of the island, draw several mountains in brown. On the key, make a brown mountain in box 5. Name the mountains and write the name on line 5.

10. West of the mountains, draw a blue lake. On the key, make a blue lake in box 6. Name the lake and write the name on line 6.

11. South of the lake, draw a small airplane symbol to represent an airport. On the key, place the symbol in box 7. Name the airport and write its name on line 7.

12. In the southwest corner of the island, draw several green trees to represent a forest. On the key, place a green tree in box 8. Name the forest and write its name on line 8.

Older students may add other features if the time permits. This activity can also be done on large sheets of butcher paper in cooperative groups.

Alternate Activity 1—Locating Places on the Globe

Materials: globe, atlas

Directions: Spend some time with the students looking for these locations. Also practice their alphabet skills by doing the search in the following order.

Amazon River	Nile River
Brazil	Oklahoma
Caribbean Sea	Puerto Rico
Denmark	Quebec, Canada
Egypt	Reykjavik, Iceland
Finland	Spain
Greenland	Tibet
Hawaiian Islands	United States of America
Italy	Vietnam
Japan	Wyoming
Kenya	Xiamen Island
Luxembourg	Yellow River
Mt. Everest	Zanzibar

World Bingo Cards

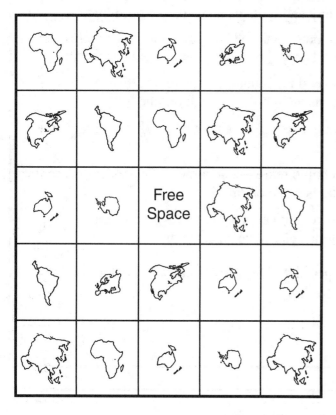

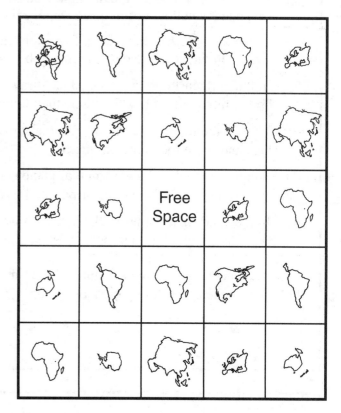

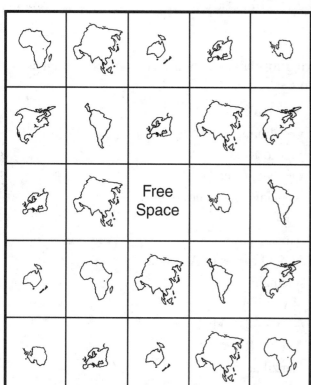

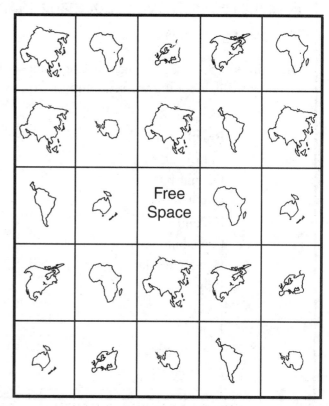

Geography

World Bingo Cards and Continent Cards

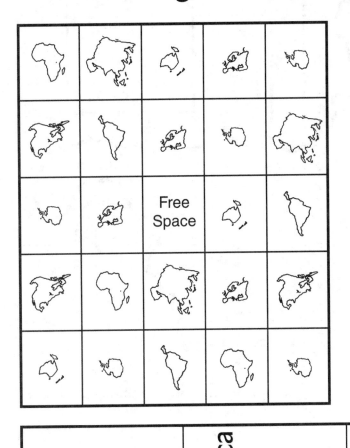

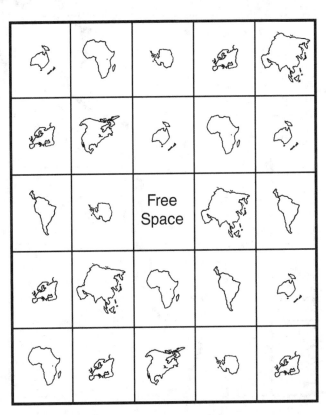

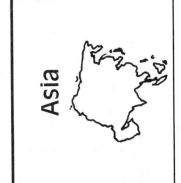 Asia / North America

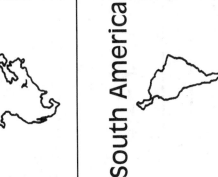 South America / Africa

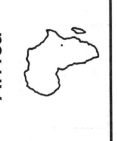 Antarctica / Europe / Australia

© Teacher Created Materials, Inc.   105   #2034 Celebrate ABC's

Island Map

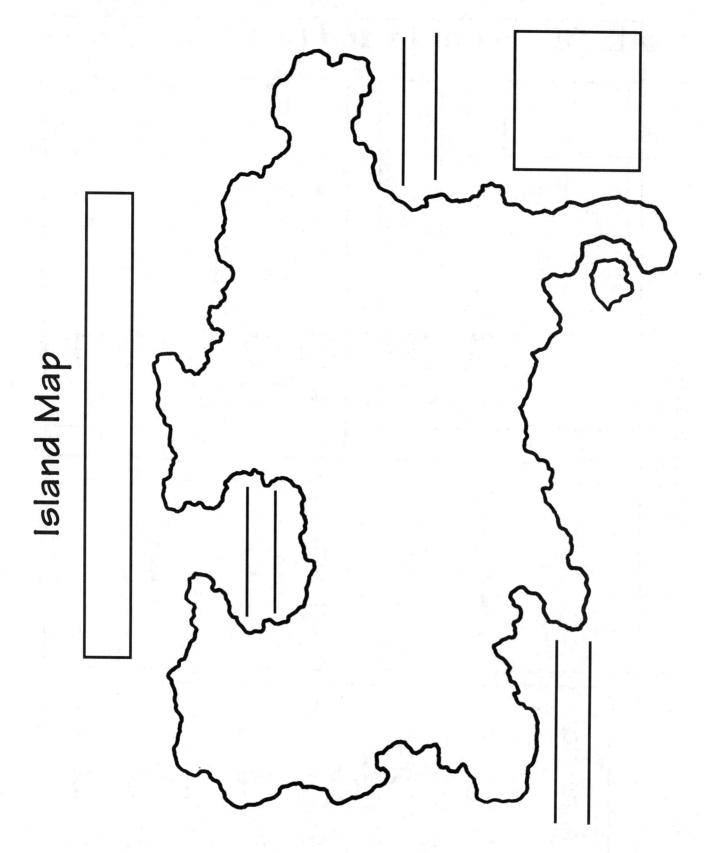

Map Keys

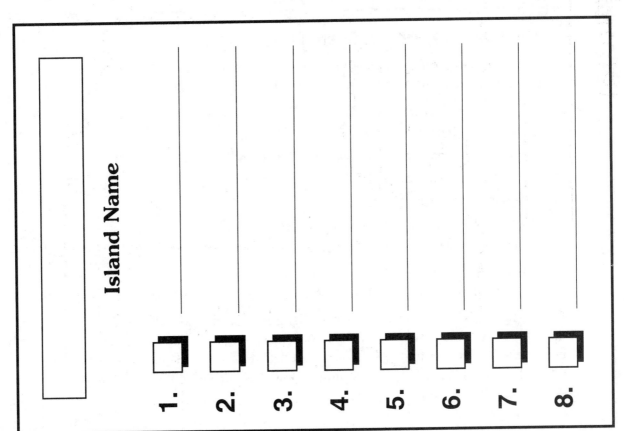

Island Name

1.
2.
3.
4.
5.
6.
7.
8.

Island Name

1.
2.
3.
4.
5.
6.
7.
8.

Alternate Activity 2—Map Referencing

Materials:

- white paper
- pencils
- blank map grids (page 109)
- crayons

Directions:

1. Give each student a blank sheet of white paper.

2. Slowly read the directions below out loud to the students. Do not let them share their work with each other. This is an exercise in listening and following directions. You may want to take them outside and spread them apart for this activity.

    a. Draw a red circle in the upper right corner of the paper.

    b. Draw a blue square in the middle of the paper.

    c. Draw a yellow star between the circle and the square.

    d. Draw two green triangles to the left of the square.

    e. Draw two purple wavy lines at the bottom of the paper.

    f. Draw an orange rectangle in the upper left corner of the paper.

    g. Draw a brown oval to the right of the purple lines.

    h. Draw a black "X" under the triangles.

3. Hold up the children's drawings to demonstrate how each child's picture differs.

4. Give each student a copy of the blank grid on page 109.

Alternate Activity 2—Map Referencing *(cont.)*

5. Help the students practice finding boxes by using the letter/number combinations. For example, have them put their fingers in box A1, A3, B2, C4, D1, and so on.

6. Slowly read the following directions.

    a. Draw a red circle in box A4.

    b. Draw a blue square where boxes B2, B3, C2, and C3 meet.

    c. Draw a yellow star in box B3.

    d. Draw two green triangles in box C2.

    e. Draw two purple wavy lines from box D3 to box D4.

    f. Draw an orange rectangle in box A1.

    g. Draw a brown oval in box D1.

    h. Draw a black "X" in box D2.

7. Collect the grids and compare these new pictures to each other. (**Note:** Do not compare these pictures to the first set. They are not supposed to look the same.) They will probably be more alike than the first set. Explain that a grid makes it easier to understand the directions. Maps and globes use a similar system of lines (longitude and latitude) to make places easier to locate.

Map Grid

	D			
C				
B				
A				
	1	**2**	**3**	**4**

Stationery

Incentives

Use the following cards for positive reinforcement during your rotations. When a student successfully demonstrates positive behavior and completion of his or her tasks, cut out a flag square and paste it onto his or her world map card. If you do not have time to cut and paste, a small star sticker or stamp would work well. Distribute awards/name tags and bookmarks where appropriate.

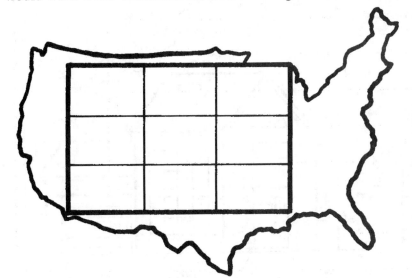

Fill in the country with flags.

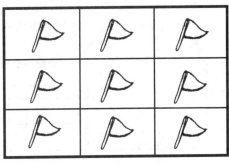

Award/Name Tag

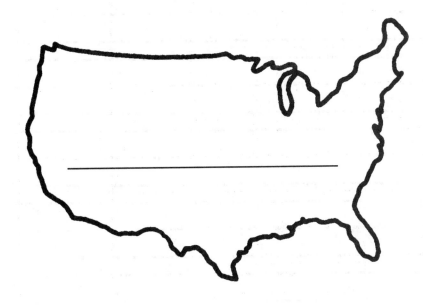

Bookmark

Houses

Teacher Note: Use this page as an introduction to the Houses theme. Have the students color the picture. Lines are provided for writing activities of your choice.

Unit Materials

Bibliography

Cutts, David. *The House That Jack Built.* Troll Books, 1979.

Dorros, Art. *This Is My House.* Scholastic, 1992.

Grifalconi, Ann. *The Village of Round and Square Houses.* Little, Brown, and Company, 1986.

Morris, Ann. *Houses and Homes.* Mulberry Books, 1994.

Spier, Peter. *People.* Doubleday, 1980.

Wood, Audrey. *The Napping House.* Harcourt Brace, 1984.

Materials Checklist

Station 1—Literature

_____ *The House That Jack Built*
_____ *The Napping House*
_____ paper
_____ crayons
_____ activity card

Station 2—Writing

_____ shape books
_____ pencils
_____ crayons
_____ activity card

Station 3—Painting

_____ blocks
_____ *This Is My House*
_____ painting paper
_____ paint
_____ brushes
_____ activity card

Station 4—Cooking

_____ bread
_____ turkey slices
_____ cheese slices
_____ rectangular crackers
_____ square crackers
_____ black olive slices
_____ paper plates
_____ mustard
_____ mayonnaise
_____ activity card

Station 5—Geometric Castles

_____ geometric patterns
_____ construction paper
_____ salt or sand
_____ glue
_____ scissors
_____ pencils
_____ markers
_____ toothpicks
_____ activity card

Station 6—Paper Bag Houses

_____ paper bags
_____ newspaper
_____ construction paper
_____ pencils
_____ markers
_____ scissors
_____ crayons
_____ glue
_____ stapler
_____ activity card

Station 7—House Graphs

_____ *The Village of Round and Square Houses*
_____ *People*
_____ graphs on butcher paper
_____ pictures of types of houses
_____ markers
_____ sticky notes
_____ activity card

Station 8—Word Problems

_____ scratch paper
_____ pencils
_____ houses from old Monopoly® sets or red and green construction paper houses
_____ activity card

Station 1 Activity Card—Literature

Materials:

- *The House That Jack Built*
- *The Napping House*
- paper
- crayons

Directions:

1. Read and compare *The House That Jack Built* and *The Napping House*. These books are two wonderful, rhyming, repetitive stories.

2. Give the children the opportunity to retell the stories through acting or discussion.

3. Finally, the children illustrate their favorite parts.

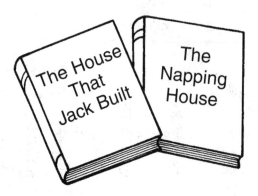

Station 2 Activity Card—Writing

Materials:

- shape books
- pencils
- crayons

Directions: Prepare a shape book for each student. Use the pattern on page 115 as a cover. Provide several sheets of paper cut in the same pattern shape. Choose one of the following activities for the group.

1. Ask the students to write a short story in their shape books beginning with, "If I could have any house I wanted, it would be . . ."

2. Write about a different type of house on each page and illustrate.

3. Write and illustrate "H" words.

4. Write and illustrate words with the "ou" sound.

Shape Book Pattern

Houses

Station 3 Activity Card—Painting

Materials:

- blocks
- *This Is My House*
- painting paper
- paint
- brushes

Directions:

1. Read *This Is My House* by Art Dorros.

2. Have the children paint their own houses on paper.

3. At the bottom of each painting, write "This is _____'s house." Tell the students to write their names in the blanks.

4. When they are dry, bind the books together for a class big book.

5. Take the children to the restrooms to wash their hands for the next activity, cooking.

Note: If you have extra time, let the children try to build houses similar to their own by using blocks.

Station 4 Activity Card—Cooking

Sandwich Houses

Materials (per child):

- 1 slice of bread
- 1 slice of turkey
- ¹/₂ slice of cheese (cut diagonally from a square to form a triangle)
- 1 rectangular cracker

- 1 small square cracker
- 1 slice of black olive
- mustard and mayonnaise in squeeze bottles
- paper plates

Directions: Give each child his or her materials. Demonstrate the following instructions for the children before they do this activity. For older students, write the instructions on a poster or sentence strips to read for themselves.

1. On a paper plate, "glue" the piece of turkey to the bread with mayonnaise. Set it towards the bottom of the plate.

2. "Glue" the cheese roof to the turkey along top edge with mustard.

3. "Glue" on a rectangular cracker for the door.

4. "Glue" on a square cracker for the window.

5. Add an olive for the doorknob.

Station 5 Activity Card—Geometric Castles

Materials:

- construction paper
- salt or sand
- scissors
- markers

- geometric patterns (page 118)
- glue
- pencils
- toothpicks

To Be Done in Advance: Make several copies, on thick paper, of the shape patterns provided. Cut out the patterns. These will be used for tracing in the activity. If you are working with younger students, use the pattern pieces to trace and cut out shapes from gray construction paper before the theme day. To save time, ask parents or older students to help in the cutting.

Directions: Show the students how to trace patterns of their choice onto gray construction paper. Explain that they will then glue the shapes onto construction paper to make castles. Then show the students how to glue salt or sand onto the castle bricks to make them shine. Then, let them add tiny banners or flags made from brightly colored construction paper and toothpicks. Finally, tell them to add doors and windows, as desired, with black or brown construction paper.

Station 6 Activity Card—Paper Bag Houses

Materials: lunch-sized paper bags, newspaper, construction paper, pencils, markers, scissors, crayons, glue, and a stapler

Directions:

1. Give each student a lunch-sized paper bag. Tell them to lay their bags flat and add doors and windows, as desired, using colored construction paper and glue.

2. Then, tell them to add flowers, curtains, and other details, using markers.

3. Have them turn over their bags and write their names on the folded bottom rectangles.

4. Next, show them how to refold the bottom side towards the decorated side of the bag to add features to the back of the house. Give them time to decorate the backs.

5. Stuff the sacks with crumpled newspaper, filling them about one-half to two-thirds full.

6. Tell the children to close their sacks by folding the tops down two or three times. Staple.

7. Ask the children to each cut out two triangular pieces of construction paper for the roofs. Staple the triangles, back to back, onto the fronts and backs of the bags.

Geometric Castle Patterns

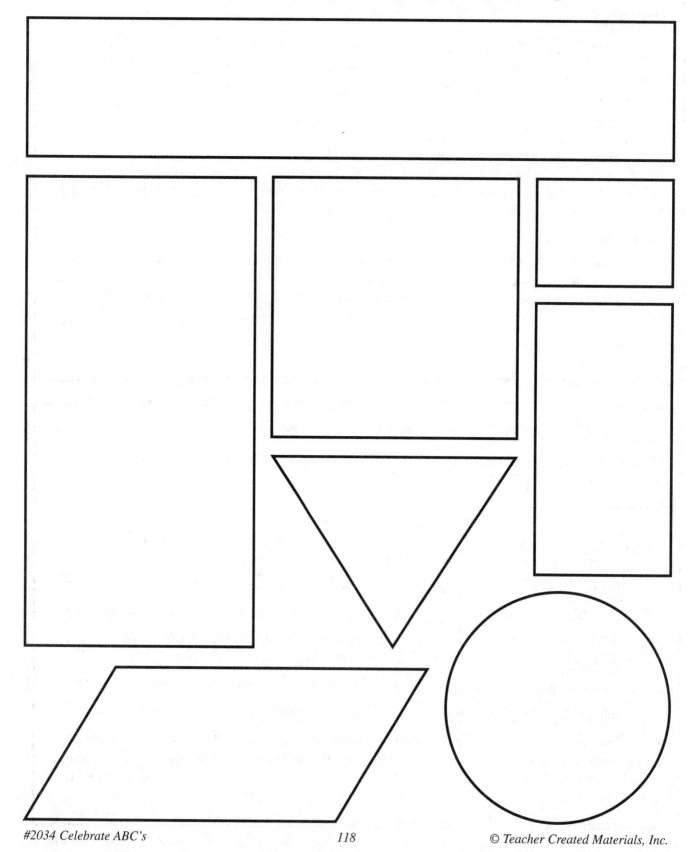

Station 7 Activity Card—House Graphs

Materials:

- *The Village of Round and Square Houses*
- *People*
- graphs on butcher paper
- pictures of types of houses
- markers
- sticky notes

To Be Done in Advance: Along the top of a piece of butcher paper, write the question, "What is your favorite type of house?" Directly under this question, list (going across) the types of houses you will be discussing with the students. Draw a column under each category.

Directions:

1. Read *The Village of Round and Square Houses*.
2. Talk about and show pictures of different types of houses. The book *People* has a section on houses around the world. Often, a children's atlas will too.
3. Ask each child what his or her favorite type of house is out of the ones you discussed. Give the children sticky notes to write their names on. Let them place their sticky notes on the butcher paper in the desired columns.

Station 8 Activity Card—Word Problems

Materials: scratch paper, pencils, and houses from old Monopoly® sets or red and green construction paper houses (see page 120 for patterns)

Directions:

Using the houses from an old Monopoly® set (or the house patterns provided), have the students do the following word problems:

1. Red houses are worth $10.00. Green houses are worth $5.00. You own 3 red houses and 2 green houses. How much are they worth all together? ($40.00)
2. You own 5 green houses and 5 red houses. How much are your houses worth all together? ($75.00)
3. Your friend owns 7 red houses. He sells two. How much are his remaining houses worth? ($50.00)
4. One red house is worth the same as two green houses. How many red houses would you need to equal 12 green ones? (6)
5. How many green houses would you need to equal 4 red ones? (8)

Throughout the time students are trying to find the answers, encourage their efforts. Guide them, but do not give them the answers. If these problems are too hard, make easier ones for the group or work through the problems with them. Give them plenty of time; they can usually figure out ways to solve these problems if they are given enough time to explore.

House Patterns

Stationery

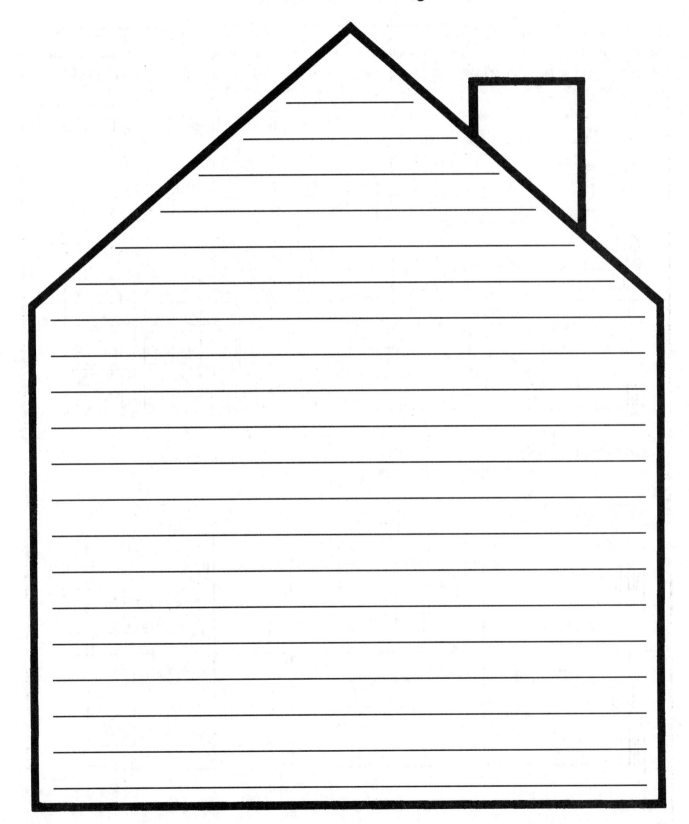

Incentives

Use the following cards for positive reinforcement during your rotations. When a student successfully demonstrates positive behavior and completion of his or her tasks, cut out a house square and paste it onto his or her neighborhood card. If you do not have time to cut and paste, a small star sticker or stamp works well. Distribute awards/name tags and bookmarks where appropriate.

Fill in the neighborhood with houses.

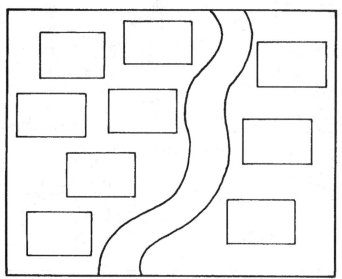

Award/Name Tag

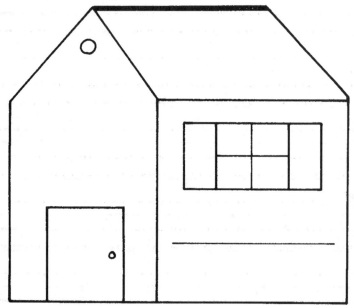

Bookmark

Feel at Home with a Book.

Insects

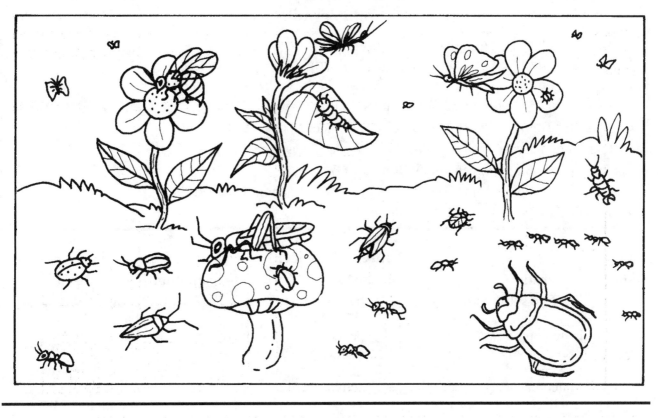

Teacher Note: Use this page as an introduction to the Insects theme. Have students color the picture. Lines are provided for writing activities of your choice.

Unit Materials

Bibliography

Bailey, Jill. *Life Cycle of a Bee.* Bookwright Press, 1990.

Bailey, Jill. *Life Cycle of a Grasshopper.* Bookwright Press, 1990.

Bailey, Jill. *Life Cycle of a Ladybug.* Bookwright Press, 1989.

Carle, Eric. *The Grouchy Ladybug.* HarperCollins, 1977.

Carle, Eric. *The Very Hungry Caterpillar.* Philomel Books, 1981.

deBourgoing, Pascale. *Ladybug and Other Insects.* Cartwheel Books, 1991.

Parker, Nancy. *Bugs.* Greenwillow Books, 1987.

Philpot, Loran and Graham. *Amazing Anthony Ant.* Random House, 1994.

Zoobooks: *Insects,* Volume #1 and Volume #2.

Materials Checklist

Station 1—Literature

_____ literature selections
_____ red ink pad
_____ damp paper towels
_____ black, fine-tip markers
_____ scratch paper
_____ pencils
_____ crayons
_____ activity card

Station 2—Music

_____ *Amazing Anthony Ant*
_____ activity card

Station 3—Cooking

_____ peanut-or finger-shaped cookies
_____ gumdrops
_____ string licorice
_____ small cinnamon candies
_____ icing in a tube
_____ activity card

Station 4—Writing

_____ beehive or butterfly shape books
_____ pencils
_____ colored pencils, markers, or crayons
_____ activity card

Station 5—Observation

_____ clear plastic cups
_____ aluminum foil
_____ craft sticks
_____ magnifying glasses
_____ paper
_____ pencils
_____ activity card

Station 6—Art

_____ newspaper
_____ paper towels
_____ butterfly pictures
_____ easel paper
_____ paint in small containers
_____ black markers
_____ black pipe cleaners
_____ brushes
_____ activity card

Station 7—Bug Racing

_____ enlarged racetrack on butcher paper
_____ magnets
_____ rulers
_____ racing bug patterns
_____ crayons
_____ scissors
_____ brass fasteners
_____ activity card

Station 8—Word Problems

_____ word problems
_____ plastic ants
_____ clear cups
_____ scratch paper
_____ insect stickers
_____ pencils
_____ activity card

Station 1 Activity Card—Literature

Materials:

- literature selections
- red ink pad
- damp paper towels
- black, fine-tip markers
- scratch paper
- pencils
- crayons

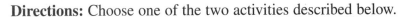

Directions: Choose one of the two activities described below.

1. Read *Bugs* and/or Zoobooks*: Insects* to the group. Discuss the parts of an insect. Ask the children to draw and label insects and the parts that they learned about.

2. Read *Ladybug and Other Insects* and/or *The Grouchy Ladybug* to the group. Help the students make thumbprint ladybugs. Demonstrate by gently pressing your thumb onto a red ink pad. Press your thumb onto a piece of paper to make a thumbprint. Wipe your thumb off on a damp paper towel. Use a marker to add the details to your ladybug. Finally, color in a background (perhaps grass, dirt, flowers) for your insect with crayons.

Station 2 Activity Card—Music

Materials:

- *Amazing Anthony Ant*

Directions:

1. Read *Amazing Anthony Ant* to the group. It is a charming little book that is great for small groups. The illustrations are wonderful.

2. This book follows "The Ants Go Marching" song. After you have finished reading the book, try doing it again except to the tune of "The Ants Go Marching." Also, try adding some hand motions.

3. Finish early so that you can take the students to the restrooms to wash their hands before moving on to the cooking station.

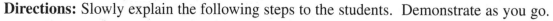

Station 3 Activity Card—Cooking

Ingredients (per child):

- 1 peanut-or finger-shaped sandwich cookie
- 3 gumdrops
- 9" (23 cm) length of string licorice
- 2 small cinnamon candies
- icing in a tube

Directions: Slowly explain the following steps to the students. Demonstrate as you go.

1. Carefully, break open a sandwich cookie so that you have two cookies, one plain and one with the filling attached. Add a little icing to the center of the cookie that has the filling on it.
2. Cut the string licorice into three equal strips. Place these strips so that six legs hang off the edge of the cookie.
3. Add more icing to cover the licorice. Place the other cookie back on top to again make a sandwich.
4. Add three icing dots to the top of the cookie. Put a gumdrop on each icing dot.
5. Add two small dots of icing to one end. Place a cinnamon candy on each dot to make eyes.
6. With the icing, make two small antennae on the gumdrop below the cinnamon candy eyes.

Station 4 Activity Card—Writing

Materials: beehive or butterfly shape books, pencils, colored pencils, markers, or crayons

Directions: Prepare shape books as described on previous cards. There are two different shape book patterns, a beehive and a butterfly. Choose one of the two shapes and then choose from the activities listed below.

1. **Beehive**

   a. Read *Life Cycle of the Bee* to the students. Have them draw and name each stage in their books.

   b. Write the following rhyme on a large piece of paper so that everyone in the group can see it. Ask the students to write one line on each page of their shape books and then illustrate.

   This is a beehive.
   Where are the bees?
   They're hiding away
   Where no one can see.

   Be still and watch,
   They'll come from the hive,
   Here they come now!
   One, two, three, four, five.
   Buzzzzzz!

2. **Butterfly**

   a. Read *The Very Hungry Caterpillar* to the group. Guide the students in drawing the stages in the life cycle of a butterfly in their shape books.

   b. Read *The Very Hungry Caterpillar* to the group. Ask the students to retell the story in their shape books, using their own words and illustrations.

Shape Book Patterns

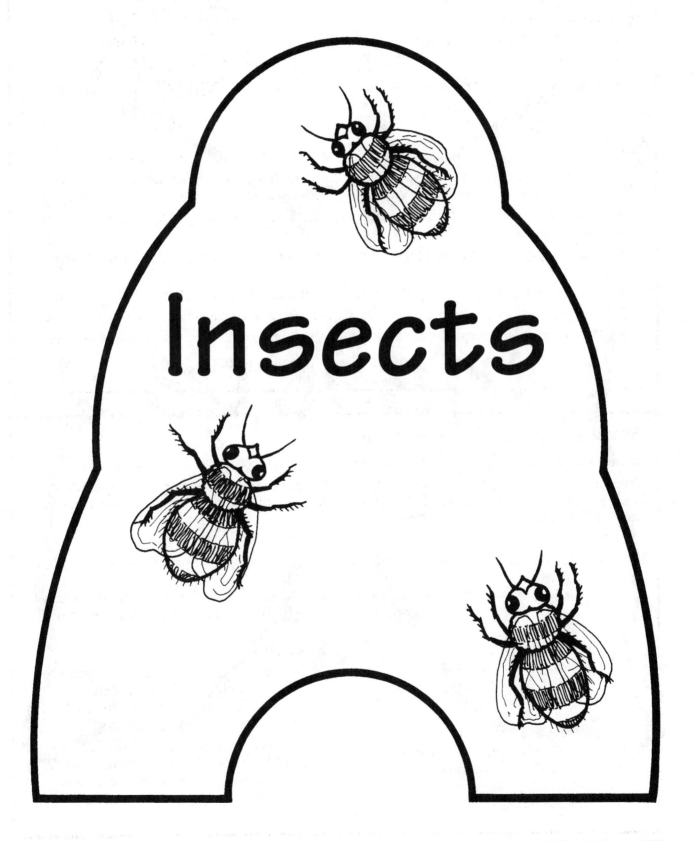

Shape Book Patterns *(cont.)*

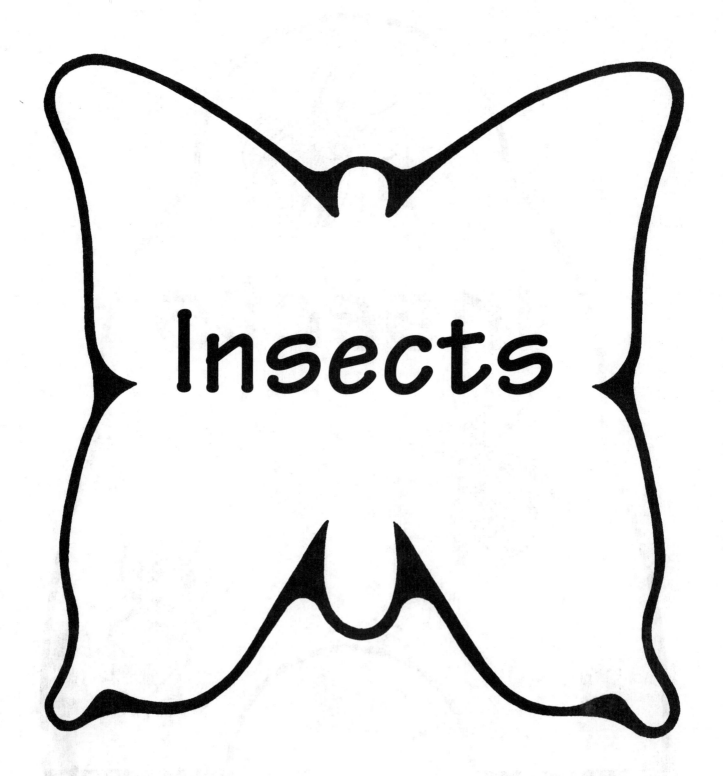

Station 5 Activity Card—Observation

Materials:
- clear plastic cups
- aluminum foil
- craft sticks
- magnifying glasses
- paper
- pencils

Directions:

1. Give each child a clear plastic cup with a lid made of foil. (If you keep the bugs longer than the 20-minute observation period, poke holes in the foil for air.)

2. Give each child a craft stick to transfer bugs to his or her cup. Take the students outside for a 10-minute bug collecting session.

3. Return to the classroom so that the students may observe their findings. Give each child a magnifying glass to look closely at the parts of the insects' bodies.

4. If there is enough time, let them illustrate their bugs on a sheet of paper. Then set the bugs free outside.

Station 6 Activity Card—Art

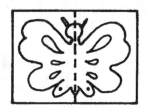

Painted Butterflies

Materials: newspaper, paper towels, butterfly pictures, easel paper, tempera paint in small containers, black markers, black pipe cleaners, and brushes

Directions: You will need at least two adults at this station. You may use easel paper or butcher paper with tempera paints. Set up the work area so that two students can share paint. Make sure the area is covered with newspaper and that you have paper towels ready for any messes which may arise. You may wish to do this project outside of the classroom on the sidewalk.

Show the students pictures of butterflies. Talk about how the pattern is the same on both wings. Tell them to each fold a piece of paper in half. Have each child paint a design on one half and then copy the design to the other half. (Or, paint a design on one half and then fold the paper and press the paint design to the other half.) Tell them to also paint a black strip down the center fold. Let the paint dry. Later, you or another helper can refold the papers and draw half butterflies, starting at the fold. Students will later cut along the outlines and then unfold their papers to find beautiful butterflies. If you add black pipe cleaners for antennae, they are perfect for hanging in the cafeteria or hall.

Station 7 Activity Card—Bug Racing

Materials: enlarged racetrack on butcher paper, magnets, rulers, racing bug patterns, crayons, scissors, and brass fasteners

To Be Done in Advance (See diagrams on page 133.)**:** Enlarge one of the racetrack patterns (pages 131 and 132) onto butcher paper. For the figure-eight track, the butcher paper should be at least 18 inches (45.7 cm) wide and 5 feet (1.5 m) long. Copy the figure-eight track onto the center of the paper to give plenty of room for two to four students to hold the ends of the paper and for one player to be placed on either side. The straight-lane track should run almost the length of the paper. It has two lanes.

Glue a magnet onto one end of each of the two rulers. Let them dry thoroughly. Make copies of the bug patterns (page 133) on white construction paper. Give one bug to each student. Students may color their bugs. Attach a brass fastener through the middle on each bug so that the round part is on the bottom side and the long pieces of brass look like antennae coming out the top of the bug.

Directions: Allow two students to race at a time while the other students hold the paper racetrack. Place two bugs on start. Give the students the chance to practice moving their bugs, using the magnetic rulers on the underside of the paper. Then begin conducting elimination tournaments.

Station 8 Activity Card—Word Problems

Materials:
- word problems (page 134)
- plastic ants
- insect stickers
- clear cups
- scratch paper
- pencils

Directions: Let the students use tiny plastic ants as manipulatives to solve the word problems. If plastic ants are not available, ask the students to draw ants to solve the problems.

Start by doing estimations with the group. Place different numbers of ants into four clear plastic cups. Ask the children to estimate (and write down) the number of ants in each cup. Count the ants in each cup together. Who was closest? Give the winners plastic ants or insect stickers.

Next, have the students solve the problems on page 134, using the manipulatives. Choose the problems that are the most age and skill appropriate for your group.

Page 134 Answers:

1. 9	3. 5	5. 14	7. 10	9. 38
2. 6	4. 4	6. 29	8. 25	10. a. 16
				b. yes

Racetrack Pattern #1

Finish | Start

Racetrack Pattern #2

Finish	**Finish**
Start	**Start**

Ii

Bug Patterns

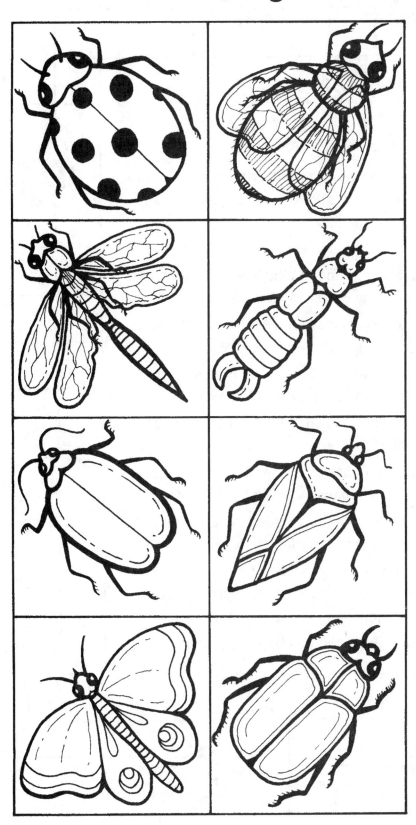

1. Glue magnets to the ends of two rulers.

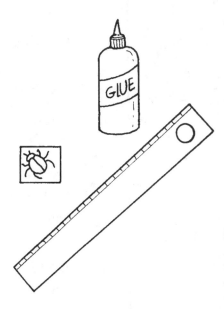

2. Attach a brass fastener through the middle of each bug.

3. Move the bugs around the racetrack, using the magnets.

Math Word Problems

Directions: Solve the following problems, using your ants.

1. 4 ants went marching down to town. They met up with 5 other ants. How many ants were marching all together?

2. 12 ants attended the Teddy Bears' picnic uninvited. Six were stepped on. How many were left?

3. 7 ants went searching for food in the forest. 2 stopped to sit on a log. How many were still searching for food?

4. 5 little red ants ran up John's leg! SMACK! 1 little red ant got away. How many did John "smack"?

5. 8 ants found Kevin's lunch. They invited 6 more to help eat it. How many ants in all ate Kevin's lunch?

6. 14 ants went marching to town. They met up with 15 others. How many ants were marching all together?

7. 33 ants attended the Teddy Bears' picnic uninvited. 27 were stepped on. How many were left?

8. 37 ants went searching for food in the forest. 12 stopped to sit on a log. How many were left searching?

9. 26 little red ants found Mari's lunch. They invited 12 more to help eat it. How many ants in all ate Mari's lunch?

10. a. If 1 ant could carry a 2-ounce marshmallow, how many ounces would 8 ants be able to carry?

   b. Could 16 ants carry a 32-ounce bag of marshmallows?

Stationery

Incentives

Use the following cards for positive reinforcement during your rotations. When a student successfully demonstrates positive behavior and completion of his or her tasks, cut out a bee square and paste it onto his or her beehive card. If you do not have time to cut and paste, an insect sticker or stamp would work well. Distribute awards/name tags and bookmarks where appropriate.

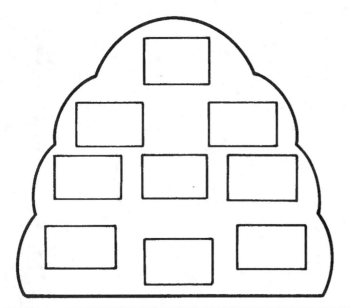

Fill the beehive with bees.

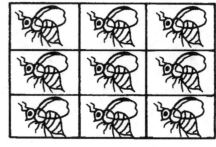

Award/Name Tag

Bookmark

Fly High with Books!

136

Jacks

Teacher Note: Use this page as an introduction to the Jacks theme. Have students color the picture. Lines are provided for writing activities of your choice.

Unit Materials

Bibliography

Aschenbrenner, Gerald (adapted by Joanne Fink). *Jack, the Seal, and the Sea.* Silver Burdett Press, 1988.

Cutts, David. *The House That Jack Built.* Troll Books, 1979.

Jack and the Beanstalk (any version).

Jack and Jill (any version).

Jack Sprat (any version).

Little Jack Horner (any version).

Other choices for this unit include any of Jack Prelutsky's poems.

Materials Checklist

Station 1—Literature

_____ *Jack and the Beanstalk*
_____ any Jack Prelutsky poems
_____ *Jack and Jill*
_____ *Little Jack Horner*
_____ *Jack Sprat*
_____ puppets for retelling
_____ activity card

Station 2—Reading and Games

_____ literature selections
_____ jacks
_____ jackstraws (pick-up-sticks)
_____ activity card

Station 3—Cooking

_____ flour tortillas
_____ butter knife
_____ butter or margarine
_____ hot plate
_____ paper plates
_____ skillet
_____ Monterey Jack cheese
_____ cheese grater
_____ spatula
_____ activity card

Station 4—Word Problems

_____ jacks or beans for manipulatives
_____ pencils or crayons
_____ scratch paper
_____ activity card

Station 5—Planting Beans

_____ milk cartons (saved from the cafeteria)
_____ potting soil
_____ rulers
_____ scissors
_____ masking tape
_____ beans
_____ permanent black markers
_____ paper towels
_____ newspapers
_____ activity card

Station 6—Writing

_____ pencils
_____ shape books
_____ crayons, markers, or colored pencils
_____ activity card

Station 7—Painting with Jacks

_____ 3–4 small flat boxes
_____ paint
_____ small paper plates
_____ jacks
_____ paper towels
_____ construction paper
_____ dish soap
_____ baby wipes
_____ activity card

Station 8—Puppets

_____ paper bag puppets
_____ patterns
_____ scissors
_____ glue
_____ crayons
_____ paper bags
_____ stick puppets
_____ markers
_____ craft sticks
_____ activity card

Station 1 Activity Card—Literature

Materials:
- *Jack and the Beanstalk*
- any Jack Prelutsky poems
- *Jack and Jill*
- *Little Jack Horner*
- *Jack Sprat*
- puppets (made ahead of time from the patterns on pages 140–146)

Directions: Choose any one of the following three activities to do at this station.

1. Read any version of *Jack and the Beanstalk.* Ask the students to retell the story, using paper bag puppets, stick puppets, or flannelboard cutouts. Use the patterns provided for the version you like. The stick puppet patterns can also be used as flannelboard figure patterns.

2. Read some poems by Jack Prelutsky. Ask the students to illustrate their favorites.

3. Read and act out nursery rhymes with Jack in them. Have some of the following props available:

    Jack and Jill—pail

    Little Jack Horner—pie pan and plum

    Jack Sprat—plates and utensils

Station 2 Activity Card—Reading and Games

Materials:
- literature selections
- jacks
- jackstraws (pick-up-sticks)

Directions: Give the children the opportunity to choose their own activities at this station. Supply Jack-related books that they may read to each other or examine on their own. Or, if some students would rather play games, teach them how to play jacks or jackstraws (pick-up-sticks).

Use the last five minutes of activity time to take the children to the restrooms to wash their hands for the next activity, cooking.

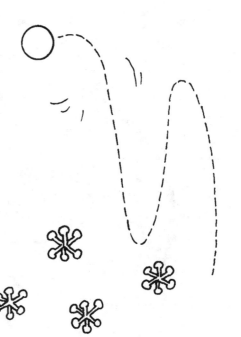

         #2034 Celebrate ABC's

Paper Bag Puppet Patterns

To make paper bag puppets, simply cut out and color the faces on pages 140–142 and glue them to the bottoms of lunch-sized paper bags. (**Note:** Use a grocery-sized paper bag for the giant's face.)

140

Paper Bag Puppet Patterns *(cont.)*

Paper Bag Puppet Patterns *(cont.)*

Stick Puppet Patterns

To make stick puppets, simply cut out and color the patterns on pages 143 and 144 and glue them onto craft sticks. (**Note:** Tape the giant's pattern onto a ruler instead.)

Stick Puppet Patterns *(cont.)*

Overhead Transparency and Flannelboard Patterns

To use the patterns on pages 145 and 146 with an overhead projector, carefully cut out the shapes and then project. To create flannelboard characters, cut out the patterns and trace them onto felt. Cut out the felt figures.

Overhead Transparency and Flannelboard Patterns *(cont.)*

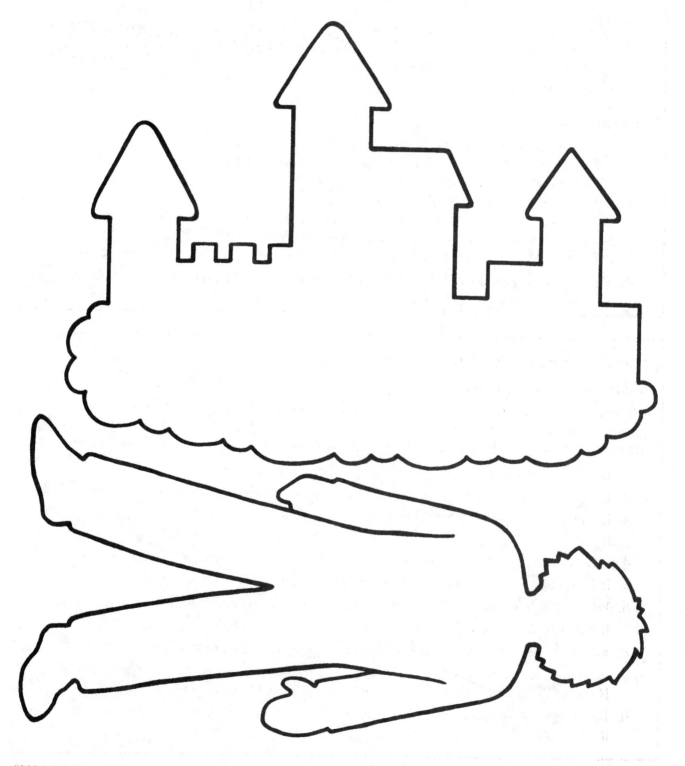

Station 3 Activity Card—Cooking

Jack Quesadillas

Materials:

- flour tortillas
- butter knife
- spatula
- butter or margarine
- cheese grater

- Monterey Jack cheese
- skillet
- hot plate
- paper plates

Directions:

1. Grate the Jack cheese or slice it into thin strips for the students.
2. Let the children butter the tortillas on one side with butter knives.
3. Place the tortillas (butter side down) into a heated skillet.
4. Put cheese on one half of each of the tortillas.
5. Fold the tortillas so that the halves with no cheese cover the halves that have cheese.
6. Fry the quesadillas until the tortillas are lightly browned and the cheese melts.
7. Remove the quesadillas from the heat. Cut them into halves or thirds and serve.

Note: As an alternative to using a hot skillet, quesadillas can also be prepared without oil, using a microwave or conventional oven.

Station 4 Activity Card—Word Problems

Materials: jacks or beans for manipulatives, pencils or crayons, scratch paper

Directions: Let the children use jacks or beans for manipulatives in solving the following problems. Also, have scratch paper and pencils available for drawing the problems. The problems get progressively more difficult, so choose which ones are the most appropriate for the group.

1. Jack had 4 beans. He found 5 more. How many does he have now? (9)
2. Jack had 6 beans. Then he lost 4 beans. How many does he have left? (2)
3. If Jack had 12 beans and his mother threw 11 out the window, how many would Jack have left? (1)
4. If Jack traded his cow for 5 beans, how many beans would he need to get 2 cows? (10)
5. If Jack's hen lays 3 golden eggs each day, how many eggs will he have in 3 days? (9)
6. Jack has 6 golden eggs. His hen lays 5 more. How many eggs does he have now? (11)
7. If Jack had 27 beans and he found 28 more, how many would he have in all? (55)
8. Jack had 43 beans. Then he lost 17 of them. How many does he have left? (26)
9. Each day Jack's hen lays 4 eggs. He gives one to his mother. He uses one to buy clothes. He saves the others. After a week, how many eggs has he saved? (14)
10. Jack's hen lays 4 eggs a day. If Jack needs 56 eggs to buy a new farm, how many weeks will it take? (2)

Station 5 Activity Card—Planting Beans

Materials:

- potting soil
- rulers
- masking tape
- permanent black markers
- newspapers
- milk cartons (from the cafeteria)
- scissors
- beans
- paper towels

To Be Done in Advance: Wash the cartons and dry them with paper towels. Make a line around the carton where it tapers to close. Cut off the top with scissors. Finally, put a strip of masking tape on the front of each carton. Write a child's name (or let them) on each carton with permanent marker.

Directions:

1. Let the students fill the cartons approximately ⅔ high with potting soil.
2. Tell them to each insert one finger (up to the first knuckle) to make a hole in the soil.
3. Allow them to plant two beans in each hole.
4. Ask the students to cover the beans with a little bit of soil and then water.
5. Set the cartons in a sunny place. Keep the soil moist.

Station 6 Activity Card—Writing

Materials: pencils, shape books, and crayons, markers, or colored pencils

Directions: Prepare shape books (see pattern on page 148) as described on previous shape books activity cards. Choose one of the three following writing activities to do with the shape books.

1. Ask the students to write about and illustrate different kinds of jacks (Jacks):

Jack and the Beanstalk	*Jack and Jill*
Little Jack Horner	Jack cheese
jack-in-the-box	jackstraws
jacks	Cracker Jacks®

2. Have the students write about and illustrate a "J" word on each page.
3. Challenge the students to write about and illustrate words that have the "ck" sound in them.

jack	jacket	nickel	buckle	neck
quack	duck	rock	truck	trick
tack	clock	sock	lucky	pick
back	block	sack	sick	pickle
black	lock	track	brick	tickle

Shape Book Pattern

Jacks

Station 7 Activity Card—Painting with Jacks

Materials:

- 3 or 4 small flat boxes, large enough to hold a 9" x 12" (22.8 x 30.4 cm) piece of construction paper
- paint
- small paper plates
- jacks (2 or 3 for each color of paint)
- paper towels
- construction paper
- dish soap
- baby wipes

To Be Done in Advance: Cover the work area with newspaper. Choose six to eight colors of paint. Put the paints on separate small plates for each color. Mix a little dish soap into each paint. Put two to three jacks in each color. Write a child's name in pencil on each piece of paper. Place each paper, name side down, in a shallow box.

Directions: Let the children carefully roll the jacks in the paint. Using their hands, they can pick up the jacks and put them on their papers. The students should then shake their boxes carefully to roll the jacks (and paint) around in the boxes. Ask them to remove the jacks but to be careful to put them back on the correct paint plates. Repeat the process with the other colors. Remove the papers and let them dry. Wash up before the next station. (Wet wipes are great if you do not have water in your classroom.)

Station 8 Activity Card—Puppets

Materials:

- paper bag puppets
- patterns
- scissors
- glue
- crayons
- paper bags
- stick puppets
- patterns
- scissors
- glue
- markers
- craft sticks

Directions: Using the patterns provided on pages 140–146, let the children make their own puppets for the *Jack and the Beanstalk* story. You may choose to make either paper bag puppets or stick puppets. (All of the puppets will require copying the patterns onto construction paper ahead of time.)

After students create the puppets, give them a couple of minutes to practice the story and then the chance to perform it.

Stationery

Incentives

Use the following cards for positive reinforcement during your rotations. When a student successfully demonstrates positive behavior and completion of his or her tasks, cut out a jack square and paste it onto his or her bag card. If you do not have time to cut and paste, a star sticker or stamp would work well. Distribute awards/name tags and bookmarks where appropriate.

Fill the bag with jacks!

Award/Name Tag

Bookmark

Reach for the Sky . . . Read!

Kites

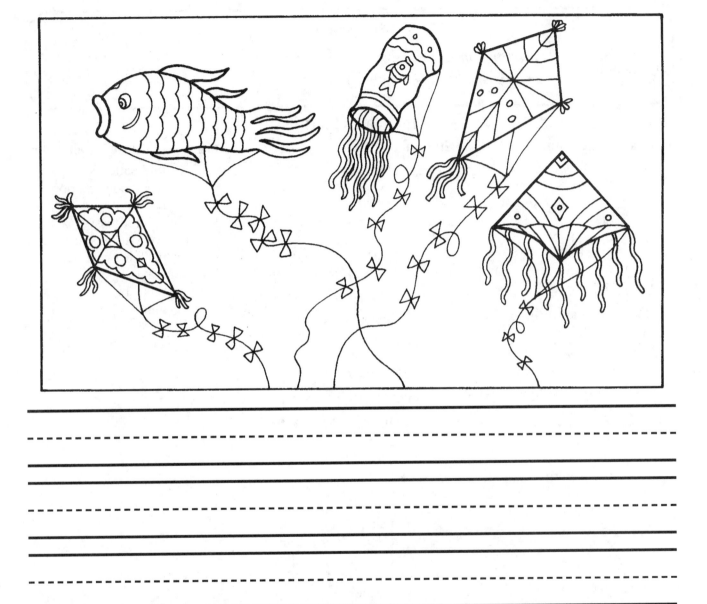

Teacher Note: Use this page as an introduction to the Kites theme. Have the students color the picture.
Lines are provided for writing activities of your choice.

Unit Materials

Bibliography

Mayer, Susan. *The Usborne Book of Kites.* Usborne Publishing, 1992.

Yolen, Jane. *The Emperor and the Kite.* Philomel Books, 1992.

Materials Checklist

Station 1—Literature

_____ *The Emperor and the Kite*
_____ 4 or more types of kites
_____ graph paper
_____ markers
_____ sticky notes
_____ activity card

Station 2—Creating Blob Kites

_____ *The Usborne Book of Kites*
_____ construction paper
_____ paint
_____ craft sticks
_____ straws
_____ scissors
_____ kite pattern
_____ yarn
_____ activity card
_____ tissue paper
_____ ruler
_____ wallpaper samples

Station 3—Cooking

_____ bread
_____ mayonnaise in a squeeze bottle
_____ mustard in a squeeze bottle
_____ cheese slices
_____ carrot sticks
_____ bow macaroni
_____ plates
_____ plastic knives
_____ paper plates
_____ activity card

Station 4—Math

_____ premade kites with bows
_____ paper
_____ pencils
_____ hole punch
_____ yarn
_____ activity card

Station 5—Writing

_____ shape books
_____ pencils
_____ crayons
_____ activity card

Station 6—Art

_____ white construction paper
_____ masking tape
_____ pencils
_____ crayons
_____ scissors
_____ paper strips
_____ crepe-paper streamers (red, orange, yellow, green, blue, and purple)
_____ activity card

Station 7—Class Big Book

_____ newspapers
_____ paint in containers
_____ brushes
_____ easel paper
_____ pencils
_____ markers
_____ activity card

Station 8—Tissue Paper Kites

_____ kite patterns
_____ black construction paper
_____ colored tissue paper
_____ colorful pipe cleaners
_____ pencils or white crayons
_____ scissors
_____ glue
_____ stapler
_____ activity card

Station 1 Activity Card—Literature

Materials:

- *The Emperor and the Kite*
- graph
- sticky notes
- 4 or more types of kites
- markers

To Be Done in Advance: On a large piece of butcher paper draw an empty graph. Draw a column for each type of kite you plan to share. At the bottom of each column, write the name or draw a simple sketch of one of the kites. At the top of the graph write the title "What Is Your Favorite Kite?"

Directions:

1. Read *The Emperor and the Kite*, or another book involving kites, to the students and discuss.

2. Share different types of kites with the students.

3. Give each child a sticky note and have him or her write his or her name on it. Ask the children to each pick a single type of kite as a favorite. Have them place their sticky notes on the graph.

4. Discuss the results.

Station 2 Activity Card—Creating Blob Kites

Materials: *The Usborne Book of Kites*, construction paper, paint, craft sticks, straws, scissors, kite pattern, wallpaper samples, ruler, yarn, tissue paper

To Be Done in Advance: Cut a large diamond shape out of construction paper for each student. Lay newspaper down around the painting area to keep surfaces clean.

Directions: Share *The Usborne Book of Kites* with the children. Give each child a diamond-shaped piece of paper. Tell the group members to dab craft sticks into one paint color at a time and drizzle the paint onto their papers. Limit each child to using three different colors of paint. Next, demonstrate how to blow through a straw at the paint to make it spread across the paper. Have the students try this and then let the paint dry. You can add tails later and hang them in the room. Throw away all of the straws after only one use so as not to spread germs.

Take the students to the restrooms to wash their hands in preparation for cooking, which is the next station.

Station 3 Activity Card—Cooking

Kite Sandwiches

Materials: bread, mayonnaise in a squeeze bottle, mustard in a squeeze bottle, cheese slices, carrot sticks, bow macaroni, plates, plastic knives, paper plates

To Be Done in Advance: Cook the bow-shaped macaroni by following the directions on the bag (or box). While the pasta is warm, butter it and roll it in Parmesan cheese, if desired. Refrigerate. Make one long carrot stick for each child.

Directions: Write the following directions on sentence strips or a poster so that older children can read the directions themselves and you can read the directions to younger children.

1. Place the bread on the plate to form a diamond.
2. Lightly apply mayonnaise.
3. Place the cheese on the bread.
4. Make a mayo stripe across the diamond.
5. Make a mustard stripe down the diamond.
6. Add a carrot tail.
7. Add bow ties to the tail.
8. Eat it right up!

Station 4 Activity Card—Math

Match the Number Sentences

Materials:

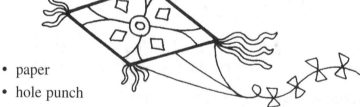

- premade kites with bows
- pencils
- yarn
- paper
- hole punch

To Be Done in Advance: Use the pattern on page 157 to make ten kites. The kites can be made out of construction paper (laminated), tagboard, or wallpaper samples. Make tails out of foot (30.4 cm) long pieces of yarn. Staple the yarn pieces onto the finished kite diamonds or punch holes in the bottom ends of the diamonds and connect the tails by tying them on. Before the bows are laminated, put a number sentence on each one. You should have three to four sentences (bows) for each number kite.

Directions: Help the students work as a group to match the correct bows to kites. Have scratch paper available for working out the problems.

To make this activity harder, you can make extra bows that do not correspond with any of the kites.

To make this activity a game, divide the class in half. Race to see who finishes his or her kite first.

Kite Patterns

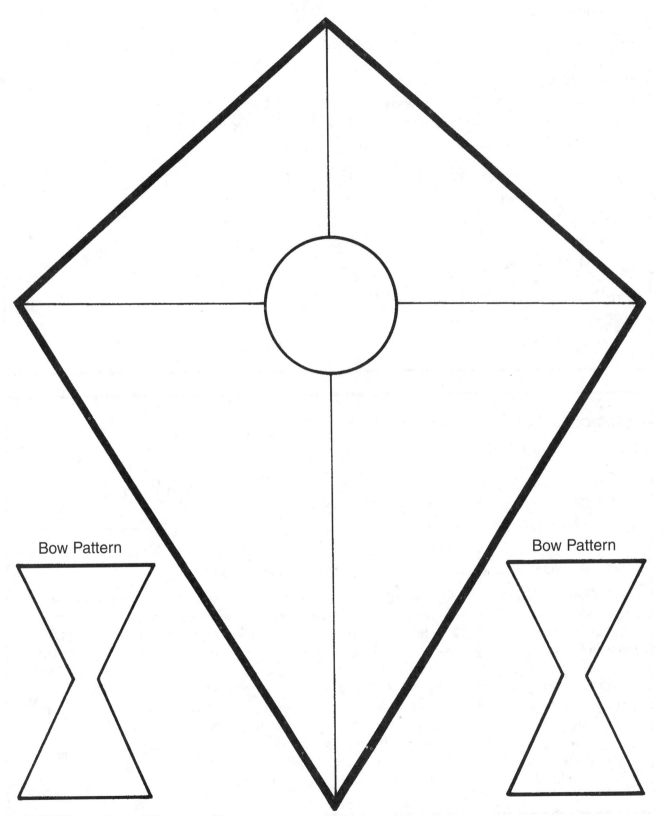

Bow Pattern

Bow Pattern

Station 5 Activity Card—Writing

Materials:

- shape books
- pencils
- crayons

Directions: Prepare shape books (see pattern on page 159) as described on previous shape book activity cards. Give each student a shape book. Ask the students to write about and illustrate one of the following:

1. "If I were a kite, I would fly to . . . ."
2. Words that begin with "K."
3. "Long i" words or words that rhyme with "kite."

bite	night	white	tight	might
fight	right	light	write	sight

(Emphasize "-ite" and "-ight" endings.)

Station 6 Activity Card—Art

Rainbow Hand Kites

Materials:

- paper strips
- masking tape
- crayons
- crepe-paper streamers (red, yellow, orange, green, blue, and purple)
- white construction paper
- pencils
- scissors

To Be Done in Advance: Cut out a large diamond shape for each student from white construction paper. Also, cut out a hand strip for each student from construction paper. These strips should measure approximately 3" x 7" (7.6 x 17.7 cm). Cut strips of crepe-paper streamers in 2 feet (60.9 cm) long pieces of each color for each student.

Directions: Give each child a construction paper diamond and tell him or her to color it completely with a rainbow pattern on it. Tape the hand strips on the backs of the kites while the students are cutting paper streamers in half lengthwise. (Younger children will need help at this step to speed up the process.) Tape the streamers to the bottom of the hand kite so that they stream from the matching colors on the kite body. Show the children how to put their hands through the hand strips to fly the kites. Watch the pretty streamers!

Shape Book Pattern

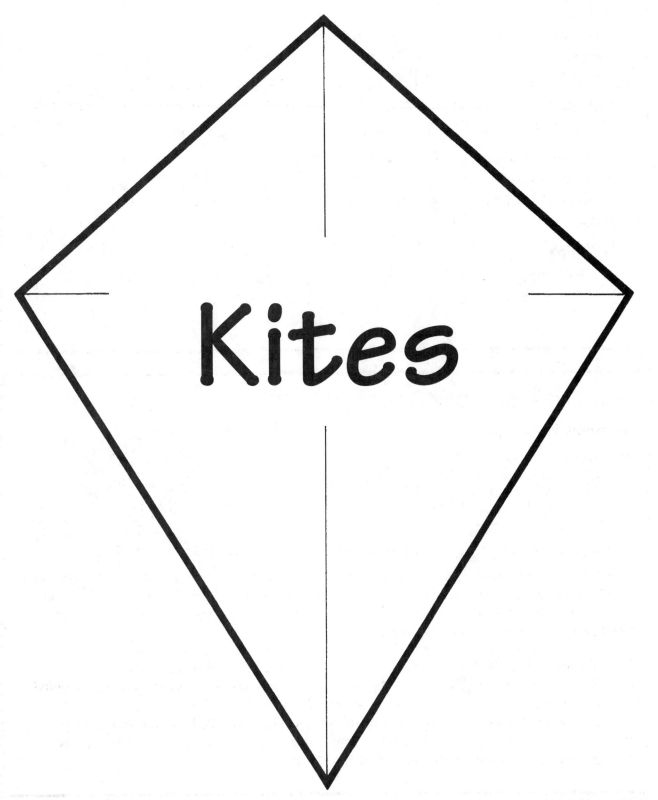

Kites

Station 7 Activity Card—Class Big Book

What Do You See?

Materials:

- paint in containers
- brushes
- pencils
- newspapers (to cover painting area)
- easel paper
- markers

Directions:

1. At the bottom of the easel paper, ask the students to complete this prompt:

   Flying high, flying high

   What do I see?

   I see a _____ looking at me.

2. Have students in the group read back what they wrote.

3. Challenge the students to paint pictures of what they wrote.

4. After all of the paintings have dried, compile them into a big book titled "Flying High, Flying High, What Do I See?"

Station 8 Activity Card—Tissue Paper Kite

Materials:

- kite patterns
- black construction paper (two 9" x 12" / 22.8 x 30.4 cm sheets and a tail strip per child)
- colored tissue paper
- colorful pipe cleaners (3 per child)
- pencils or white crayons
- scissors
- glue
- stapler

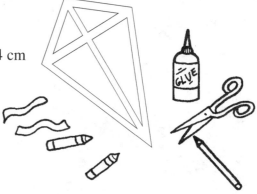

Directions: Staple or tape two pieces of black construction paper together at the top and bottom for each child. Have the students carefully trace the kite patterns onto the black construction paper in pencil or white crayon. Then help them cut the two papers out at the same time. Next, tell them to place the kite patterns onto the tissue paper, trace around the outside edges only, and cut out the shape. Let them glue, using only small amounts of glue, the tissue paper between the already cut out black kite patterns. Attach the tail strips with staples. Show them how to shape pipe cleaners into bows and staple these onto the tail.

Tissue Paper Kite Pattern

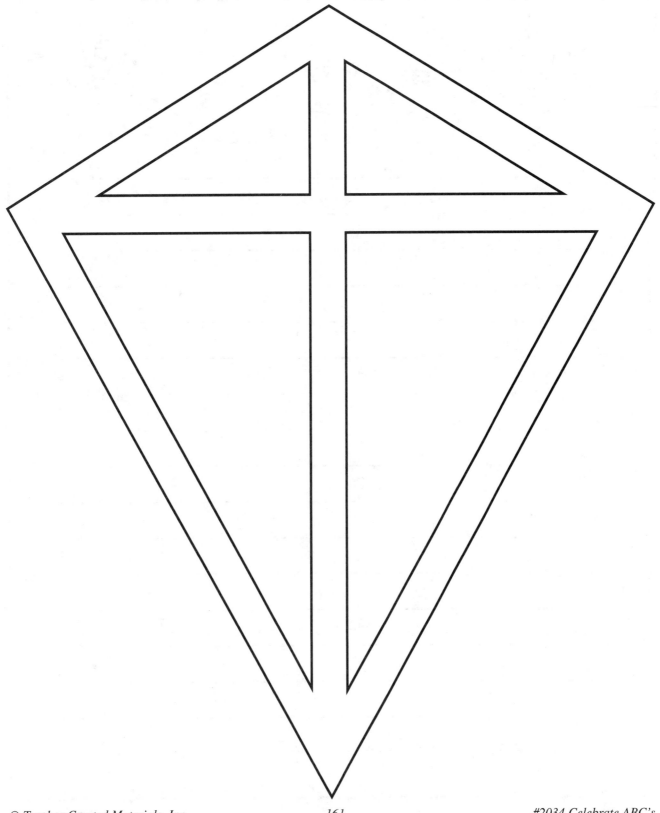

Stationery

Incentives

Use the following cards for positive reinforcement during your rotations. When a student successfully demonstrates positive behavior and completion of his or her tasks, cut out a bow square and paste it onto his or her kite card. If you do not have time to cut and paste, a star sticker or stamp would work well. Distribute awards/name tags and bookmarks where appropriate.

Tie the bows onto the kite!

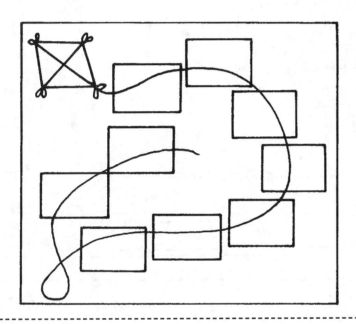

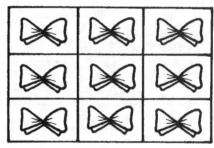

Award/Name Tag

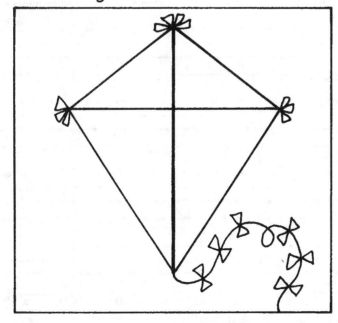

Bookmark

Leaves, Logs, and Lumberjacks

Teacher Note: Use this page as an introduction to the Leaves, Logs, and Lumberjacks theme. Have the students color the picture. Lines are provided for writing activities of your choice.

Unit Materials

Bibliography

Cherry, Lynne. *The Great Kapok Tree.* Harcourt Brace Jovanovich, 1990.

Ehlert, Lois. *Red Leaf, Yellow Leaf.* Harcourt Brace, 1991.

Gile, John. *The First Forest.* John Gile Communications, 1989.

Kellogg, Steven. *Paul Bunyan.* Morrow, 1992. (or any other version)

Silverstein, Shel. *The Giving Tree.* HarperCollins, 1964.

Materials Checklist

Station 1 Activity Card— Literature

_____ *Paul Bunyan* (any version) or other literature selection
_____ pencils
_____ drawing paper
_____ crayons
_____ pictures of trees
_____ activity card

Station 2—Writing

_____ shape books
_____ pencils
_____ crayons
_____ activity card

Station 3—Building

_____ toy building logs
_____ activity card

Station 4—Cooking

_____ 3 or more kinds of lettuce or spinach
_____ alphabet pasta
_____ pitted black olives
_____ hard-boiled egg
_____ Parmesan cheese
_____ butter or margarine
_____ small paper plates or bowls
_____ croutons
_____ salad dressing
_____ paper towels
_____ plastic knives
_____ lemon pepper
_____ measuring cup
_____ activity card

Station 5—Classifying Leaves

_____ 30–40 assorted leaves
_____ activity card

Station 6—Word Problems

_____ word problems
_____ pencils
_____ paper
_____ crayons
_____ activity card

Station 7—Art

_____ newspapers
_____ small paper plates
_____ yellow, brown, red, orange, and green paints
_____ white paper
_____ damp and dry paper towels
_____ paintbrushes
_____ activity card

Station 8—Literature/Art

_____ leaf patterns (make ahead)
_____ *Red Leaf, Yellow Leaf*
_____ 12" x 18" (30.4 x 45.7 cm) brown or orange construction paper
_____ crayons, markers, or paint in containers (yellow, orange, gold, brown, and red)
_____ brushes for paint
_____ black permanent marker
_____ activity card

Station 1 Activity Card—Literature

Materials:

- *Paul Bunyan* (any version) or other literature selection
- pictures of trees
- pencils
- drawing paper
- crayons

Directions:

1. Read to the children and discuss *Paul Bunyan, The Great Kapok Tree, The Giving Tree*, or *The First Forest*.

2. Share with the group pictures of different types of trees. Many children have not had the experience of seeing a colorful fall landscape, and others may never have seen desert trees.

3. Talk about trees that shed their leaves and those that do not.

4. Allow the students to color a fall landscape if time permits.

Station 2 Activity Card—Writing

Materials:

- shape books
- pencils
- crayons

Directions: Prepare shape books (see pattern on page 167) as described on previous shape book activity cards. Give each child a leaf shape book. Assign one of the following activities:

1. Write about and illustrate words beginning with the letter "l" in the leaf shape book.

2. Write about and illustrate words that have the "long e" sound in them. Here are some ideas:

tree	wheat	sea
leaf	seed	me
bead	read	key
meat	bee	

3. On the first page of the book write, "Trees give us . . . ." On each page draw and label one thing that trees produce.

Shape Book Pattern

Leaves

Station 3 Activity Card—Building

Materials:

- toy building logs

Directions:

1. Give the children the opportunity to build log structures as a group or individually.

2. Have the students clean up a little early so that you can take them to the restrooms to wash their hands in preparation for the next activity, cooking.

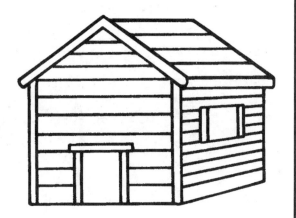

Station 4 Activity Card—Cooking

Letter Salad

Ingredients:

- 3 or more kinds of lettuce or spinach (5–6 heads or bunches per class), rinsed and dried
- alphabet pasta (2–3 bags per class, precooked)
- pitted black olives (2 olives per child)
- hard-boiled egg ($\frac{1}{2}$ egg per child)
- Parmesan cheese
- butter or margarine (for macaroni)
- measuring cup ($\frac{1}{4}$ cup/60 mL)

- small paper plates or bowls
- croutons
- salad dressing
- paper towels
- plastic knives
- lemon pepper (if desired for macaroni)

To Be Done in Advance: Hard-boil the eggs. Cook the pasta by following the directions on the bag. Drain. Butter the pasta while it is warm and then liberally sprinkle Parmesan cheese on it. Also, if desired, sprinkle lightly with lemon pepper. Cool and store the pasta in a plastic, resealable bag and refrigerate. (You may wish to ask parents to help by doing this for you.)

Directions: Give each child a paper towel to cover his or her own work area. Direct students through the process making a salad of edible leaves, starting with torn leaves, and adding the remaining ingredients.

Station 5 Activity Card—Classifying Leaves

Materials:

- 30–40 leaves (collected ahead and stored in plastic bags)

To Be Done in Advance: At least one week ahead, have the students help you collect different kinds of leaves and bring them back to class. (Send plastic bags home for collecting.)

Directions: Pile the leaves on a table. Ask the students to stand or sit around the table to classify the leaves. Have them classify the leaves according to categories such as shape, size, color, fresh and dry, ridges, edges, and number of points. Choose one or two categories to classify at a time. Once classified, change the characteristics you are looking for and reclassify. For example, if the group chose to classify according to size the first time, have them reclassify according to the number of points on the leaves this time. How do the groupings change? Give them plenty of time to explain the new classifications.

Station 6 Activity Card—Word Problems

Materials:

- word problems (page 170)
- paper
- pencils
- crayons

Directions:

1. Give a copy of page 170 to each student. (An answer key is provided at the bottom of this card.) Assign the problems which are the most age and ability appropriate for the groups.

2. Provide pencils and paper for the students to complete the word problems.

3. Have the students illustrate the word problems to help find the solutions.

4. If they finish early, challenge the students to make up more problems for each other.

Page 170 Answers:

1. 13	3. 9	5. 16	7. 25	9. 12
2. 26	4. 16	6. 5	8. 9	10. 7 feet, 9 inches

Word Problems

Directions: Make drawings to help solve the following math problems.

1. Paul Bunyan cut down 6 trees by himself. Babe helped him with 7 more. How many trees did they cut in all?

2. If Paul cut down 12 trees yesterday and 14 trees today, how many did he cut down in all?

3. Paul has 20 trees he needs to cut down. He was able to cut 11 down today. How many will he need to cut down tomorrow in order to finish?

4. If a tree has 9 big branches and 7 little branches, how many branches does the tree have?

5. Paul and Babe ate 8 flapjacks each. How many did they eat in all?

6. If a tree has 17 leaves on a certain branch and 4 leaves drop to the ground each day for 3 days in a row, how many leaves would be left on the branch?

7. The cook is making 40 flapjacks. Paul can eat 8 flapjacks in 5 minutes. How many minutes will it take Paul to eat all of the flapjacks?

8. Mr. Jackson has hired Paul to cut down the trees on his land so that he can build a new house. There are 111 trees on the land. He wants 3 large trees left standing. If Paul cuts 12 trees each day, how many days will it take for him to finish?

9. Paul's ax weighs 60 pounds (27 kg). Your ax weighs 5 pounds (2.25 kg). How many of your axes would it take to make one as heavy as Paul's?

10. If Paul is 12 feet (3.6 m) tall and you are 4 feet and 3 inches (1.28 m) tall, how much taller is Paul than you?

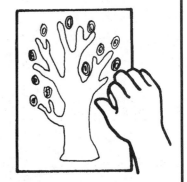

Station 7 Activity Card—Art

Materials:

- newspapers
- white paper
- paintbrushes
- small paper plates
- damp and dry paper towels
- yellow, brown, red, orange, and green paints

Directions:

1. Pour a little bit of each paint color onto separate plates.

2. Lay down the newspapers to protect the work area.

3. Give each child a piece of paper and a paintbrush. Show them how to paint a simple tree trunk and some branches, using brown paint. Tell them to do the same on their papers.

4. Have the students dip their thumbs into a paint color. Then tell them to make thumbprint leaves on their trees.

5. Hand out damp paper towels to wipe the paint off of their thumbs. Next, allow them to dip their thumbs into another color.

6. Have them repeat this process until the trees are full of brightly colored leaves.

Station 8 Activity Card—Literature/Art

Materials:

- leaf patterns (make ahead)
- *Red Leaf, Yellow Leaf*
- 12" x 18" (30.4 x 45.7 cm) brown or orange construction paper
- crayons, markers, or paint in containers (yellow, orange, gold, brown, and red)
- brushes for paint
- black permanent marker

To Be Done in Advance: Make patterns from tagboard, using the leaf patterns provided on pages 172 and 173.

Directions:

1. Read *Red Leaf, Yellow Leaf* to the students. Discuss.

2. Give each student a piece of construction paper. Ask the students to write their names in the bottom right-hand corners of their papers.

3. Show the students how to trace the pattern leaves onto their construction paper, using either crayons or paint. Create bright, overlapping designs.

Leaf Patterns

Leaf Patterns *(cont.)*

Stationery

Incentives

Use the following cards for positive reinforcement during your rotations. When a student successfully demonstrates positive behavior and completion of his or her tasks, cut out a leaf square and paste it onto his or her tree card. If you do not have time to cut and paste, a star sticker or stamp would work well. Distribute awards/name tags and bookmarks where appropriate.

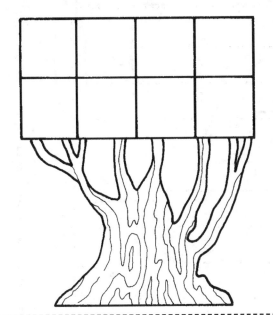

Fill the tree with leaves!

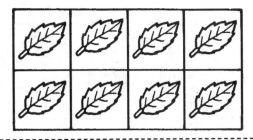

Award/Name Tag

Bookmark

Leave No Leaf Unturned . . . Read a Book.

Measurement

Teacher Note: Use this page as an introduction to the Measurement theme. Have the students color the picture. Lines are provided for writing activities of your choice.

Unit Materials

Bibliography

Carle, Eric. *The Grouchy Ladybug.* HarperCollins, 1977.

Materials Checklist

Station 1—Literature

_____ *The Grouchy Ladybug*
_____ large instructional clock with movable hands
_____ small instructional clocks with movable hands
_____ scratch paper
_____ crayons
_____ activity card

Station 2—Writing

_____ shape books
_____ pencils
_____ crayons
_____ activity card

Station 3—Measuring M's

_____ measuring tapes or rulers
_____ activity sheet
_____ pencils
_____ activity card

Station 4—Cooking

At least four or five of the following:
_____ minimarshmallows
_____ granola
_____ raisins
_____ peanuts
_____ sunflower seeds (no shells)
_____ chocolate chips
_____ dried fruits
_____ round toasted oat cereal
_____ other trail mix ingredients
_____ a variety of volume measuring tools
_____ a large bowl
_____ pencils
_____ note cards
_____ activity card

Station 5—Measuring Length

_____ 6–8 packages of different sizes, wrapped (with tags)
_____ yardstick and meterstick activity sheets (pages 183 and 184)
_____ scissors
_____ tape
_____ scratch paper
_____ pencils
_____ activity card

Station 6—Measuring Temperature

_____ two indoor/outdoor thermometers
_____ one oral thermometer
_____ temperature strips (thermometers that you put on the forehead to take body temperature)
_____ activity card

Station 7—Measuring Weight

_____ 4 different sizes of letters and envelopes
_____ a small letter or card
_____ medium (business-sized) letters
_____ 9" x 12" (22.8 cm x 30.4 cm) manila envelopes
_____ small packages
_____ a bathroom scale
_____ a letter scale
_____ a balance scale
_____ activity card

Station 8—Measuring Volume

_____ measuring cup
_____ measuring spoons
_____ containers (cup, pint, quart, half-gallon, gallon)
_____ assorted containers to measure capacity rice, beans, and water (to measure)
_____ activity card

Station 1 Activity Card—Literature

Materials:

- *The Grouchy Ladybug*
- large instructional clock with movable hands (one for the group)
- small instructional clocks with movable hands (one for each child)
- scratch paper
- crayons

Directions:

1. Read *The Grouchy Ladybug* to the group.

2. Give each child a small instructional clock. Talk about hours and how they are a measurement of time. Show them how to move the hands of the clocks to show different times.

3. Reread the book; however, this time stop periodically to position the hands on the individual clocks and the group clock in positions which follow the story.

4. Ask the students to draw pictures of their favorite parts.

Station 2 Activity Card—Writing

Materials:

- shape books
- pencils
- crayons

Directions: Prepare shape books (see pattern on page 179) as described on previous shape book activity cards. Give each student a shape book and then assign one of the activities below.

1. Write about and illustrate words that begin with the letter "m."

2. On each page write "I use a _____ to measure _____." Fill in the blanks differently on each page and illustrate.

3. Write and illustrate the steps of a favorite recipe. Be sure to include the measurements.

Shape Book Pattern

Measurement

Station 3 Activity Card—Measuring M's

Materials:

- measuring tapes or rulers

- activity sheet (page 181)

- pencils

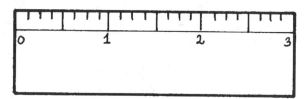

Directions: This activity can be done in pairs or individually.

1. Give each student or each pair of students a copy of page 181 and a measuring tape.

2. Show the students how to use the measuring tapes and then let them measure the M items on the activity sheet.

3. Compare the students' answers.

4. Leave a little extra time to take the students to the restrooms to wash their hands in preparation for the next activity, cooking.

Station 4 Activity Card—Cooking

Trail Mix

Materials:

- a variety of volume measuring tools (e.g., measuring cup, measuring spoons, cleaned and dried milk carton)

- a large bowl

- pencils

- note cards

- at least four or five of the following:

    minimarshmallows
    granola
    raisins
    peanuts
    sunflower seeds (no shells)
    chocolate chips
    dried fruits
    round toasted oat cereal
    other trail mix ingredients

Directions: Explain to the students that the group is going to create its own recipe for trail mix. Lay out the measuring tools and ingredients so that the students can see them. Put the large bowl in the center of the group. Give each child a pencil and a note card. Discuss how much of each ingredient should go into the trail mix. Allow each student the opportunity to use a measuring tool to add an ingredient to the bowl. As the children create the trail mix, have them keep track of how much of each ingredient they are adding by writing down the recipe on the note cards. When they are finished measuring, creating, and writing, let them enjoy their creations.

Measuring M's

Measure the items below which all begin with the letter M. Write your answers in the boxes provided.

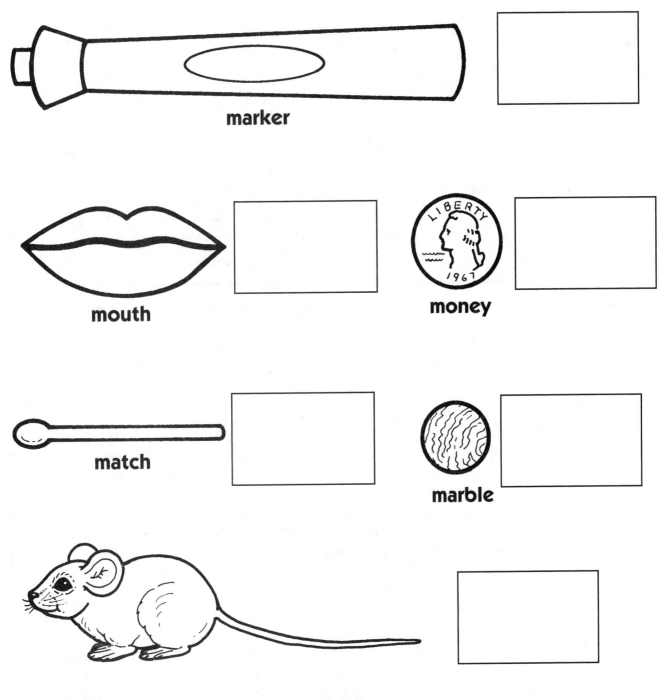

marker

mouth

money

match

marble

mouse

Station 5 Activity Card—Measuring Length

Materials:

- 6–8 packages of different sizes, wrapped (with tags)
- yardstick and meterstick activity sheets (pages 183 and 184)
- scissors
- scratch paper
- tape
- pencils

To Be Done in Advance: Wrap 6–8 packages with pretty wrapping paper. Make sure that each box is a different size. Put a tag on each one that says "Measure me."

Directions:

1. Ask the students to cut out the yardstick and meterstick pieces and put them together with tape. Be sure that they do this carefully and precisely, or their measurements will be wrong.

2. Give each student a package to measure. Tell the children to measure the lengths, heights, and widths with the yardsticks and then record their measurements on scratch paper.

3. Ask them to do the same thing, this time using the metersticks.

4. Stop for a moment to compare. Ask why the answers are different. Help them understand why we label measurement and why it is important to have common measuring tools.

5. Allow students to switch packages and continue measuring until the activity time is over.

Station 6 Activity Card—Measuring Temperature

Materials: two indoor/outdoor thermometers, one oral thermometer, temperature strips (thermometers that you put on the forehead to take body temperature)

To Be Done in Advance: Place one of the indoor/outdoor thermometers outside in a sunny spot.

Directions: Show the students an indoor/outdoor thermometer, a temperature strip, and an oral thermometer. Ask the students what they have in common. (They measure temperature.) Then, show them the differences among the thermometers by doing the following:

a. Take your own temperature with the oral thermometer. Show the students the correct way to do it. Have each student look at the number where the line stops. Tell them that the normal oral temperature is 98.6°F. Is your temperature normal?

b. Explain that the outside of your body is a little cooler than the inside. Measure your temperature with a temperature strip. What temperature does it say? How does it compare to the normal temperature?

c. Show the indoor/outdoor thermometer that you kept inside. What temperature does it show? Write the temperature down.

d. Take children outside. What does the outside thermometer say? Write it down. Compare the two numbers. (You may wish to have a second outdoor thermometer in the shade to also compare.)

Yardstick

Cut out the yardstick pieces and follow the taping directions.

| 1 | 2 | 3 | 4 | 5 | 6 | Attach next piece here. ← |

| 7 | 8 | 9 | 10 | 11 | 12 | Attach next piece here. ← |

| 13 | 14 | 15 | 16 | 17 | 18 | Attach next piece here. ← |

| 19 | 20 | 21 | 22 | 23 | 24 | Attach next piece here. ← |

| 25 | 26 | 27 | 28 | 29 | 30 | Attach next piece here. ← |

| 31 | 32 | 33 | 34 | 35 | 36 |

#2034 Celebrate ABC's

Meterstick

Cut out the meterstick pieces and follow the taping directions.

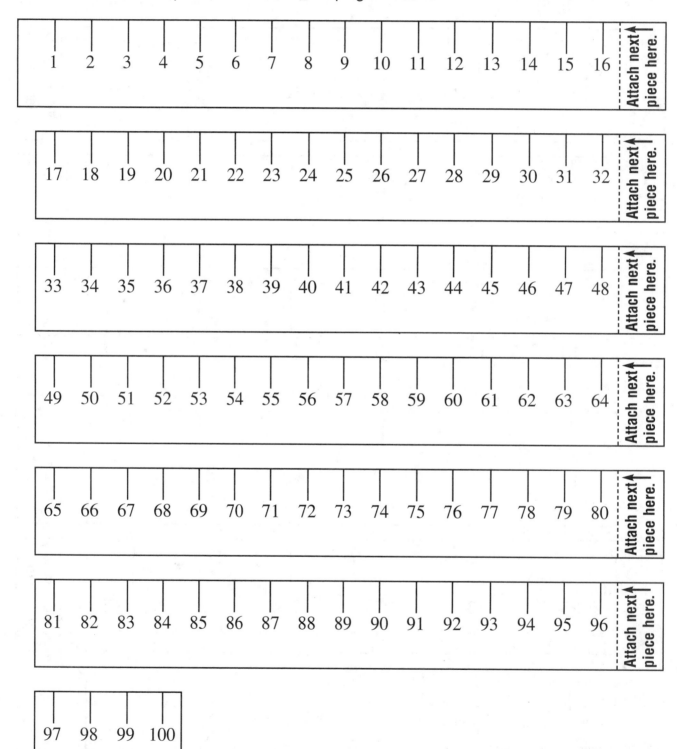

184

Station 7 Activity Card—Measuring Weight

Materials: 4 different sizes of letters and envelopes, a small letter or card, medium (business-sized) letters, 9" x 12" (22.8 x 30.4 cm) manila envelopes, small packages, a bathroom scale, a letter scale, a balance scale

Directions: Demonstrate and discuss how to use the three types of scales by doing the following and then allow the children to experiment with the scales on their own.

1. **Bathroom Scale:** Talk about what the scale is used for. (What does it measure?) Ask, "Who would like to be weighed?" Weigh the students who volunteer. Explain that this scale weighs in pounds.

2. **Letter Scale:** Talk about what this scale is used for. ("What does it weigh? Does it also weigh in pounds?") Ask the students to guess which letter or package will weigh the most and why. Weigh the items. Did they guess right?

3. **Balance Scale:** With the balance scale, have students measure (weigh) items from around the room. If you have a set of weights for the scale, they can actually find out the weights. If you do not have a weight set, they can find out such things as which items weigh the same or how many of a small item it takes to weigh the same as a large one, etc. Let the kids have fun drawing inferences and making conclusions.

Station 8 Activity Card—Measuring Volume

Materials:
- measuring cup
- measuring spoons
- containers (cup, pint, quart, half-gallon, gallon)
- assorted containers to measure capacity
- rice, beans, and water (to measure)

Directions:

1. Allow the students to explore with measuring volume. Ask them to look for relationships like how many of one measuring container it takes to fill another or how the shape of a container makes a difference in capacity.

2. After ten minutes of exploration, stop them and ask them to try to explain the things they have learned.

3. Show them the relationships among cups, pints, quarts, etc.

4. Clean up the area for the next group.

Stationery

Incentives

Use the following cards for positive reinforcement during your rotations. When a student successfully demonstrates positive behavior and completion of his or her tasks, color in or shade a section of the thermometer card, starting at the bottom. Challenge the students to get their entire thermometers filled to the top. Distribute awards/tags and bookmarks where appropriate.

Rise to the top!

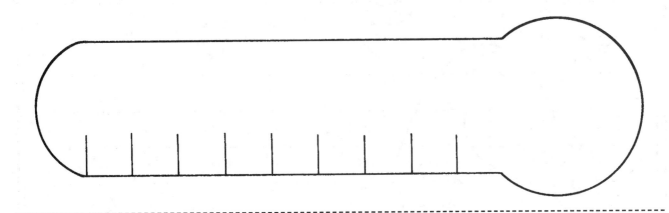

Award/Name Tag

Bookmark

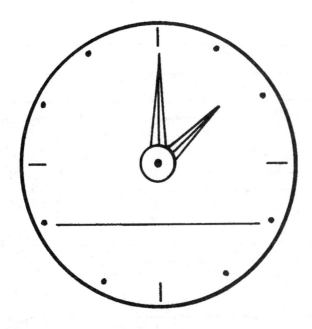

Measure Up . . . Read!

Numbers

Teacher Note: Use this page as an introduction to the Numbers theme. Have students color the picture. Lines are provided for writing activities of your choice.

Unit Materials

Bibliography

Count Your Way Through . . . (series). Lerner Publications.

Crews, Donald. *Ten Black Dots.* Greenwillow Books, 1986.

Ehlert, Lois. *Fish Eyes.* Harcourt Brace, 1990.

Feelings, Muriel. *Moja Means One.* Dial Books for Young Readers, 1971.

Hague, Kathleen. *Numbears.* Henry Holt and Company, 1986.

Kellogg, Steven. *How Much Is a Million?* Lothrop, Lee, and Shepard, 1985.

Materials Checklist

Station 1—Literature

_____ *How Much Is a Million?*
_____ small "n" things (noodles, nuts, nails, napkins, nickels, etc.)
_____ containers
_____ activity card

Station 2—Stamps

_____ small rubber stamps
_____ stamp pads
_____ crayons or colored pencils
_____ paper
_____ activity card

Station 3—Cooking

_____ tortilla chips
_____ sliced olives
_____ green onions (sliced into rings)
_____ grated Monterey Jack cheese
_____ grated cheddar cheese
_____ small paper plates
_____ napkins
_____ toaster oven
_____ aluminum foil
_____ activity card

Station 4—Word Problems

_____ real or play money:
40 or more pennies
20 or more nickels
6 or more dimes
_____ pencils
_____ paper
_____ activity card

Station 5—Writing

_____ shape books
_____ pencils
_____ crayons, markers, or colored pencils
_____ activity card

Station 6—Fish Art

_____ *Fish Eyes*
_____ 9" x 12" (22.8 x 30.4 cm) sheets of dark blue paper
_____ fluorescent colored copier paper, several colors
_____ scissors
_____ pencils
_____ hole punch
_____ glue
_____ activity card

Station 7—Math

_____ code chart
_____ pencils
_____ paper
_____ activity card

Station 8—Flip Books

_____ *Moja Means One* or one of the Count Your Way Through . . . series
_____ 12" x 18" (30.4 x 45.7 cm) white construction paper
_____ scissors
_____ pencils
_____ crayons or colored pencils
_____ activity card

Alternate Activities:

1. Menu Word Problems
_____ children's menus from local restaurants
_____ pencil
_____ paper
_____ activity card

2. Counting Books—*Numbears*
_____ shape book pattern on page 29
_____ pencils
_____ paper
_____ crayons, markers, or colored pencils
_____ activity card

Station 1 Activity Card—Literature

Materials:

- *How Much Is a Million?*

- small "n" things (noodles, nuts, nails, napkins, nickels, etc.)

- containers

To Be Done in Advance: Place random amounts of the "n" items in separate containers, such as jars or resealable bags.

Directions:

1. Read and discuss *How Much Is a Million?*

2. Place the containers of "N" items in front of the students. Ask them to estimate the number of "N" things you have put in each container. Have them write their guesses on scratch paper.

3. Count the items to see who was the closest.

Station Activity Card 2—Stamps

Materials:

- small rubber stamps
- stamp pads

- crayons or colored pencils
- paper

Directions:

1. Let the students each stamp or draw 100 things. Have them make 10 rows of 10 things.

2. Next, ask them to use a different stamp to make (or draw) another 100 things.

3. Show the children what 1,000 things look like by lining up 10 of their stamp pictures. Have them imagine what 1,000,000 (1,000 x 1,000) would look like. How much of the room would it take?

4. Take the students to the restrooms to wash their hands in preparation for the next activity, cooking.

5. Before they leave for their next activity, collect all of their papers.

6. When the theme day is over, tape the papers end to end. Unroll them outside. Estimate how much larger 1,000,000 would have to be.

Station 3 Activity Card—Cooking

Nacho Numeros

Materials:

- tortilla chips
- toaster oven
- green onions (sliced into rings)
- sliced olives
- grated cheddar cheese
- small paper plates
- napkins
- grated Monterey Jack cheese
- aluminum foil

Directions:

1. Teach the children how to count to five in Spanish: uno, dos, tres, quatro, cinco.
2. Give each child a small square of aluminum foil. (Make the square large enough to accommodate the ingredients in number 3.)
3. Read the following instructions to the students:
   a. Place uno tortilla chip on your foil.
   b. Put dos olives on top of your chip.
   c. Place tres onion slices on your chip.
   d. Sprinkle quatro pieces of grated Jack cheese on top of your chip.
   e. Sprinkle cinco pieces of grated cheddar cheese on top of your chip.
4. Carefully place the foil squares in an oven or toaster oven and bake until the cheese has just melted.
5. Let the nachos cool until they are safe to eat and then enjoy!

Station 4 Activity Card—Word Problems

Materials: real or play money (40 or more pennies, 20 or more nickels, 6 or more dimes), pencils, paper

Directions:

Read the problems below and decide which ones are appropriate for the ages and abilities in your group. Write these problems on cards for the children to solve. If necessary, allow them to have partners or work as a group with them.

1. I have 3 nickels. How much is that? (15¢)
2. If I have 6 nickels, how much money do I have? (30¢)
3. How much are 10 nickels worth? (50¢)
4. How much are 20 nickels worth? ($1.00)
5. How much are 5 pennies and 4 nickels worth? (25¢)
6. How many pennies do I need to equal 8 nickels? (40)
7. How many dimes do I need to equal 8 nickels? (4)
8. If one dime equals 2 nickels, how many nickels will it take to equal 6 dimes? How much money is that? (12) (60¢)
9. I have 2 dimes and a nickel. How much is it worth? (25¢)
10. I have 4 dimes, 3 nickels, and 5 pennies. How much is it worth? (60¢)
11. If I can get 4 nuts for a nickel, how many nuts can I get for 4 nickels? (16)

Station 5 Activity Card—Writing

Materials:

- shape books
- pencils
- crayons, markers, or colored pencils

Directions for Option 1:

1. Prepare shape books (see pattern on page 193) as described on previous shape book activity cards. Give each student a shape book.

2. Ask the students to number the pages.

3. On each page, tell the children to draw anything they want in the amount denoted by the page number. For example, on the first page a child may draw one cat, on the second page he or she may draw two hearts, on the third page draw three cookies, and so on.

Directions for Option 2:

1. Give each child a shape book.

2. Discuss words that start with the letter "n."

3. Direct the students to draw a picture of an "n" thing on each page of their books.

4. Finally, have the students label each item or write a sentence about each picture.

Station 6 Activity Card—Fish Art

Materials:

- *Fish Eyes*
- 9" x 12" (22.8 x 30.4 cm) sheets of dark blue paper
- fluorescent colored copier paper, several colors
- scissors
- pencils
- hole punch
- glue

Directions:

1. Read the book *Fish Eyes* by Lois Ehlert. This is a wonderful rhymed counting book. Ask the children to pay special attention to Ehlert's colorful fish.

2. Let the children make their own fish. Show them how to draw, cut, and glue fish, using fluorescent copier paper. They may each make one big fish or several small ones. Give each child a piece of blue construction paper to which they can glue their fish.

Shape Book Pattern

Station 7 Activity Card—Math

Materials:

- code chart
- pencils
- paper

Directions:

1. Give each child a copy of the code chart below or write the code on a chalkboard or poster so that everyone may read it. Also, hand out pencils and paper.

2. Brainstorm a list of words that begin with the letter "N" with the students. For younger students you may wish to choose words from the following prepared list of short words:

   no   not   nag   nod   nap   nut   nun   now   nob   new   nest

   near   nice   none   note   nose   neon   neck   navy   nail   name   net

3. Have the children decode the letters of each word and add the numbers together. (**Note:** There are two codes. The first one is meant for the younger students. The second code is more challenging. Choose which code is the more appropriate for the group.)

   Examples (using the first code):
   numbers . . . 5 + 3 + 4 + 2 + 5 + 9 + 1 = ?
   nuts . . . 5 + 3 + 2 + 1 = ?

   Examples (using the second code):
   numbers . . . 14 + 21 + 13 + 2 + 5 + 18 + 19 = ?
   nuts . . . 14 + 21 + 20 + 19 = ?

4. Check their answers as a group.

Station 7 Activity Card—Math *(cont.)*

Code A												
A	B	C	D	E	F	G	H	I	J	K	L	M
1	2	3	4	5	6	7	8	9	1	2	3	4
N	O	P	Q	R	S	T	U	V	W	X	Y	Z
5	6	7	8	9	1	2	3	4	5	6	7	8

Code B												
A	B	C	D	E	F	G	H	I	J	K	L	M
1	2	3	4	5	6	7	8	9	10	11	12	13
N	O	P	Q	R	S	T	U	V	W	X	Y	Z
14	15	16	17	18	19	20	21	22	23	24	25	26

194

Station 8 Activity Card—Flip Books

Materials: *Moja Means One* or one of the Count Your Way Through . . . series, 12" x 18" (30.4 x 45.7 cm) white construction paper, scissors, pencils, crayons or colored pencils

Directions:

1. Read *Moja Means One* or one of the Count Your Way Through . . . series.
2. Help the children make flip books that show numbers written in English and other languages. Here is how to make a book.
   a. Fold a 12" x 18" (30.4 x 45.7 cm) sheet of white construction paper in half lengthwise.
   b. Fold it in half again, this time widthwise.
   c. Fold it once more widthwise.
   d. Open the last two folds.
   e. Cut on the three folded lines on the top flap only. Cut all the way to the top fold. The bottom piece should still be one piece while the top should now be four flaps.
   f. Open the first flap and write "ONE." Then write the word for one in another language on the first flap. Repeat this process for flaps two, three, and four.
   g. Simple drawings to match the numbers may be added if there is enough time (for example, one star, two hearts, three circles, four diamonds).

Alternate Activity Card

1. **Menu Word Problems**
   Materials:
   - children's menus from local restaurants
   - pencil
   - paper

   Directions: Make up word problems, using children's menus from local restaurants. Ask the students to solve these yummy problems with paper and pencils. If there is extra time, challenge them to make up their own word problems to ask each other.

2. **Counting Books**
   Materials:
   - *Numbears*
   - shape book pattern on page 29
   - pencils
   - paper
   - crayons, markers, or colored pencils

   Directions: Read *Numbears* to the group. Make number counting books, using the bear pattern from the Bears theme (page 29) to make book covers.

Stationery

Incentives

Use the following cards for positive reinforcement during your rotations. When a student successfully demonstrates positive behavior and completion of his or her tasks, cut out a nickel square and paste it onto his or her gumball machine card. If you do not have time to cut and paste, a star sticker or stamp would work well. Distribute awards/name tags and bookmarks where appropriate.

Fill the gumball machine with nickels!

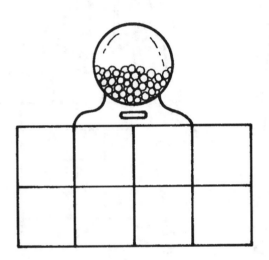

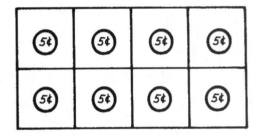

Award/Name Tag

Bookmark

Occupations

Teacher Note: Use this page as an introduction to the Occupations theme. Have your students color the picture. Lines are provided for writing activities of your choice.

Unit Materials

Bibliography

Geringer, Laura. *A Three Hat Day.* HarperCollins, 1985.

Morris, Ann. *Hats, Hats, Hats.* Mulberry Books, 1993.

Morris, Ann. *Tools.* Lothrop, Lee, and Shepard, 1992.

Roy, Ron. *Whose Hat Is That?* Clarion Books, 1990.

Smith, William J. *Ho for a Hat!* Little, Brown, and Company, 1989.

Materials Checklist

Station 1—Literature
- _____ *Ho for a Hat!, Whose Hat Is That?,* or *A Three Hat Day*
- _____ chalkboard
- _____ chalk
- _____ activity card

Stations 2 and 3— Job Experience
- _____ menus
- _____ clipboards
- _____ aprons
- _____ order forms
- _____ trash bags
- _____ small plastic bags
- _____ napkins
- _____ lemonade
- _____ water
- _____ punch
- _____ milk
- _____ chocolate chip cookies
- _____ chocolate sandwich cookies
- _____ sugar wafers
- _____ graham crackers
- _____ barbecue chips
- _____ potato chips
- _____ corn chips
- _____ tortilla chips
- _____ apples
- _____ carrot sticks
- _____ oranges
- _____ seedless grapes
- _____ activity card

Station 4—What Is in the Box?
- _____ several items representing different occupations
- _____ a large box
- _____ activity card

Station 5—Flip Book
- _____ white construction paper
- _____ pencils
- _____ crayons
- _____ scissors
- _____ activity card

Station 6—Writing
- _____ shape books
- _____ pencils
- _____ crayons
- _____ activity card

Station 7—Stick Puppets
- _____ puppet patterns
- _____ tongue depressors or craft sticks
- _____ scissors
- _____ tape
- _____ crayons
- _____ activity card

Station 8—Occupation Match
- _____ 3" x 5" (7.6 cm x 12.7 cm) cards
- _____ permanent marker
- _____ legal-sized envelopes
- _____ activity card

Alternate Activity:
Tools of the Trade
- _____ *Tools* by Ann Morris
- _____ briefcase page
- _____ pencils
- _____ crayons
- _____ various tools
- _____ activity card

Station 1 Activity Card—Literature

Materials:

- *Ho for a Hat!, Whose Hat Is That?,* or *A Three Hat Day*
- chalkboard
- chalk

Directions:

1. Read and discuss one of the listed books.

2. Ask the children what they want to be when they grow up and why. On the chalkboard draw a graph with one column for each of the occupations the children mentioned. At the top of each column, write the name of the occupation it represents.

3. One at a time, allow the children to come to the board and write their names in the columns. Tell the children that they can only choose one job each.

4. Do not erase the graph in between groups. Simply add on new columns if different occupations are mentioned. By the end of the theme day, the graph will represent the occupational aspirations of all the students.

Stations 2 and 3 Activity Card—Job Experience

Materials:

Use the following materials to complete stations 2 and 3 activities:

- menu (page 201)
- clipboards
- aprons
- order forms (page 202)
- trash bags
- small plastic bags
- napkins
- lemonade

- water
- punch
- milk
- chocolate chip cookies
- chocolate sandwich cookies
- sugar wafers
- graham crackers

- barbecue chips
- potato chips
- corn chips
- tortilla chips
- apples
- carrot sticks
- oranges
- seedless grapes

To Be Done in Advance: Divide the snacks into small serving sizes and separate them into paper cups or plastic bags.

Stations 2 and 3 Activity Card—Job Experience

Directions: This activity will occupy two groups at one time. The idea is to give the children a simple notion of what it would be like to work in a restaurant. The students who are supposed to be at station 2 will be the waiters and waitresses (give them the aprons to wear). The students who are supposed to be at station 3 will be the customers.

1. Ask the customers to find a seat at the table. Let the waiters and waitresses give menus to the customers. While the customers are trying to decide what to order, have the servers wash their hands since they will be handling food. Next, tell the servers to take the customers' orders on the forms provided on clipboards. (Allow each customer to order one drink and one or two snacks.)

2. Let the customers wash their hands while the food is being prepared. Help the waiters and waitresses pour the drinks and distribute the food. Let the customers eat their snacks.

3. While the customers are eating, the waiters and waitresses are to remain attentive. They may hand out napkins, clean up small messes, clear away trash, etc.

Menu

Welcome to the Students' Snack Bar!

Drinks

lemonade
water
fruit juice
milk

Fruits and Vegetables

apples
carrot sticks
oranges
grapes

Snacks

Chips

barbecue chips
potato chips
corn chips
tortilla chips

Sweets

chocolate chip cookies
chocolate sandwich cookies
sugar wafers
graham crackers

Enjoy your snack!

Order Forms

Check the items your customer orders.

Drinks

— lemonade   — water
— fruit juice   — milk

Fruits and Vegetables

— apples
— carrot sticks
— oranges
— grapes

Snacks

Sweets
— chocolate chip
— cookies
— chocolate
— sandwich cookies
— sugar wafers
— graham crackers

Chips
— barbecue chips
— potato chips
— corn chips
— tortilla chips

Check the items your customer orders.

Drinks

— lemonade   — water
— fruit juice   — milk

Fruits and Vegetables

— apples
— carrot sticks
— oranges
— grapes

Snacks

Sweets
— chocolate chip
— cookies
— chocolate
— sandwich cookies
— sugar wafers
— graham crackers

Chips
— barbecue chips
— potato chips
— corn chips
— tortilla chips

Station 4 Activity Card—What Is in the Box?

Materials:

- items representing different occupations

- a large box

To Be Done in Advance: Gather a collection of clothing or tools used by people of different occupations. Place the items in a box with a lid and cover.

Directions:

1. Explain to the students that inside the box you have items that represent different occupations.

2. Say "The first item I have in the box is . . . . " Then give one descriptive hint about the item.

3. Let the students ask yes or no questions and give more hints, if necessary, until someone guesses the item.

4. When a student guesses the correct answer, show him or her the item. Pass it around.

5. Repeat this process with each item in the box. After each round, give the children some time to explore and ask questions.

Station 5 Activity Card—Flip Book

Materials:

- white construction paper   • pencils   • crayons   • scissors

Directions: Help the students make flip books about occupations. The directions below are for making one flip book.

1. Fold two 12" x 18" (30.4 cm x 45.7 cm) sheets of white construction paper in half lengthwise. Place one paper inside the other along the folds and staple the folded edge to make a long, four-page book.

2. Fold the book into thirds.

3. Cut the top three pages along the folded lines (up to about 1 inch /2.5 cm from the top fold). Each section should have four pages.

4. On the left flap, write the name of an occupation.

5. On the middle flap, write or draw special clothes or tools a person in this occupation would use.

6. On the right flap, write about what a person in this occupation does.

7. Repeat this process with the second, third, and fourth pages of each section.

Station 6 Activity Card—Writing

Materials:

- shape books
- pencils
- crayons

Directions: Prepare shape books (see page 205 for patterns) as described on previous shape book activity cards. Give each child a shape book and then assign one of the following activities:

1. Ask the students to write the name of an occupation on each page. Then, tell them to draw a picture of a person working at the occupation on each page. Older students may write a sentence describing each occupation also.

2. Have the students draw a hat on each page of their books. At the top of the pages ask them to write "This is my hat; who am I?" Then at the bottom of the pages let them write the occupations.

3. Tell the students to write a different word beginning with the letter "O" on each page and illustrate. Older students can write a sentence that includes the word.

Station 7 Activity Card—Stick Puppets

Materials:

- stick puppet patterns (pages 206–210)
- tongue depressors or craft sticks
- scissors
- tape
- crayons

Directions:

1. Make available several of each of the stick puppet patterns.

2. Let the students pick out one pattern each. (It is best if each student in the group has a different puppet.) Give them time to color and cut out the patterns. Tape each pattern onto a craft stick.

3. One at a time, give the children the opportunity to tell (through their puppets) who they are and what they do.

Shape Book Pattern

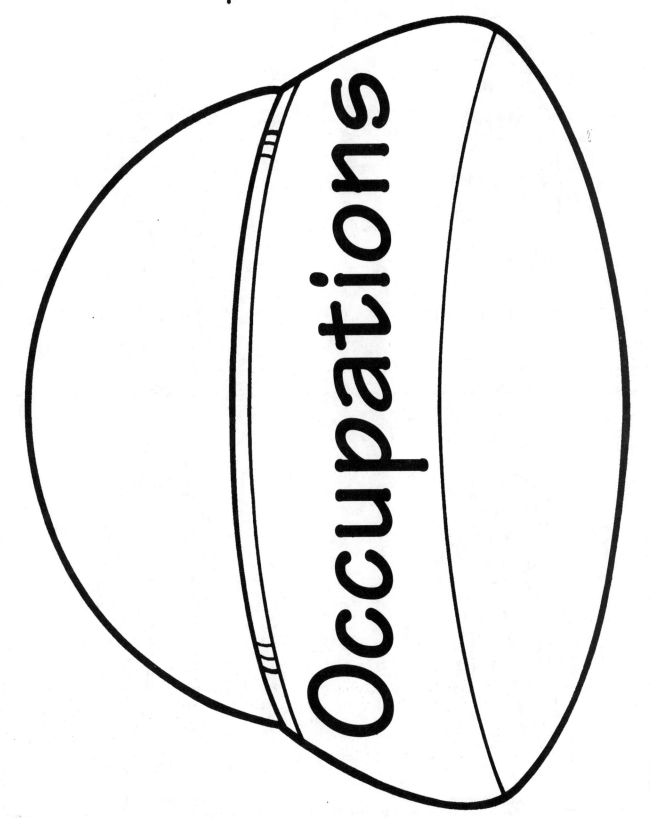

Occupations

Stick Puppet Patterns

Nurse

Doctor

Mechanic

Astronaut

Stick Puppet Patterns *(cont.)*

Teacher

Reporter

Waitress

Chef

Stick Puppet Patterns *(cont.)*

Flight Attendant

Pilot

Business Person or Lawyer

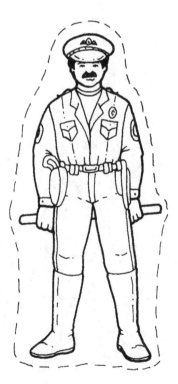

Police Officer

Stick Puppet Patterns *(cont.)*

Firefighter

Construction Worker

Veterinarian

Athlete

Stick Puppet Patterns *(cont.)*

Writer

Artist

Actor

Dancer

210

Station 8 Activity Card—Occupation Match

Materials:

- 3" x 5" (7.6 cm x 12.7 cm) cards, such as index cards, note cards, or heavy paper cut to size
- permanent marker
- legal-sized envelopes

To Be Done in Advance: Write the name of an occupation on an envelope. On eight note cards write words (or draw simple pictures for younger students) related to the occupations. For example, if the envelope is labeled firefighter, eight related words might be: fire, ladder, alarm, hydrant, hose, truck, blaze, water. Repeat this process for seven to nine more envelopes.

Directions:

1. Lay out all of the envelopes so that the children can see them. Mix up the cards from all of the envelopes.

2. Deal the cards out to the students.

3. Tell the students to try to place their cards in the correct envelopes. Give them the option of asking each other for help.

4. When the children are finished, count the cards in each envelope to see if there are eight. Discuss why certain cards were matched to certain envelopes.

Alternate Activity—Tools of the Trade

Materials:

- *Tools* by Ann Morris
- briefcase outline (page 212)
- pencils
- crayons
- various tools

Directions:

1. Read the book *Tools* by Ann Morris. It shows different tools from around the world.

2. Discuss the fact that different jobs demand different tools. For example, a teacher may need a piece of chalk, a doctor may need a thermometer, and a seamstress may need a needle.

3. Give each child a copy of page 212. Ask the students what they would like to do when they grow up. Have them write their dream occupations at the top of the page.

4. Now ask the students to imagine that they are getting ready to go to work. What types of "tools" would they need to take to work? Have them draw these items in their briefcases.

5. Ask the children to share what they drew and why.

My Briefcase

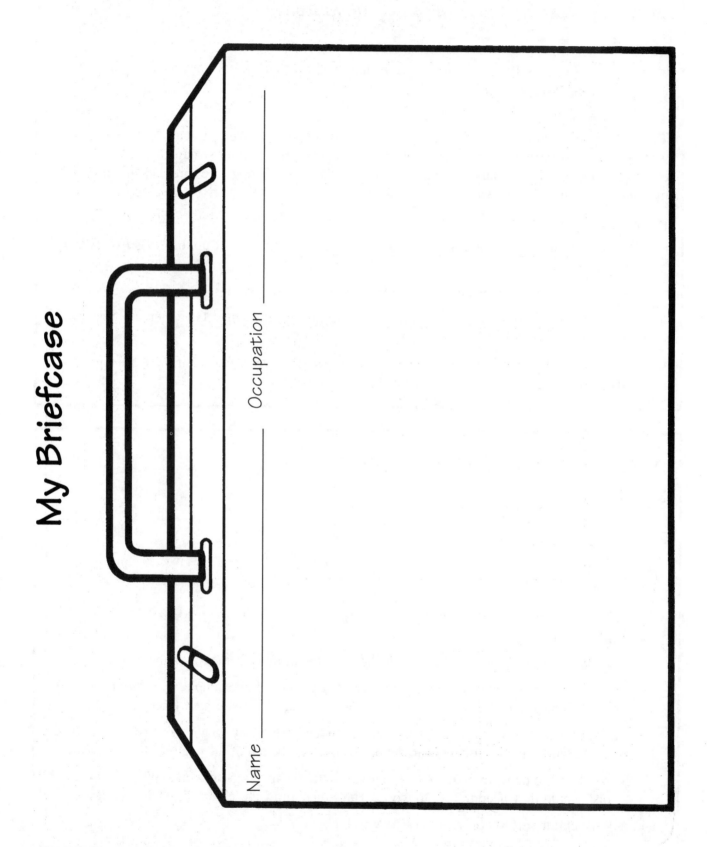

Occupation

Name

Stationery

Incentives

Use the following cards for positive reinforcement during your rotations. When a student successfully demonstrates positive behavior and completion of his or her tasks, cut out a book square and paste it onto his or her bookcase card. If you do not have time to cut and paste, a star sticker or stamp would work well. Distribute awards/name tags and bookmarks where appropriate.

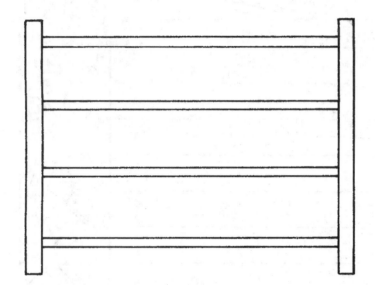

Help the librarian get his books back on the shelves!

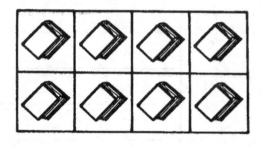

Awards/Name Tags

Bookmark

Pirates

Teacher Note: Use this page as an introduction to the Pirates theme. Have your students color the picture. Lines are provided for writing activities of your choice.

Unit Materials

Bibliography

Fox, Mem. *Tough Boris.* Harcourt Brace, 1994.

Lloyd, David. *Grandma and the Pirates.* Scholastic, 1992.

Walt Disney Staff (originated by J. M. Barrie). *Peter Pan and the Pirates.* Viking Books, 1987.

Other fiction or nonfiction books about pirates

Materials Checklist

Station 1—Literature
_____ any pirate book
_____ crown pattern
_____ construction paper
_____ glue
_____ string
_____ yarn
_____ pipe cleaners
_____ glitter
_____ paper plates
_____ scissors
_____ activity card

Station 2—Writing
_____ shape books
_____ pencils
_____ crayons
_____ activity card

Station 3—Pirate Hats
_____ newspaper
_____ skull and crossbones
       pattern
_____ scissors
_____ pencils
_____ tape
_____ stapler
_____ activity card

Station 4—Cooking
_____ large bowl
_____ plastic knives
_____ paring knives
_____ plastic sword
_____ appetizer skewers
_____ paper towels
_____ cantaloupe
_____ lemon juice
_____ sliced pineapple
_____ grapes
_____ bananas
_____ apples
_____ cherries
_____ mandarin oranges
_____ activity card

Station 5—Group Treasure Map
_____ butcher paper
_____ crayons
_____ black markers
_____ pencils
_____ activity card

Station 6—Math
_____ note cards
_____ tape
_____ pencils
_____ scratch paper
_____ treasure key
_____ treasure patterns
_____ activity card

Station 7—Indoor Treasure Hunt
_____ note cards
_____ tape
_____ classroom maps
_____ treasure patterns
_____ crayons
_____ activity card

Station 8—Outdoor Treasure Hunt
_____ note cards
_____ clear packing tape
_____ crayons
_____ treasure patterns
_____ school maps
_____ activity card

Alternate Activities:
1. Treasure Clues
_____ tally sheets
_____ note cards
_____ treasure patterns
_____ clues
_____ pencils
_____ crayons
_____ activity card
2. Pirate Flags
_____ example flags
_____ black construction
       paper
_____ pencils
_____ white chalk
_____ activity card

Station 1 Activity Card—Literature

Materials:

- any pirate book
- construction paper
- glitter
- yarn
- scissors
- crown pattern (page 218)
- glue
- paper plates
- pipe cleaners
- string

To Be Done in Advance: Use the pattern on page 218 to trace and cut out construction paper crowns for the students.

Directions: Read one of the following books (or any other book about pirates) to the students.

1. *Tough Boris*
2. *Grandma and the Pirates*
3. *Peter Pan and the Pirates*

Discuss what the word booty means in relation to pirates. Help the children make some booty or treasure. Have construction paper crowns available to color. Use glue and glitter for a jeweled effect. Size the crowns on the students' heads and tie the strings to the right sizes. They can also make coins, bracelets, necklaces, rings, etc., using paper, yarn, ribbon, and pipe cleaners.

Station 2 Activity Card—Writing

Materials:

- shape books
- pencils
- crayons

Directions: Prepare shape books (see page 219 for patterns) as described on previous shape book activity cards. Give each child a shape book. Then assign one of the following activities:

1. On the first page tell the children to write, "In my treasure chest I found . . . ." On each of the following pages, ask the children to write the name of and draw a picture of an item that might be found in a treasure chest.

2. Ask the students to write a word that starts with the letter "p" on each page. (Older students may try writing sentences which are made of primarily "p" words.) Then ask the students to illustrate the pages.

Crown Pattern

1. Start with a large piece of construction paper.

2. Fold the paper in half and place this pattern along the fold. You may be able to cut two from one piece.

3. Punch a hole in both ends of the crown. Add strings to the ends.

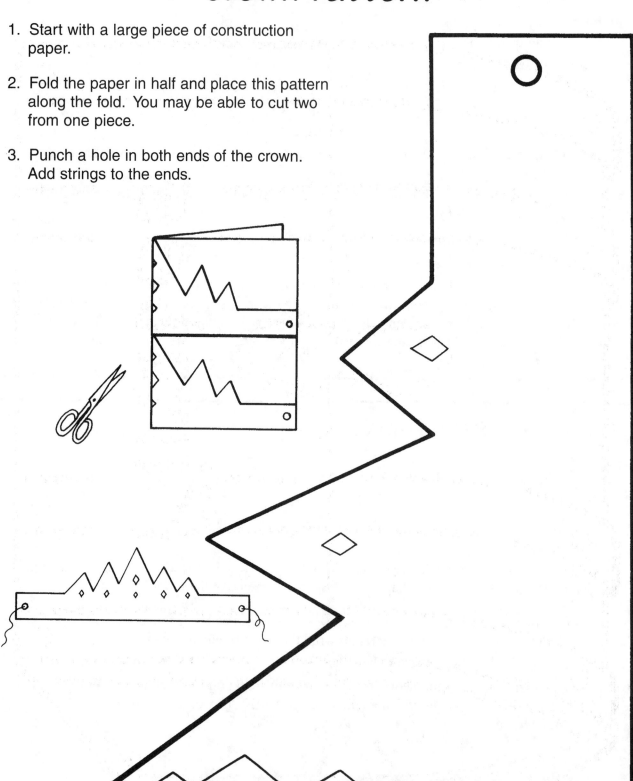

Place this edge on the fold.

Shape Book Pattern

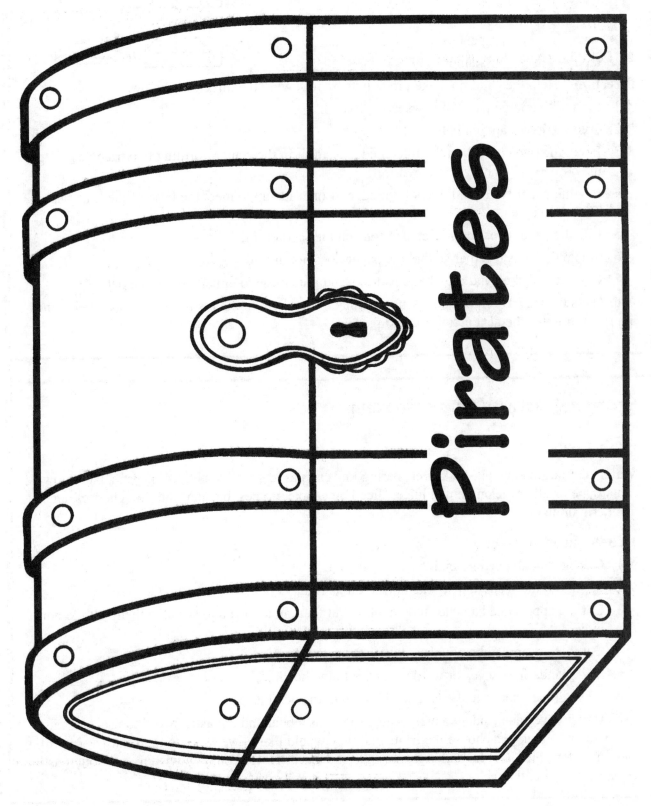

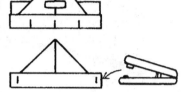

Station 3 Activity Card—Pirate Hats

Materials:

- newspaper
- scissors
- tape
- skull and crossbones pattern (page 221)
- pencils
- stapler

Directions: Help the children make pirate hats by following the directions below.

1. Start with a large piece of newspaper, folded.
2. Fold the newspaper in half.
3. Bring the two corners on the folded edge to meet in the center, forming two triangles. Tape the corners together where they meet.
4. Lay the paper flat. Fold the bottom edge of one side up to meet the base of the triangles. Then fold again.
5. Flip the paper over and repeat step four on the second side.
6. Staple the ends together so that the paper does not unfold.
7. Cut out two skull and crossbone patterns and glue these to either side of the hat.

After the students have finished making their hats, take them to the restrooms to wash their hands in preparation for the next activity, cooking.

Station 4 Activity Card—Cooking

Fruit Boats

Materials: large bowl, plastic knives, paring knives, plastic sword appetizer skewers, paper towels, cantaloupe or other melon, lemon juice, sliced pineapple, grapes, bananas, apples, cherries, and mandarin oranges

To Be Done in Advance:

1. Cut the cantaloupe into eighths.
2. Clean out the seeds and set each piece on its rind.
3. Cut the apples and bananas into chunks. Put them in a bowl and sprinkle them with lemon juice.
4. Cut the pineapple into chunks. Add them to the bowl.
5. Add mandarin oranges or whole cherries to the bowl.
6. Wash grapes, separate them, and add them to the bowl also.

Directions: Give each student a melon slice to use as a boat and a plastic sword to use as a mast. Allow them to pick and choose the fruits that they would like to weave onto their masts. Insert the masts into the ship. Let the children enjoy their snacks. (**Note:** You may wish to hand out plastic utensils for eating the melon.)

Skull and Crossbones Patterns

Station 5 Activity Card—Group Treasure Map

Materials: one 6-foot (1.8 m) section of butcher paper per group, crayons, black markers, and pencils

Directions: Ask the students to work together to create a treasure map by carefully following your instructions. Read the instructions below to the group. (**Note:** You may need to help the younger students with some of the instructions.)

1. Draw a large island in the middle of the paper.
2. Name your island and write its name at the top or side of the paper.
3. Draw a river on your island.
4. Create a lake on your island.
5. Make a swamp forest on your island.
6. Draw a haunted forest on your island.
7. Next to the coast, make mountains.
8. Draw a secret cave.
9. Create a waterfall on the river.
10. Show a boat landing area.
11. Put a big X where your treasure is buried.
12. Draw a dashed line to show how to get from the boat landing to the treasure.
13. Finish the map by coloring in the water and landmarks.

If there is any extra time, let the older students write directions for the map (for example, take 10 paces to the north . . .).

Station 6 Activity Card—Math

Materials: note cards, tape, treasure patterns (pages 223 and 224), pencils, scratch paper, and treasure key (page 225)

To Be Done in Advance:

1. Make several copies of the treasure patterns on pages 223 and 224.
2. Color and cut out the treasure patterns.
3. Glue each piece of treasure to a note card. Laminate.

Directions:

1. Lay the laminated note cards upside down on the table. Ask the students to mix them up.
2. Let each student pick three to five cards (depending on their math levels). Ask them to refer to the treasure key (page 225) to find out the worth of their individual treasures. Then challenge them to each add up the total worth of their treasures.
3. Mix up the cards and ask the children to draw again.
4. Continue until the activity time is up. You may choose to give the student with the largest "catch" a sticker or other small prize.

222

Treasure Patterns

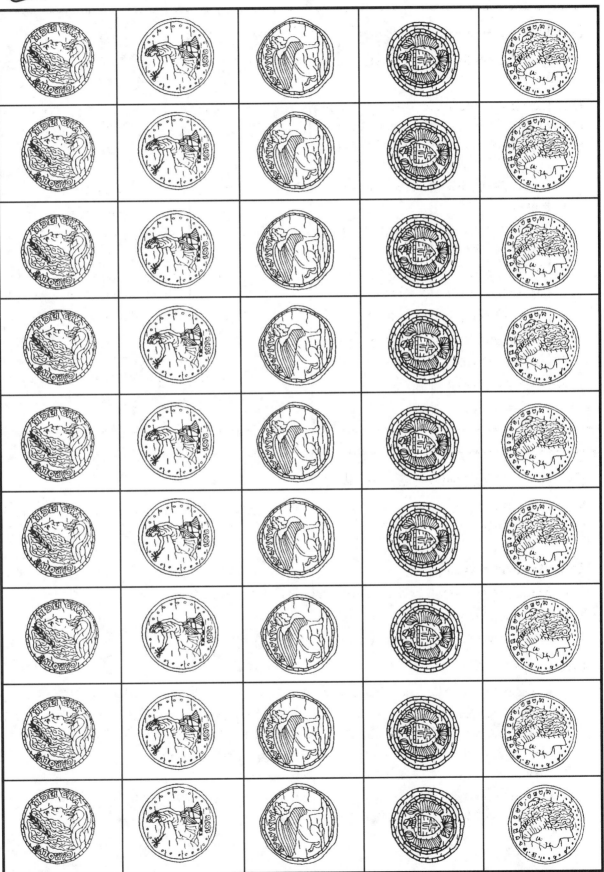

Treasure Patterns *(cont.)*

Treasure Key

$10.00	$1,000.00
$5.00	$500.00
$1.00	$100.00
$.50	$50.00
$.25	$20.00

     #2034 Celebrate ABC's

Station 7 Activity Card—Indoor Treasure Hunt

Materials: note cards, tape, classroom maps, treasure patterns, and crayons

To Be Done in Advance:

1. Make copies of the treasure patterns on pages 223 and 224.
2. Color and cut out 25 of the treasure patterns.
3. Glue each piece of treasure to a note card. Laminate.
4. Number the cards 1–25.
5. Make a map of your classroom.
6. Write the numbers 1–25 on the map on items of furniture, windows, etc., around the room.
7. Tape the corresponding numbered card to the item in the room.

Directions: It is very important that the groups do not see what is going on at this station until it is their turn. You might use another room for this activity, perhaps another classroom, the library, or the multipurpose room.

Give each student or pair of students a map to find the treasures (note cards). When they find a piece of treasure, tell them to mark an X on their maps where they found it. If you let them collect the treasure pieces, you will have to replace the cards before each rotation. (Younger children will need help with the map. Perhaps upper-grade buddies would be useful.)

Station 8 Activity Card—Outdoor Treasure Hunt

Materials: note cards, clear packing tape, crayons, treasure patterns, and school maps

To Be Done in Advance:

1. Make copies of the treasure patterns on pages 223 and 224.
2. Color and cut out 25 of the treasure patterns.
3. Glue each piece of treasure to a note card. Laminate.
4. Number the cards 1–25.
5. Make a map of the school.
6. Write the numbers 1–25 on the map on buildings, play equipment, etc., around the school.
7. Tape the corresponding numbered cards to the items around the school. Use clear packing tape to tape the cards high enough that other students will not be able to reach them.

Directions: Give each student or pair of students a map to find the treasures (note cards). When they find a piece of treasure, tell them to mark an X on their maps where they found it. If you let them collect the treasure pieces, you will have to replace the cards before each rotation. (Younger children will need help with the map. Perhaps upper-grade buddies would be useful.)

(**Note:** It may be fun to combine this activity with a class field trip to the park. Ask parent helpers to visit the park ahead of time to hide the treasure pieces and make the maps.)

Alternate Activity 1—Treasure Clues

Materials:

- note cards
- clues
- crayons
- treasure patterns
- pencils
- tally sheets

To Be Done in Advance:

1. Make copies of the treasure patterns on pages 223 and 224.
2. Color and cut out one to three of each of the treasure patterns (depending on how many treasure pieces you want to hide).
3. Glue each piece of treasure to a note card. Laminate.
4. Hide the treasure pieces in the classroom and around the school.
5. Write a clue on a note card for each piece of hidden treasure. (See page 228 for examples.)

Directions: This activity is meant to be a variation of activity 7 (see page 226). Instead of using maps to find the treasure pieces, challenge the students to use the clues you give them. Younger children may need some help during this activity; older student buddies work well. After the children have been given enough time to search for the treasure pieces, gather everyone together and discuss where the pieces were hidden.

Alternate Activity 2—Pirate Flags

Materials:

- example flags (page 229)
- black construction paper
- pencils
- white chalk

Directions: Show the children some examples of pirate flags (page 229). Explain that the most commonly used pirate flag was the skull and crossbones; however, many pirates designed their own flags. Ask the students to design their own pirate flags on black construction paper. First, have the students draw the shapes of their flags in pencil. Ask the students to cut the flags out. Then, in chalk, let them create their own pirate designs. Encourage students to draw things that represent themselves, for example, hobbies and personality traits. Finally, remind the students to write their names on the backs of the flags and post the flags around the room.

Sample Treasure Hunt Clues

The following are example clues for alternate activity 1 (see page 227).

Library	Books, books, books! Check them out!
Detention	If a ticket you receive, in this room you will be (at lunch, that is)!
Bathrooms	If you visit this room during class, you have to put your name on the chalkboard with a circle around it.
Basketball Court	Throw the ball through the hoop and score two points!
Monkey Bars	Run, slide, pull up, climb; where do you begin?
Computer Lab	This room is loaded with keys.
Bike Rack	This is the place you lock your bike.
Music Room	There are a lot of notes in this room.
Front Steps	Step down here on your way home!
Flag Pole	Salute to me as I wave in the breeze!
Office	If you are absent, you must go through me to get your pink slip.
Lunch Tables	If you bring your lunch, you eat here.
Cafeteria Door	You pass through me when you are hungry.
Bus Gate	If you ride a bus, you pass through me!

228

Pirate Flag Samples

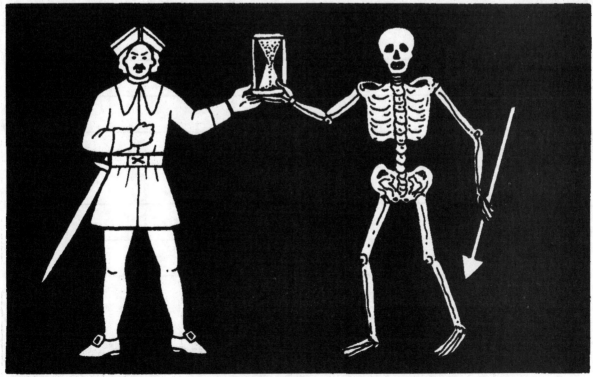

Stationery

Incentives

Use the following cards for positive reinforcement during your rotations. When a student successfully demonstrates positive behavior and completion of his or her tasks, cut out a treasure piece square and paste it onto his or her treasure chest. If you do not have time to cut and paste, a star sticker or stamp would work well. Distribute awards/name tags and bookmarks where appropriate.

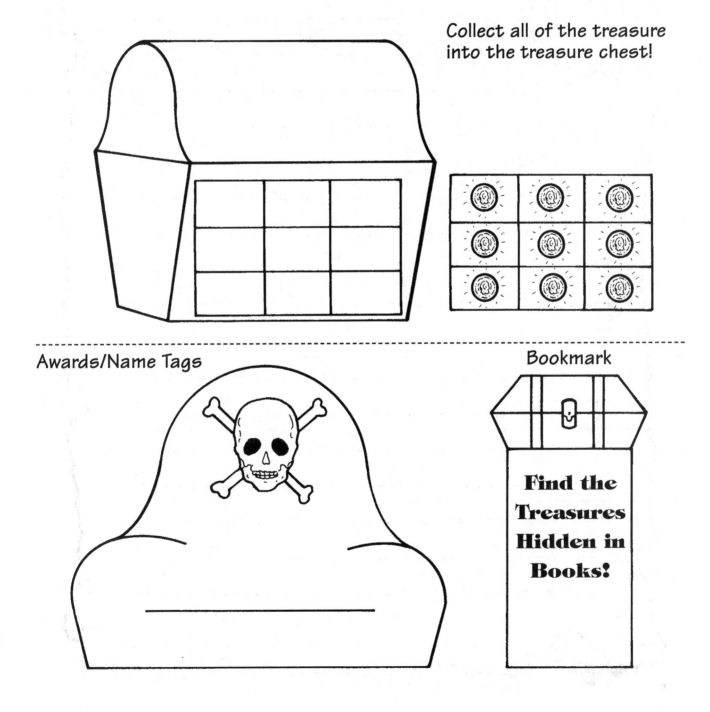

Collect all of the treasure into the treasure chest!

Awards/Name Tags

Bookmark

Find the Treasures Hidden in Books!

Quilts

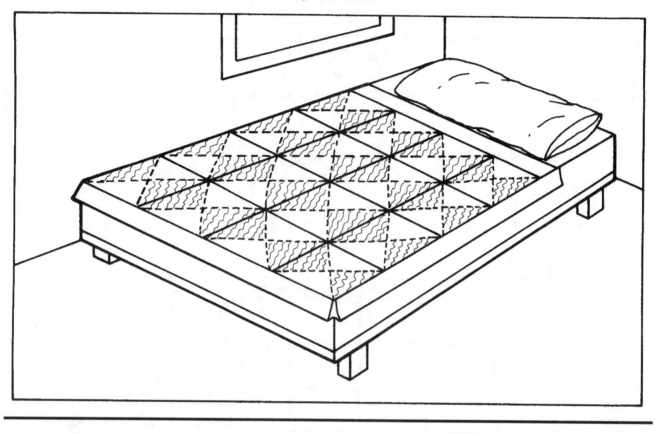

Teacher Note: Use this page as an introduction to the Quilts theme. Have your students color the picture. Lines are provided for writing activities of your choice.

Unit Materials

Bibliography

Flourney, Valerie. *The Patchwork Quilt.* Dial Books for Young Readers, 1985.

Jonas, Ann. *The Quilt.* Greenwillow Books, 1984.

Palacco, Patricia. *The Keeping Quilt.* Simon and Schuster, 1988.

Materials Checklist

Station 1—Literature
_____ any of the suggested literature selections
_____ quilts
_____ activity card

Station 2—Writing
_____ fabric scraps (brought from children's homes)
_____ quilt stationery
_____ pencils
_____ crayons
_____ construction paper
_____ activity card

Station 3—Crazy Quilt Art
_____ construction paper
_____ pencils
_____ black markers
_____ crayons, colored pencils, or markers
_____ activity card

Station 4—Quilt Coloring
_____ quilt block patterns
_____ pencils
_____ crayons
_____ tape
_____ scissors
_____ activity card

Station 5—Cooking
_____ paper plates
_____ napkins
_____ bread
_____ sandwich meat
_____ Monterey Jack cheese
_____ American cheese
_____ cream cheese
_____ pickle relish
_____ sliced olives
_____ mayonnaise
_____ mustard
_____ catsup
_____ activity card

Station 6—Writing
_____ shape books
_____ quilting books for reference
_____ pencils
_____ crayons
_____ activity card

Station 7—Quilt Block Math
_____ geometric pattern pieces
_____ construction paper squares
_____ pencils
_____ scratch paper
_____ scissors
_____ activity card

Station 8—Geoboard Patterns
_____ geoboards (one per student)
_____ rubber bands
_____ pattern cards
_____ activity card

Station 1 Activity Card—Literature

Materials:

- any of the suggested literature selections
- quilts

Directions:

1. Read *The Keeping Quilt, The Patchwork Quilt,* or *The Quilt* to the students.

2. Share a collection of real quilts with the children. Borrow as many different types as you can. Talk about how each type is made, how much they are worth, and how their value is measured.

3. Ask the students if their families have any quilts. Ask them to describe the quilts and where they are from.

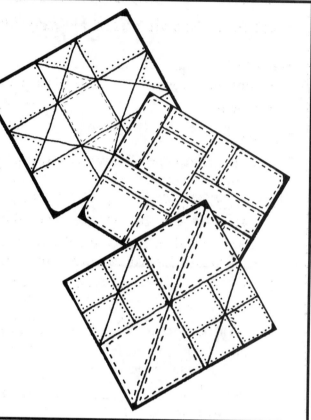

Station 2 Activity Card—Writing

Materials:

- quilt stationery (page 250)
- pencils
- construction paper
- fabric scraps (brought from children's homes)
- crayons

Directions:

1. Ask each child to bring to school a piece of cloth from home.
2. Talk about where each fabric piece came from.
3. Give each child a sheet of quilt stationery.
4. Ask them to write about their fabric pieces.
5. Have them draw their fabric pieces (or staple on the actual fabric) on a blank 9" x 12" (22.8 x 30.4 cm) piece of construction paper.
6. Compile the group's papers for a group quilt book.

Note: As a variation to this activity, you may wish to make an actual quilt from the pieces. If so, be sure to specify the size of the fabric pieces ahead of time so that they are all the same. Sew the pieces together to make a Super Star quilt. Whoever is the Super Star of the Week may take it home.

Station 3 Activity Card—Crazy Quilt Art

Materials:

- construction paper
- pencils
- black markers
- crayons, colored pencils, or markers

Directions:

1. Discuss what crazy quilts are. Explain that they are made out of fabric scraps and use random shapes. The shapes are usually sewn together with a variety of special stitches.
2. Give each child a 9" x 12" (22.8 x 30.4 cm) sheet of white paper. Show the students how to divide the paper into large geometric shapes to look like a crazy quilt.
3. Tell the children to color the shapes with colored pencils, markers, or crayons. They may wish to give the fabrics different patterns.
4. Go over the lines, using a black marker. Make the lines look like fancy stitches. Some examples are below.

 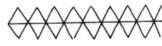 

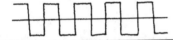  

Station 4 Activity Card—Quilt Coloring

Materials:

- quilt block patterns (pages 236–243)
- pencils
- crayons
- scissors
- tape

Directions:

1. Let each child choose one of the block patterns to color.
2. Ask the children to color the quilt patterns. Challenge them to create stripes, calicos, polka dots, etc., not just solid colors.
3. Tell the students to cut out the blocks along the outer edges.
4. Tape the blocks together to create a small paper quilt.
5. Take the students to the restrooms to wash their hands in preparation for the next activity, cooking.

Quilt Block Patterns

Pinwheel

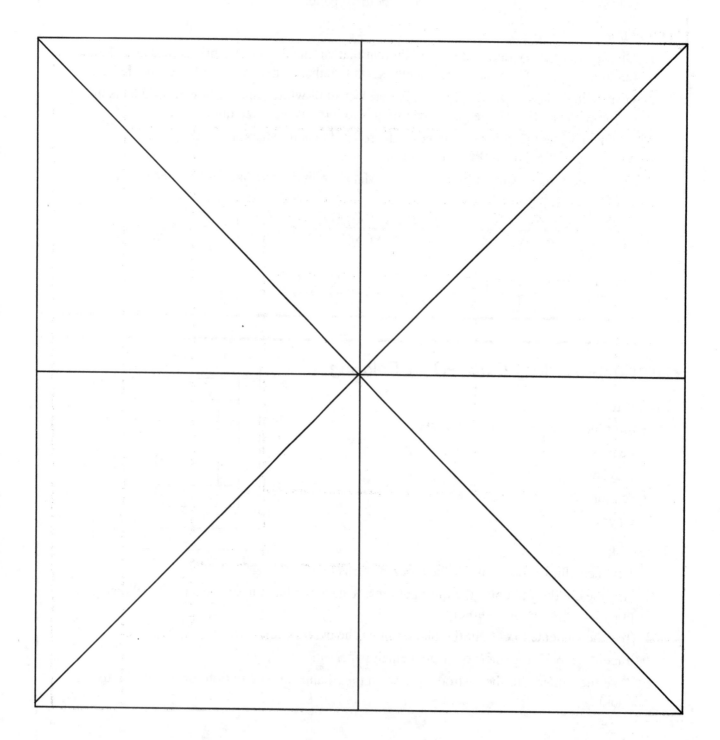

236

Quilt Block Patterns (cont.)

Log Cabin

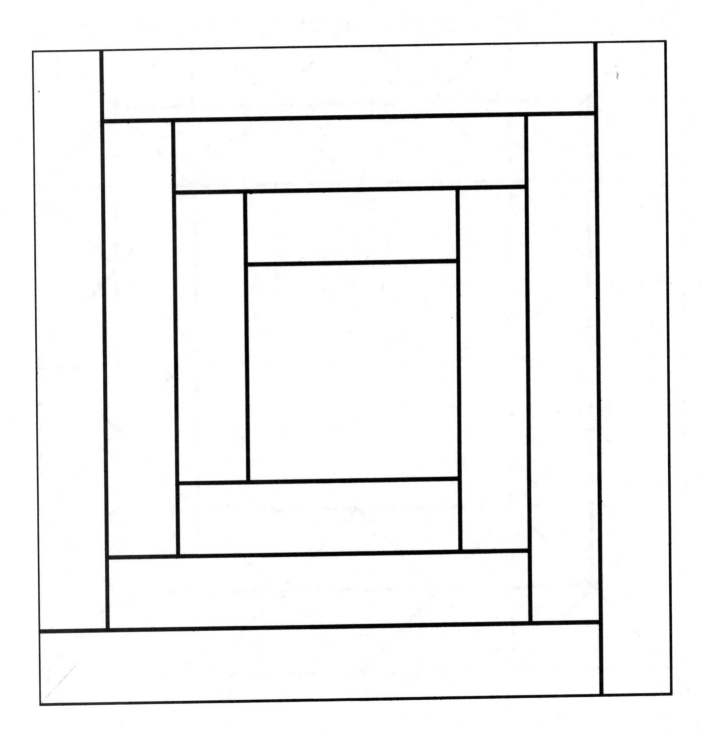

Quilt Block Patterns (cont.)

Ocean Waves

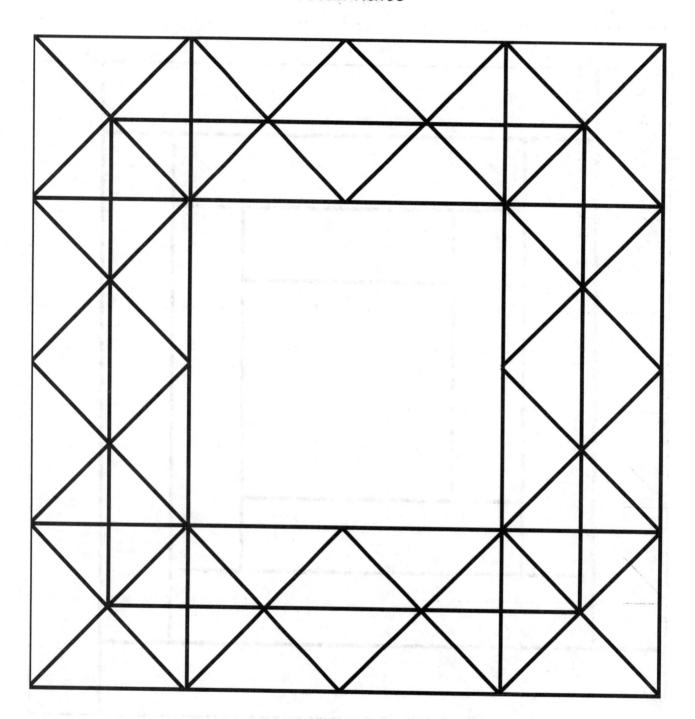

238

Quilt Block Patterns *(cont.)*

Bear's Paw

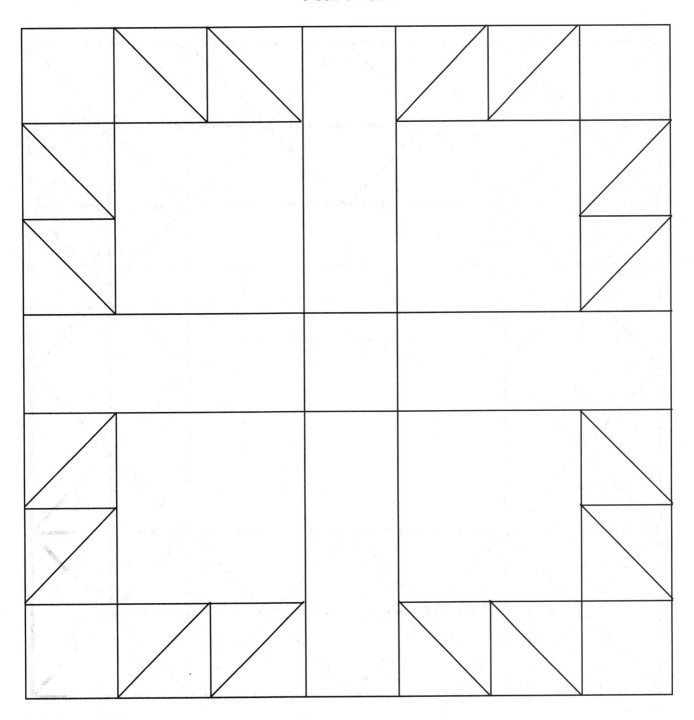

Quilt Block Patterns *(cont.)*

Double Nine Patch

Quilt Block Patterns (cont.)

Tumbling Blocks

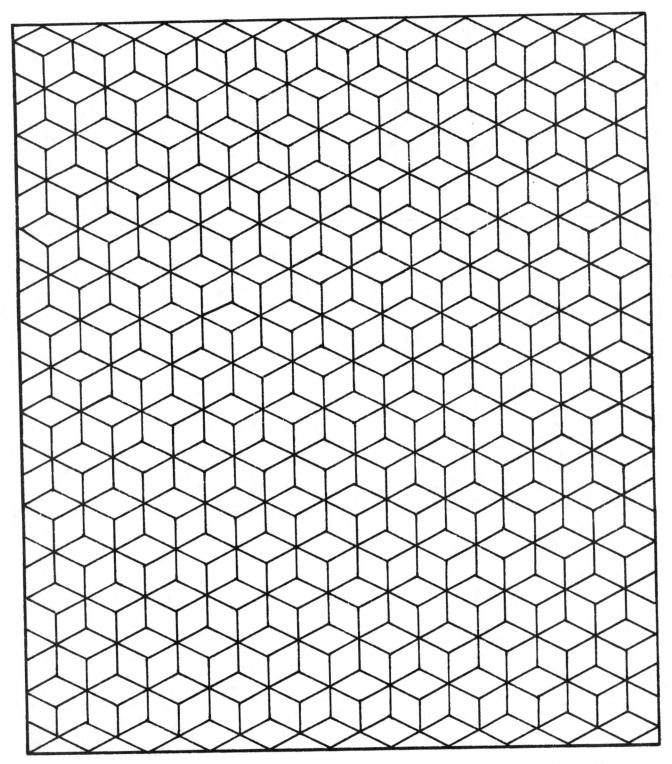

Quilt Block Patterns (cont.)

Sawtooth Star

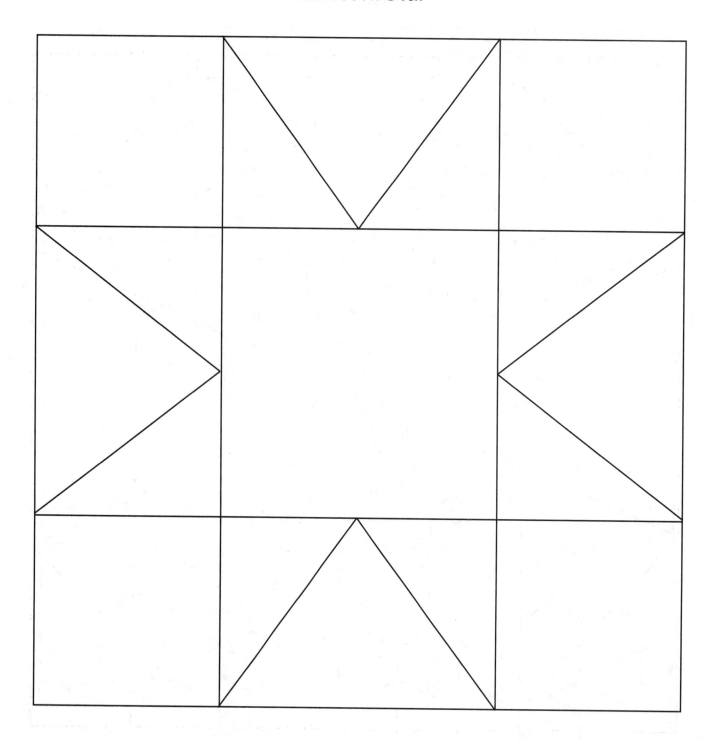

Quilt Block Patterns *(cont.)*

Kaleidoscope

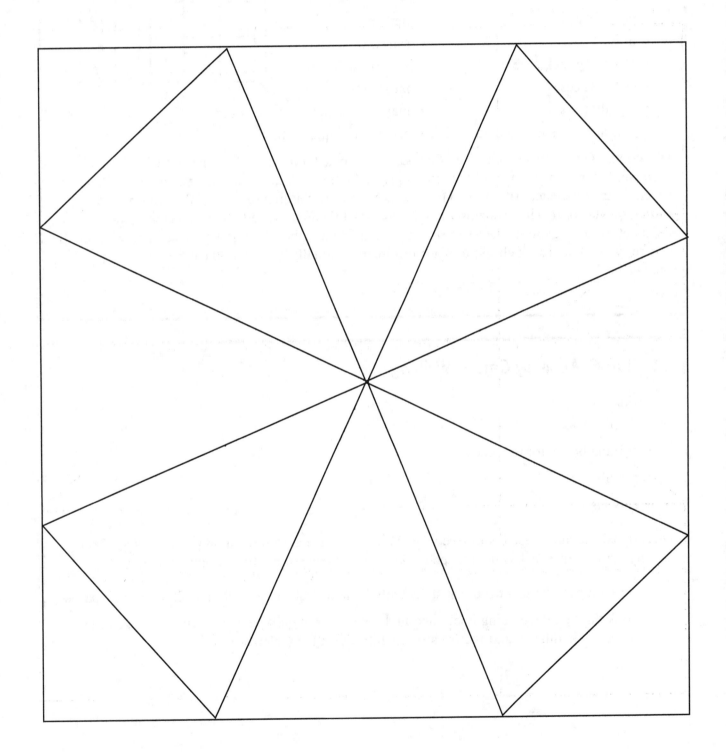

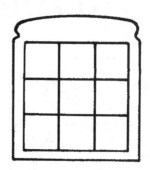

Station 5 Activity Card—Cooking

Nine Patch Quilt Sandwiches

Materials:

- paper plates
- bread
- Monterey Jack cheese
- cream cheese
- sliced olives
- mustard in a squeeze bottle

- napkins
- sandwich meat
- American cheese
- pickle relish
- mayonnaise in a squeeze bottle
- catsup in a squeeze bottle

Directions: Give each child a slice of bread. Lay a piece of meat on each person's bread. Let each child choose one or two of the three squeeze bottles (mustard, mayonnaise, or catsup) and squeeze the Nine Patch pattern onto their bread. Ask the children to "color" the quilt blocks by adding pickles or relish to squares 1 and 2. Then, let them put sliced olives in squares 3 and 4. Help out by adding cream cheese to squares 5 and 6. Give the children American cheese to add to squares 7 and 8 and Jack cheese to place in square 9. Finally, tell them to eat their quilt sandwiches!

Station 6 Activity Card—Writing

Materials:

- shape books
- quilting books for reference
- pencils
- crayons

Directions: Prepare shape books (see page 245 for pattern) as described on previous shape book activity cards. Give each child a shape book and assign one of the following activities.

1. On each page write a word that starts with the letter "q" or has a Q in it. Illustrate the pages.

2. Look through the quilting books and find your favorite quilt patterns. On each page of your shape book, draw a quilt pattern and label it. Color the patterns.

Shape Book Pattern

Station 7 Activity Card—Quilt Block Math

Materials: geometric pattern pieces, construction paper squares, pencils, scratch paper, and scissors

To Be Done in Advance: Make 25–30 copies of pages 247 and 248 on sturdy paper or on regular paper that can then be laminated. Carefully cut out the shapes. Also, cut out enough 7" x 7" (17.7 x 17.7 cm) squares of construction paper so that each child may have one.

Directions:

1. Give each child a construction paper square. Lay out the dozens of geometric figures on the table.

2. Ask the students to use any combination of the geometric figures to create blocks on top of the construction paper squares.

3. After the children have practiced working with the shapes, tell them you are going to play a math game. Explain that each shape will be worth one point. Ask the students, "Who can make a block worth the fewest number of points?" Once the children have created their blocks, ask them to add up their points. For example, a block made up of four geometric figures would be worth four points. Congratulate the person with the fewest points.

4. Continue challenging the students with other questions, such as "Who can make a block worth the most points?" and "Who can make a block worth exactly 10 points?"

5. If there is any extra time, have half of the students create blocks and then ask the other half to try to replicate them.

Station 8 Activity Card—Geoboard Patterns

Materials:

- geoboards (one per student)
- rubber bands
- pattern cards (page 249)

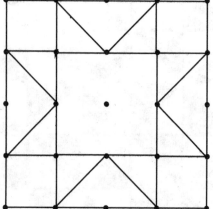

Directions:

1. Pair the students. If one person is left without a partner, you may be the partner or make one group of three.

2. Give each set of partners a geoboard, some rubber bands, and a pattern card (page 249). Ask them to recreate the patterns on the cards on the geoboards. Tell the students to trade the pattern cards among themselves and try again.

3. After the students have worked for 10 minutes or so, take the patterns away and have them model and copy patterns for each other. (One set of partners will make a pattern, and another will copy it.)

Math Pattern Pieces

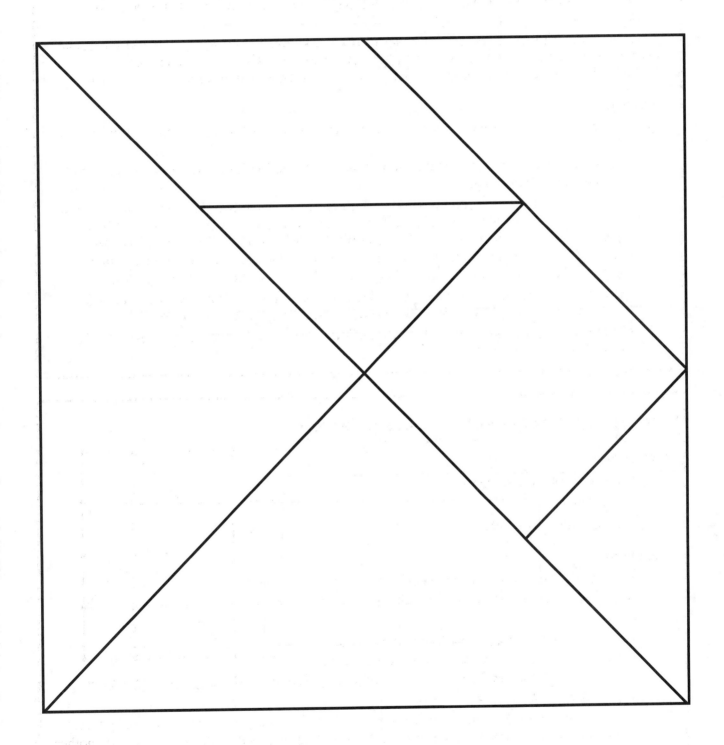

Math Pattern Pieces *(cont.)*

Geoboard Patterns

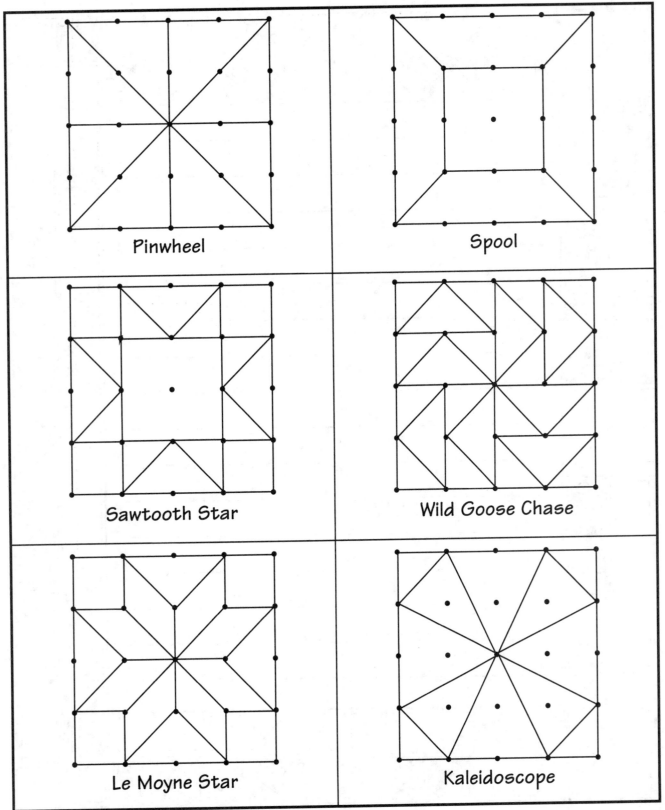

Pinwheel

Spool

Sawtooth Star

Wild Goose Chase

Le Moyne Star

Kaleidoscope

#2034 Celebrate ABC's

Stationery

Incentives

Use the following cards for positive reinforcement during your rotations. When a student successfully demonstrates positive behavior and completion of his or her tasks, cut out a quilt block square and paste it onto his or her quilt. If you do not have time to cut and paste, a star sticker or stamp would work well. Distribute awards/name tags and bookmarks.

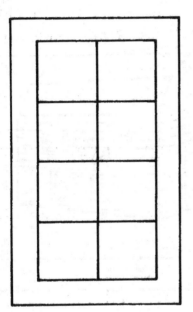

Make a quilt out of the quilt blocks!

Award/Name Tag

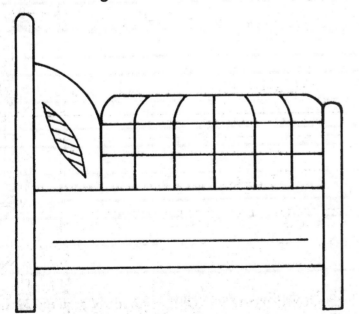

Bookmark

Reading Is Sew Much Fun!

Red

Teacher Note: Use this page as an introduction to the Red theme. Have your students color the picture. Lines are provided for writing activities of your choice.

Unit Materials

Bibliography

Bridwell, Norman. *Clifford, the Big Red Dog.* Scholastic, 1985.
Grimm, Jakob and Wilhelm. *The Little Red Hen* (any version).
Grimm, Jakob and Wilhelm. *Little Red Riding Hood* (any version).

Materials Checklist

Station 1—Literature

_____ *Little Red Riding Hood*
_____ *The Little Red Hen*
_____ overhead outline patterns
_____ overhead projector
_____ paper
_____ felt
_____ flannelboard
_____ scissors
_____ activity card

Station 2—Paper Bag Puppets

_____ *Little Red Riding Hood*
_____ *The Little Red Hen*
_____ puppet patterns
_____ construction paper
_____ lunch-sized paper bags
_____ crayons
_____ scissors
_____ glue
_____ activity card

Station 3—Writing

_____ shape books
_____ pencils
_____ crayons
_____ activity card

Station 4—Remembering Red Game

_____ red construction paper
_____ item cards
_____ activity card

Station 5—Cooking

_____ clear plastic dessert cups
_____ plastic spoons
_____ 2–3 large spoons
_____ canned cherry pie filling
_____ instant vanilla pudding mix
_____ milk
_____ angel food cake
_____ canned whipped cream
_____ napkins
_____ activity card

Station 6—Watermelon Mosaics

_____ 12" x 18" (30.4 x 45.7 cm) royal blue construction paper
_____ pencils
_____ glue
_____ construction paper (red, dark green, light green, and black)

_____ activity card

Station 7—Math

_____ red item cards
_____ red item codes
_____ pencils
_____ scrap paper
_____ activity card

Station 8—Writing

_____ sentence strips
_____ note cards
_____ pencils
_____ crayons
_____ stapler
_____ tape
_____ pocket chart
_____ activity card

Station 1 Activity Card—Literature

Materials:

- *Little Red Riding Hood*
- overhead projector
- felt
- scissors
- *The Little Red Hen*
- paper
- flannelboard
- overhead outline patterns (pages 255 and 256)

To Be Done in Advance: Use the patterns on pages 255 and 256 to create one of the following:

1. paper cutouts to be used on an overhead projector
2. felt cutouts to be used on a flannelboard

Directions:

1. Read a favorite version of *Little Red Riding Hood* or *The Little Red Hen*.

2. Retell the story by using an overhead projector and the characters on pages 255 and 256 or by using a flannelboard and felt cutouts from the same page.

Station 2 Activity Card—Paper Bag Puppets

Materials:

- *Little Red Riding Hood*
- puppet patterns (pages 257–260)
- lunch-sized paper bags
- scissors
- *The Little Red Hen*
- construction paper
- crayons
- glue

Directions:

1. Let each child choose one puppet to make. Encourage them to choose different characters so that when they are finished they will be able to do a puppet skit with all of the characters.

2. Hand out the puppet faces. Ask the children to color and cut out the character faces. Then, have them glue the faces to the bottoms of the paper bags.

3. Give the children enough time to decorate the bodies of the puppets.

4. Provide the opportunity for the children to perform the fairy tales with their puppets.

Overhead/Flannelboard Patterns

Little Red Riding Hood

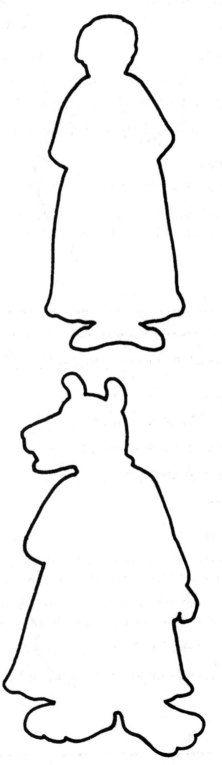

Overhead/Flannelboard Patterns *(cont.)*

Little Red Hen

Rr

Puppet Patterns

Little Red Riding Hood

Puppet Patterns *(cont.)*

Little Red Riding Hood

Puppet Patterns (cont.)

The Little Red Hen

259

Puppet Patterns *(cont.)*

The Little Red Hen

260

Station 3 Activity Card—Writing

Materials:

- shape books
- pencils
- crayons

Directions: Choose one of the shape book covers, either a heart or a stop sign, and prepare shape books. Prepare shape books (see pages 262 and 263 for patterns) as described on previous shape book activity cards. Give each child a shape book and then assign one of the following activities.

1. Ask the children to write about red things in their shape books and then illustrate each page. The younger children may just put one word on each page while the older students may write whole sentences.

2. Teach the children how to make number books of red things. On the first page have them write the number one and a red object and illustrate, for example, one red heart. On the second page ask them to write the number two and another red object, for example, two red shoes. Continue this format on the third page: three red tulips. Fill in the rest of the book, using the same format.

3. Ask the students to write about and illustrate a word that starts with the letter "r" on each page.

Station 4 Activity Card—Remembering Red Game

Materials:

- red construction paper
- two sets of item cards (pages 264 and 265), laminated

To Be Done in Advance: Make two sets of the item cards. Cut them out, color, and laminate. (**Note:** Before laminating, turn the cards over and check to see that they are not see-through. If you can see the items from the back sides, mount the cards on red construction paper before laminating.)

Directions:

1. Mix up the cards and lay them in rows, face down.

2. Let the first player turn over two cards. If, by chance, he or she makes a match (for example, two hearts), he or she may keep the cards. When a match is made, the player will continue taking more turns until he or she does not make a match.

   If a match is not made the first time, the player must replace the cards upside down in the original positions. The next player will then take a turn.

3. Let the game continue until all of the matches have been made and all of the cards are gone.

4. With the extra time, take the students to the restrooms to wash their hands in preparation for the next activity, cooking.

Shape Book Patterns

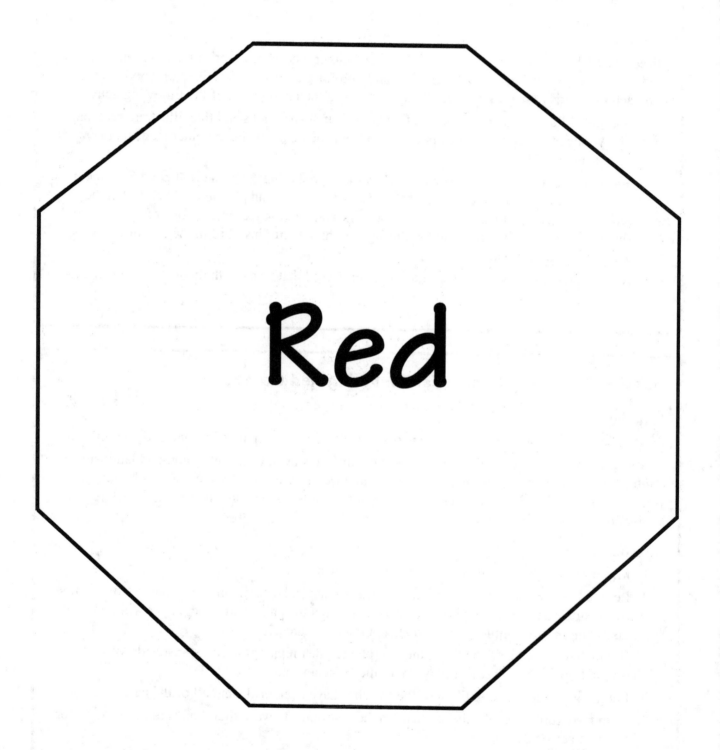

Red

Shape Book Patterns *(cont.)*

Red Item Cards

Crayon

Flower

Ladybug

Heart

Candy Cane

Stop Sign

Apple

Strawberry

Fire Truck

Red Item Cards *(cont.)*

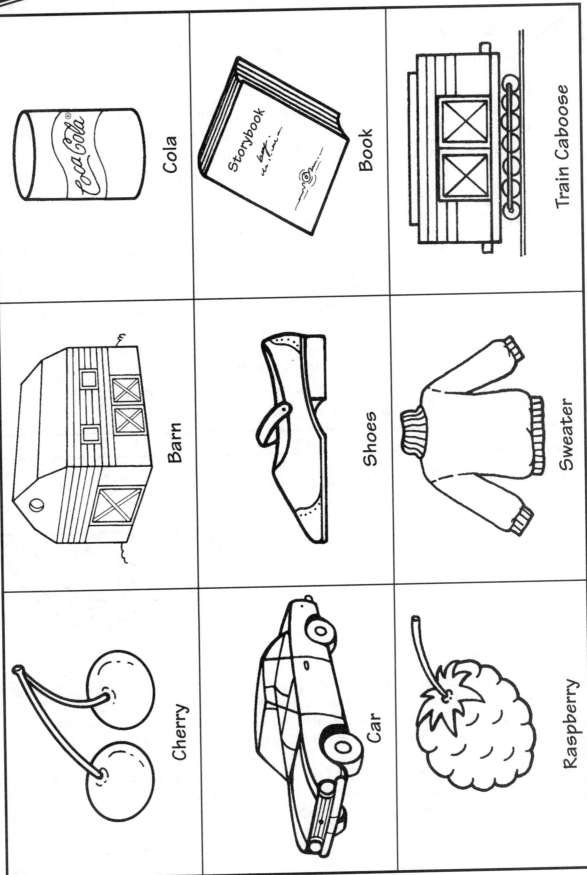

Cola

Book

Train Caboose

Barn

Shoes

Sweater

Cherry

Car

Raspberry

Station 5 Activity Card—Cooking

Cherries Jubilee

Materials:

- clear plastic dessert cups (one per student)
- plastic spoons
- canned cherry pie filling
- milk
- canned whipped cream
- napkins (one per student)
- 2–3 large spoons
- instant vanilla pudding mix (enough for class)
- angel food cake

Directions:

1. Give each student a chunk or slice of cake. Have them tear the cake into smaller pieces and put the pieces into the dessert cups (filling the cups about halfway).

2. Mix the pudding mix with milk (use the amount suggested on the package) in a bowl. Make sure that the pudding is well mixed, but do it quickly. You do not want it to begin to set before the next step.

3. Pour the pudding over the cake in the cups. The pudding will fill in the spaces between the cakes pieces. Pour in enough pudding so that the top of the cake is just covered.

4. Have the children spoon cherry mix on top of the cake and pudding mixture.

5. Add whipped cream, if desired, and enjoy!

Station 6 Activity Card—Watermelon Mosaics

Materials:

- 12" x 18" (30.4 x 45.7 cm) royal blue construction paper

- pencils

- glue

- construction paper (red, dark green, light green, and black)

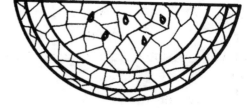

Directions: Give the children pieces of large blue paper (one per student) and have them write their names on the backs. Next, ask them to each draw a large half-oval shape (the watermelon outline) in pencil. Tell them to make another line about an inch away from the bottom line. Finally, ask them to make still another line a half inch in from the last line.

To decorate the watermelon outlines, tell the children to tear small pieces of dark green paper for the bottom area (the rind) and glue them in place. They should then tear tiny strips of light green paper for the next area and glue them in place. Now they may tear medium-sized chunks of red paper and glue them to the rest of the watermelon. To finish off the mosaic, ask the children to tear tiny black "seeds" from the paper and glue them randomly onto the red.

Station 7 Activity Card—Math

Materials:

- red item cards (pages 264 and 265)
- red item codes (page 268)
- pencils
- scrap paper

To Be Done in Advance: Make several copies of the red item cards on pages 264 and 265. Cut out the cards and laminate them.

Directions: Use the red item cards to make up addition equations. Display one of the two codes (page 268) where the children can read it. Younger children will need to use Code A while older, more advanced students may use Code B. The codes give numerical values to each of the red symbols. Start by holding up two cards. Ask, for example, how much a heart plus a flower equals. Tell the children to refer to the code and then solve the problem on scratch paper. Discuss the answer. Continue creating more problems of increasing difficulty (try adding three or four cards at a time). After awhile, let the children use the cards to make up problems for each other.

Station 8 Activity Card—Writing

Materials:

- sentence strips
- stapler
- note cards
- tape
- pencils
- pocket chart
- crayons

To Be Done in Advance: On four sentence strips write the following lines and illustrations:

1. "Who will help me?"
2. "Not I," said the duck.
3. "Then I will do it myself."
4. And so she did.

On two note cards write and draw the following.

cat

pig

Staple the two cards on top of each other on strip #2 over the word "duck" and the duck picture. Place the strips in a pocket chart.

Directions: Give each of the students four sentence strips and two note cards. Ask them to prepare their sentence strips and cards the same way you did the pocket chart example. Arrange their strips in the correct order and then staple them into a book. Read the story aloud three times with the students. Each time change the animal on the second page by flipping up the cards.

Math Symbol Codes

Code A

1 ___

2 ___

3 ___

4 ___

5 ___

6 ___

7 ___

8 ___

9 ___

Code B

5 ___

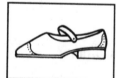

10 ___

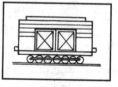

15 ___

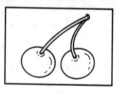

20 ___

25 ___

30 ___

35 ___

40 ___

45 ___

Stationery

Incentives

Use the following cards for positive reinforcement during your rotations. When a student successfully demonstrates positive behavior and completion of his or her tasks, cut out a strawberry square and paste it onto his or her basket card. If you do not have time to cut and paste, a star sticker or stamp would work well. Distribute awards/name tags and bookmarks where appropriate.

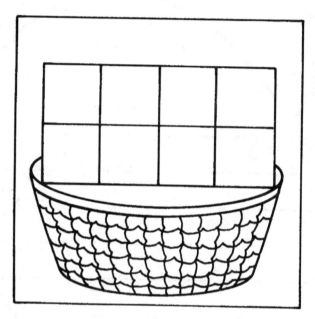

Fill the basket with strawberries!

Award/Name Tag

Bookmark

Space

Teacher Note: Use this page as an introduction to the Space theme. Have your students color the picture. Lines are provided for writing activities of your choice.

Unit Materials

Bibliography

Hirst, Robin. *My Place in Space.* Orchard Books, 1992.

Lovejoy, Pamela. *If I Were an Astronaut.* Learn-Abouts Publications, 1994.

Marshall, Edward. *Space Case.* Dial Books for Young Readers, 1982.

Simon, Seymour. *Our Solar System.* Morrow Jr. Books, 1992.

If you cannot find these books, substitute any good nonfiction books about the solar system or space flight for *Our Solar System* and *If I Were an Astronaut.* Other fiction books can be substituted for *Space Case* and *My Place in Space.*

Materials Checklist

Station 1—Literature

- _____ *Our Solar System* and/or other nonfiction space books
- _____ blackboard
- _____ chalk
- _____ activity card

Station 2—Shape Books

- _____ shape books
- _____ pictures of the nine planets in our solar system
- _____ pencils
- _____ crayons
- _____ activity card

Station 3—Art

- _____ white or light blue construction paper
- _____ pencils
- _____ brushes
- _____ crayons
- _____ black tempera paint, in containers (watered down)
- _____ pictures or a model of the solar system
- _____ activity card

Station 4—Math

- _____ 4–5 sets of laminated Astronaut and Spaceship Cards
- _____ scratch paper
- _____ pencils
- _____ activity card

Station 5—Sun Mosaics

- _____ sun patterns
- _____ black, yellow, and orange construction paper
- _____ pencils
- _____ paste or glue
- _____ activity card

Station 6—Strip Book

- _____ *My Place in Space*
- _____ pencils
- _____ sentence strips or adding machine tape
- _____ example sentence strips
- _____ crayons
- _____ stapler
- _____ activity card

Station 7—Puzzle

- _____ word search puzzles
- _____ pencils
- _____ activity card

Station 8—Cooking

- _____ bread
- _____ American cheese
- _____ sliced olives
- _____ pickle slices
- _____ mustard in a squeeze bottle
- _____ mayonnaise in a squeeze bottle
- _____ bologna
- _____ carrot sticks
- _____ activity card

Station 1 Activity Card—Literature

Materials:

- *Our Solar System* and/or other nonfiction space books
- blackboard
- chalk

Directions:

1. Read *Our Solar System* or any other good nonfiction book on the solar system.

2. Discuss the order of the planets. If this station is near a blackboard, put a portion of the sun on one side of the board and draw the planets in the correct order, starting at the sun.

3. Note their order, size, and distance from each other.

4. Have several extra books available for students to explore if you finish a little early.

Station 2 Activity—Shape Books

Materials:

- shape books
- pictures of the nine planets in our solar system
- pencils
- crayons

Directions: Choose one of the shape book cover patterns (pages 274 and 275). Prepare shape books as described on previous shape book activity cards. Give each child a shape book and then assign one of the following activities.

1. Ask the students to write a story about traveling in outer space. On the first page have them write, "If I had a rocket, I would fly it to . . . ." Tell them to write at least one sentence per page and then illustrate the pages. This can be done as a group or individually.

2. List the names of the nine planets. Ask the students to write a planet name on each page of their books and then illustrate the pages. Pictures of the planets would be helpful for this activity.

3. Tell the students to write a word that begins with the letter "s" on each page and then illustrate.

Shape Book Patterns

Shape Book Patterns (cont.)

Space

Station 3 Activity Card—Art

Materials:

- white or light blue construction paper
- pencils
- brushes
- crayons

- black tempera paint, in containers (watered down)
- pictures or a model of the solar system

Directions:

1. Share a chart or model of the solar system with the students.

2. Ask the children to draw and color the solar system onto white or light blue construction paper, using crayons. Tell them to do the coloring heavily, leaving no spaces. Also, ask them not to color in their backgrounds.

3. When the coloring is finished, let the students paint over their pictures with black tempera paint that has been slightly watered down. This needs to be done quickly. Do not allow the students to use too much paint. The crayon drawings should reappear from underneath the paint.

Station 4 Activity Card—Math

Materials:

- 4–5 sets of laminated math cards (pages 277–280)
- scratch paper
- pencils

To Be Done in Advance: Make four or five copies of pages 277 and 278. Cut out the cards and laminate them. Choose the cards which would be the most age- and ability-appropriate for your group; younger students will not be able to do them all.

Directions:

1. Pair each student with a partner (you may need to make one group of three). Give each pair of students a set of Astronaut and Spaceship Cards.

2. Tell the students to lay out the Spaceship Cards.

3. Challenge the students to see which pair can work together to match all of the Spaceship Cards to the Astronaut Cards the most quickly. They may use scratch paper and pencils to help.

4. Congratulate the winning pair.

Note: With younger children you may want to do this activity as a group. Lay out the Spaceship Cards so that they can see all of the possible answers. Then work through the math problems on the Astronaut Cards together.

Astronaut Cards

If an astronaut spends 7 days on her first mission and 4 days on her second mission, how many total days will she have spent in space?

5 + 3 =

An astronaut counted 5 stars out of one window and 5 stars out of another window. How many stars did he count in all?

Before leaving the earth, the astronauts heard a countdown . . . "10, 9, 8, 6, 5, 4, 3, 2, 1, Blast-Off!" What was wrong with the countdown?

An astronaut had 3 pockets on each sleeve of his suit. How many pockets did the suit have all together?

If 4 astronauts go on a mission and 2 are women, how many are men?

10 − 5 =

If 5 astronauts plan to go on a mission and 1 gets sick and can't go, how many are left?

Astronaut Cards (cont.)

15 + 3 = 	If 6 astronauts go on a mission and each astronaut needs a pair of boots, how many boots will they need to pack? 
If 10 Russian astronauts are working on a space station and 3 American astronauts join them, how many astronauts would be on the space station all together? 	Each astronaut eats 3 meals a day. There are 3 astronauts on a flight. How many meals will be eaten each day on this flight? 
Out of a 10-day mission, the astronaut has spent 9 days. How many days does she have left? 	17 + 2 = 
17 - 2 = 	An astronaut spent 7 days on his first flight, 4 days on his second, and 6 more on his third flight. How many total days did he spend in space? 

Spaceship Cards

Spaceship Cards *(cont.)*

Station 5 Activity Card—Sun Mosaics

Materials:

- sun patterns
- black, yellow, and orange construction paper
- pencils
- paste or glue

To Be Done in Advance: Make several copies of the patterns on page 282 onto thick paper or tagboard. Cut out the patterns.

Directions:

1. Give each child a piece of black construction paper.
2. Show the children how to draw a sun outline by first tracing the circle pattern and then by tracing triangles around the curves of the circle. Tell the children to draw their own suns on their black construction paper, using pencils.
3. Help the children tear small pieces of yellow and orange construction paper (try to use more than one shade of each color) to glue to their sun designs. The colors can be glued in a pattern, such as orange in the circle and yellow in the triangles, or the colors may be mixed.

Station 6 Activity Card—Strip Book

Materials: *My Place in Space*, pencils, sentence strips or adding machine tape, "Our Place in Space" example sentence strips (page 282), crayons, and a stapler

To Be Done in Advance: Use a large piece of paper or the chalkboard to write the example sentence strips.

Directions:

1. Read the book *My Place in Space* (if you do not have this book, you can still conduct the rest of this activity).
2. Discuss how vast our solar system is. Emphasize that we each live in only a tiny part of the solar system.
3. Give each child a sentence strip. (**Note:** For younger children you may want to write out the strips in advance and just let them fill in the blanks.) The completed sentence strip book will have eight sentence strip pages; so, if you have fewer than eight children in the group, some students will have to do two strips.
4. Ask the first child to write the following title, "Our Place in Space." Ask the next child to write the next line that you wrote on the chalkboard. Assign each child a line to write and discuss what should be written in the blanks. If there is enough time, let the children illustrate their sentences.
5. Staple the strips together to make a book.

Sun Patterns

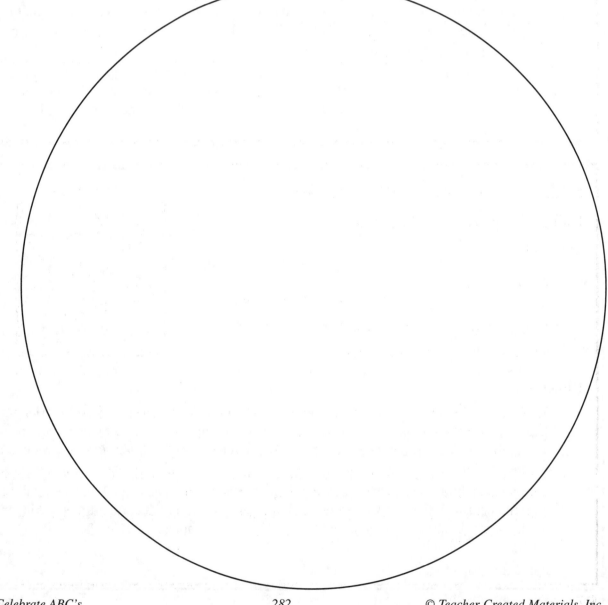

Our Place in Space

We are in the _____ grade

in _____ class

at _____ school

in the city of _____

in the county of _____

in the country of _____

on the continent of _____

on the planet of _____

in the solar system.

Station 7 Activity Card—Puzzle

Materials:

- word search puzzle (page 284)
- pencils

Directions:

1. Give each child a word search puzzle.

2. Discuss the meanings of the words in the word bank.

3. Let the children do their puzzles individually or in pairs. The words can be found going across and down only.

4. With any extra time, take the children to the restrooms to wash their hands in preparation for the next activity, cooking.

```
A T E D Q X Y M O N S A T J P
J N V P T U R A D S E E F C O
R S O J P Y F R A C O T A J T
M X U R A N U S C I M   M R E
R E R H S W O F B E S U N X Y
S A M Y T R E V O N P L U T O
T R M F R Y A S N C A L P E P
A T W   O D R E O E C O J E F
R H M R N E P T U N E M U F P
S U M P A U S P R E R D P E A
Y V E N U S A M O O N A I B O
E F S A T U R N C A N D T M U
U N W T H D O F K A X E E F G
A M X R L C A M E R C U R Y X
M O T G P A T   T P Y A F O Z
```

Station 8 Activity Card—Cooking

Bologna and Cheese Sunwich

Materials:

- bread
- sliced olives
- pickle slices
- bologna
- American cheese
- mustard in a squeeze bottle
- mayonnaise in a squeeze bottle
- carrot sticks

Directions:

1. Give each child a piece of bread, a slice of bologna (or other round sandwich meat), and two slices of cheese.

2. Tell the children to place the bologna on top of the bread.

3. Using plastic knives, help the children cut the cheese slices into triangles. Show them how to add the cheese triangles to the bologna circle to make a sun.

4. Using mustard and/or mayonnaise, let the children attach olive eyes and pickle noses.

5. Finally, give them carrot sticks to use as mouths.

Space Word Search

```
A T E D Q X Y M O N S A T U R
J N V P T U R A D S E E F C O
R S O J P Y F R A C O T A U T
M X U R A N U S C I M I M R E
R E R H S W O F B E S U N X Y
S A M Y T R E V O N P L U T O
T R M F R Y A S N C A L P E R
A T W I O D R E O E C O J E F
R H M R N E P T U N E M U F P
S U M P A U S P R E R D P E A
Y V E N U S A M O O N A I B O
E F S A T U R N C A N D T M U
U N W T H D O F K A X E E F G
A M X R L C A M E R C U R Y X
M O T G P A T E T P Y A F O Z
```

Word Bank

astronaut	Jupiter
rocket	Saturn
moon	Uranus
sun	Neptune
Mercury	Pluto
Venus	science
Earth	space
Mars	stars

Stationery

Incentives

Use the following cards for positive reinforcement during your rotations. When a student successfully demonstrates positive behavior and completion of his or her tasks, cut out a planet square and paste it onto his or her solar system card. If you do not have time to cut and paste, a star sticker or stamp would work well. Distribute awards/name tags and bookmarks where appropriate.

Put the planets back in their orbits!

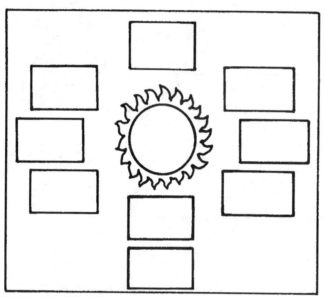

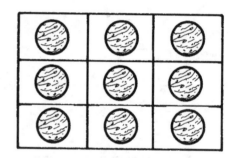

Awards/Name Tag

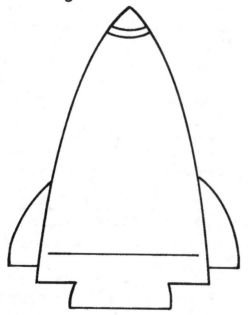

Bookmark

Soar
to the
Stars . . .
Read!

Tales of Three

Teacher Note: Use this page as an introduction to the Tales of Three theme. Have your students color the picture. Lines are provided for writing activities of your choice.

Unit Materials

Bibliography

The Three Bears (any version)

The Three Billy Goats Gruff (any version)

The Three Little Pigs (any version)

Three Little Kittens (any version)

Materials Checklist

Station 1—Literature

_____ *The Three Billy Goats Gruff*

_____ stick puppets patterns

_____ flannelboard patterns

_____ a flannelboard

_____ felt

_____ craft sticks

_____ crayons or markers

_____ scissors

_____ glue

_____ activity card

Station 2—Writing

_____ white construction paper

_____ chalkboard and chalk or butcher paper and a marker

_____ stapler

_____ pencils

_____ markers or crayons

_____ activity card

Station 3—Puzzle

_____ *Three Little Kittens*

_____ mitten puzzles

_____ pencils

_____ crayons or markers

_____ activity card

Station 4—Cooking

_____ butter

_____ marshmallows

_____ evaporated milk

_____ sugar

_____ nuts

_____ salt

_____ semi-sweet chocolate chips

_____ vanilla

_____ hot plate

_____ large saucepan

_____ wooden spoon

_____ loaf pan

_____ measuring cups and spoons

_____ activity card

Station 5—Math

_____ manipulatives patterns

_____ scratch paper

_____ pencils

_____ crayons

_____ scissors

_____ activity card

Station 6—Literature

_____ *The Three Little Pigs*

_____ construction paper, light colors

_____ scissors

_____ crayons

_____ activity card

Station 7—Pig Sequencing

_____ *The Three Little Pigs*

_____ sequencing cards

_____ crayons

_____ scissors

_____ activity card

Station 8—Writing

_____ shape books

_____ pencils

_____ crayons

_____ activity card

Station 1 Activity Card—Literature

Materials:

- *The Three Billy Goats Gruff*
- stick puppets patterns (page 290)
- flannelboard patterns (page 291)
- craft sticks
- scissors
- a flannelboard
- felt
- glue
- crayons or markers

Directions for Option A:

1. Read a favorite version of *The Three Billy Goats Gruff.*
2. Give each child a stick puppet pattern to color and cut out.
3. Instruct the children to glue their puppet patterns to wooden craft sticks to make stick puppets.
4. Give the children several minutes to practice and then have them perform *The Three Billy Goats Gruff* story.

Directions for Option B:

1. Read a favorite version of *The Three Billy Goats Gruff.*
2. Using felt figures made from the flannel pattern and a flannelboard, retell the story.

Station 2 Activity Card—Writing

Materials: white construction paper, chalkboard and chalk or butcher paper and a marker, stapler, pencils, and markers or crayons

To Be Done in Advance: Write the following lines on a chalkboard or a piece of butcher paper.

1. Who's that trapping on my bridge? It is I, the littlest Billy Goat Gruff.
2. I'm going to eat you up. No, please. Wait for my bigger brother. Okay. You may pass to the other side.
3. Who's that trapping on my bridge? It is I, the medium-sized Billy Goat Gruff.
4. I'm going to eat you up. No, please. Wait for my bigger brother. Okay. You may pass to the other side.
5. Who's that trapping on my bridge? It is I, the biggest Billy Goat Gruff.
6. I'm going to eat you up. I'd like to see you try!
7. Yeowww! The biggest Billy Goat Gruff knocked the troll right off that bridge, and they were able to eat on the other side as often as they wished.

Directions: Assign each student one or two sets of sentences to copy onto white construction paper. Every piece of paper should have only one of the numbered sets of sentences. Let the children illustrate their pages. Collect the pages and staple them together as a book. (**Note:** For younger children, you may want to write the sentence sets on the pages ahead of time and just let them trace the letters and illustrate.)

Stick Puppet Patterns

Flannelboard Patterns

Station 3 Activity Card—Puzzle

Materials:

- *Three Little Kittens*
- pencils
- mitten puzzles
- crayons or markers

Directions:

1. Read the nursery rhyme below or read the same rhyme out of a book.

   Three Little Kittens
   Three little kittens,
   They lost their mittens,
   And they began to cry,
   Oh, mother dear, we sadly fear
   Our mittens we have lost.
   What, lost your mittens, you naughty kittens!
   Then you shall have no pie.

2. Give each child a copy of the puzzle on page 293. Tell students to help the kittens find their mittens by circling each mitten in pencil. Then let them color the rest of the page.

3. After the children have finished the puzzles, take them to the restrooms to wash their hands in preparation for the next activity, cooking.

Station 4 Activity Card—Cooking

Three-Minute Fudge

Materials:

- 1 cup (250 mL) marshmallows
- $5/6$ teaspoon (4 mL) sugar
- $1/4$ teaspoon (1.3 mL) salt
- $1/4$ cup (60 mL) nuts
- hot plate
- large saucepan
- loaf pan
- $1/3$ cup (80 mL) evap. milk
- $1/2$ teaspoon (3 mL) vanilla
- $3/4$ cup (180 mL) semi-sweet chocolate chips
- butter (to grease the loaf pan)
- measuring cups and spoons
- wooden spoon

Directions: (Note: This recipe will make about 1 $1/2$ dozen pieces of fudge per group.) Involve the students in this activity by asking them to help with the measurements and help watch the cooking time. In a saucepan mix the sugar, salt, and milk. Bring the mixture to a boil over low heat. Boil for three minutes, stirring constantly. Remove the mixture from the heat and add the rest of the ingredients. Stir until the chips and marshmallows have melted. Pour the mixture into a greased loaf pan. Refrigerate until set. Cut into squares and share. Have plenty of the fudge made up ahead of time so that the students can sample it during the activity. You can divide the fudge equally among your students. Wrap it to take it home as a gift. Their families will love it too!

Missing Mittens

Directions: Help the kittens find their mittens! Circle the six mittens in pencil and then color the picture.

Station 5 Activity Card—Math

Materials: manipulative patterns (page 295), scratch paper, pencils, crayons, and scissors

Directions: Give each child a copy of the manipulatives on page 295. Ask the students to quickly color the manipulatives and cut them out. Challenge the students to use the manipulatives to practice adding and, for older students, multiplying with the number 3. For example, let them make up problems which look like these:

$$3 \times \underline{\hspace{1cm}} = \underline{\hspace{1cm}}$$
$$3 + \underline{\hspace{1cm}} = \underline{\hspace{1cm}}$$

Also, let the children use paper, pencils, and the manipulatives to solve the following problems: (Younger children will need your help.)

1. Three people are buying 3 tickets each. How many do they buy in all? (9)

2. Sue has 3 mama turtles. If each mama has 3 baby turtles, how many turtles will Sue have in all? (Do not forget to count the mama turtles too!) (12)

3. Tom gave his mother and his 4 sisters 3 tulips each. How many tulips did he give them in all? (15)

4. Jim colored 3 purple triangles, 3 orange triangles, 3 red triangles, 3 blue triangles, 3 yellow triangles, and 3 green triangles. How many triangles did he color in all? (18)

5. Mr. Johnson had 3 small turkeys. Mr. Jones and Mrs. Morgan came to visit. Each brought Mr. Johnson 3 turkeys. How many did he have in all? (9)

Station 6 Activity Card—Literature

Materials: *The Three Little Pigs*, construction paper (light colors), scissors, crayons, stapler

Directions: Read *The Three Little Pigs* to the children and help them make flip books about the story. Give each child two pieces of construction paper. Tell the group to fold each piece in half lengthwise and place one folded piece inside the other. Staple the four long pages along the fold. Then ask the students to fold their strips of paper into thirds. Help them cut the top three pieces of paper along the fold lines (near the top fold). At this point the books should each have three sections of four pages. Ask the children to write "Three Little Pigs" on the top three flaps. On the second flap in each section, tell them to draw one of the little pigs. On the third flap in each section, ask them to draw the corresponding pig's house (straw, sticks, or bricks). On the final flap of each section, tell them to show what becomes of the house. Let the children use their finished books to retell the story. (**Note:** For young children, you can have the books made or partially made ahead of time.)

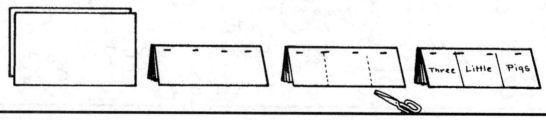

"T" Manipulatives

Station 7 Activity Card—Pig Sequencing

Materials:

- *The Three Little Pigs*
- sequence cards (pages 297 and 298)
- crayons
- scissors

Directions:

1. Read the story of *The Three Little Pigs* to the children. If the group just came from Station 6, just review the story, since they will have just heard it.
2. Give each child a copy of page 297 and page 298. Ask them to color the pictures and cut out the cards.
3. Let the children put their card sets in the correct sequence. You may need to help the younger children read the captions.
4. Discuss with the group the sequencing experience. How did they know what went where? Does anyone have a different order?
5. Read the cards, in order, together.

Station 8 Activity Card—Writing

Materials:

- shape books
- pencils
- crayons

Directions: Give each child a shape book. Help them write and illustrate a "t" phrase on each page. The phrases should be used as page titles and should follow this pattern: Three *(adjective)* *(noun)*. Some such phrases might be . . .

Three Tiny Trees
Three Ticklish Turkeys
Three Tired Turtles
Three Tall Triangles
Three Terrible Trolls
Three Torn Tickets
Three Tinted Tulips
Three Turquoise Taxis

Pig Sequence Cards

Directions: Color and cut out the cards. Then put them in the correct order.

The wolf tried to sneak into the brick house through the chimney.

The third pig spent a long time building his house out of brick.

The wolf could not blow down the brick house.

The wolf fell into the fireplace.

Once upon a time there were three little pigs.

The hungry wolf blew down the house made of straw.

Pig Sequence Cards *(cont.)*

Directions: Color and cut out the cards. Then put them in the correct order.

The pig knew the wolf was trying to sneak into the brick house through the chimney, so he built a large fire in the fireplace.

The first pig built his house out of straw.

The wolf tried to trick the third pig into coming out of his house, but the pig was too smart to be fooled.

The third little pig lived happily ever after.

The wolf blew down the house made out of sticks.

The second pig built his house out of sticks.

Shape Book Pattern

Stationery

Incentives

Use the following cards for positive reinforcement during your rotations. When a student successfully demonstrates positive behavior and completion of his or her tasks, cut out a brick square and paste it onto his or her house card. If you do not have time to cut and paste, a star sticker or stamp would work well. Distribute awards/name tags and bookmarks where appropriate.

Build a house brick by brick!

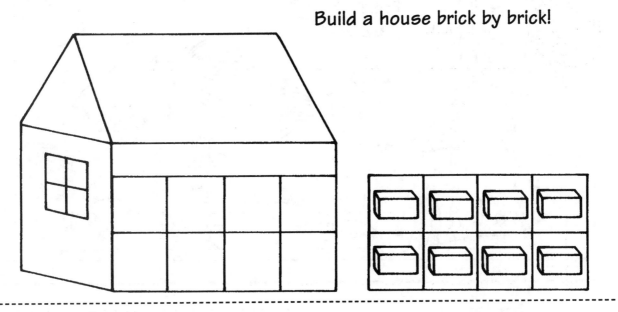

Award/Name Tag

Bookmark

Pig

Out

on

Books!

Under the Sea

Teacher Note: Use this page as an introduction to the Under the Sea theme. Have your students color the picture. Lines are provided for writing activities of your choice.

Unit Materials

Bibliography

Lionni, Leo. *Swimmy.* Knopf Books for Young Readers, 1963.

Milton, Joyce. *Whales, the Gentle Giants.* Random House, 1989.

Pfister, Marcus. *The Rainbow Fish.* North-South Books, 1992.

Sheldon, Dyan. *The Whale's Song.* Dial Books for Young Readers, 1991.

Provide several nonfiction books about sea life.

Materials Checklist

Station 1—Literature

_____ *The Rainbow Fish*
_____ *Swimmy*
_____ fish pattern
_____ pencils
_____ crayons
_____ scissors
_____ activity card

Station 2—Writing

_____ shape books
_____ pencils
_____ crayons
_____ vocabulary list
_____ activity card

Station 3—Compound Word Game

_____ game cards
_____ activity card

Station 4—Cooking

_____ bread
_____ pickle relish
_____ tuna
_____ mayonnaise
_____ crackers
_____ fish-shaped crackers
_____ blue gelatin
_____ jelly worms
_____ punch or other drink

_____ paper plates
_____ clean plastic cups
_____ 2 fish bowls
_____ mixing bowl
_____ can opener
_____ mixing spoon
_____ plastic knives and spoons
_____ activity card

Stations 5 and 6—Art

_____ light blue construction paper
_____ construction paper for matting
_____ fish pattern
_____ foil
_____ wiggle eyes
_____ scissors
_____ yellow construction paper
_____ paint (shades of blue, purple, fuschia, pink, and green)
_____ paper plates for paint
_____ brushes
_____ glue
_____ crayons
_____ pencils
_____ activity card

Station 7—Literature

_____ *Whales, the Gentle Giants* (or another nonfiction book about whales)
_____ chalkboard or butcher paper for Venn diagrams
_____ chalk or a marker
_____ activity card

Station 8—Math

_____ octopus activity sheet
_____ crayons
_____ pencils
_____ activity card

Station 1 Activity Card—Literature

Materials:

- *The Rainbow Fish*
- *Swimmy*
- fish pattern (page 305)
- pencils
- crayons
- scissors

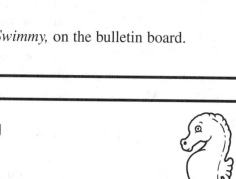

Directions:

1. Read *The Rainbow Fish* to the children.
2. Next, read *Swimmy.*
3. Compare the two books.
4. Let each student cut out the fish outline. Ask them to write on their fish: *I can, I will.* Tell them to also write their names on their fish.
5. Ask the children to decorate their fish.
6. Use the fish to form a large fish, as in *Swimmy,* on the bulletin board.

Station 2 Activity Card—Writing

Materials:

- shape books
- vocabulary list (page 308)
- pencils
- crayons

Directions: Prepare shape books (see pages 306 and 307) as described on previous shape book activity cards. Give each child a shape book (choose from the whale or underwater shapes) and assign one of the following activities.

1. Ask the children to draw a picture of an underwater creature on each page. Have them include labels and challenge the older children to also include an interesting fact about each creature.
2. Have the students write one word which starts with the letter "u" on each page (see page 308 for ideas). Ask them to then illustrate the pages.
3. Let the students write different short "u" words (see page 308 for ideas) in their shape books and then illustrate the words.
4. Discuss the meanings of the vocabulary words listed on page 308. Tell the children to write one word on each page of their books and then illustrate. Ask the older students to write the words in sentences.

Fish Pattern

Shape Book Patterns

Under
the
Sea

Shape Book Patterns (cont.)

Vocabulary List

Thematic	Short "u" Sound	Begins with "u"
1. fish	1. duck	1. up
2. whale	2. hug	2. under
3. baleen	3. lunch	3. use
4. toothed	4. plum	4. uncle
5. mammal	5. bump	5. umbrella
6. blow	6. jump	6. ugly
7. shark	7. puppy	7. umpire
8. coral	8. cup	8. unicorn
9. reef	9. tub	9. uniform
10. ocean	10. husband	10. union
11. hook	11. hunt	11. unit
12. sea	12. hut	12. universe
13. fluke	13. puddle	13. unplug
14. dive	14. summer	14. upset
15. waves	15. sun	15. Uranus
16. seaweed	16. mud	16. usher
17. starfish	17. grubby	17. upstairs
18. sand	18. gum	18. unique
19. shell	19. cut	19. unicycle
20. octopus	20. bus	20. UFO (unidentified flying object)

Station 3 Activity Card—Compound Word Game

Materials:

- game cards (pages 310–313)

To Be Done in Advance: Make copies of pages 310–313. Cut out the star and fish boxes.

Directions:

1. Explain to the students that the word "starfish" is called a compound word because it is made up of two smaller words, star and fish. Brainstorm with the children other compound words until you are sure they understand the concept.

2. Randomly lay out the star and fish cards for the students. Give each child a turn to match a star card (the first part of a word) to a fish card (the second part of a word). Continue until all of the matches have been made. For younger children, you may have to read the cards out loud and help the group make the matches.

3. With any extra time, take the students to the restrooms to wash their hands in preparation for the next activity, cooking.

Station 4 Activity Card—Cooking

Materials:

- bread
- pickle relish
- tuna
- mayonnaise
- crackers
- fish-shaped crackers

- blue gelatin
- jelly worms, optional
- punch or other drink
- paper plates
- clean plastic cups
- 2 fish bowls

- mixing bowl
- can opener
- mixing spoon
- plastic knives and spoons

To Be Done in Advance: Ask a few parents to prepare blue gelatin for this theme day. Ask them to bring the gelatin in round fish bowls if possible.

Directions: This small seafood feast will consist of tuna salad on crackers, blue gelatin, and fish-shaped crackers.

1. Allow the students to mix the tuna, mayonnaise, and pickle relish to make tuna salad.

2. Spread a spoonful of the mixture on a cracker for each child.

3. Serve a spoonful of gelatin (garnished with jelly worms, if you wish), fish-shaped crackers, and a drink with the tuna salad.

Star Cards

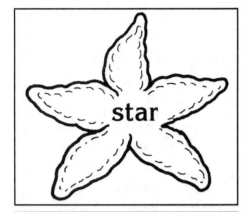

Star Cards *(cont.)*

candle

hand

dog

mail

door

rain

hair

sail

Fish Cards

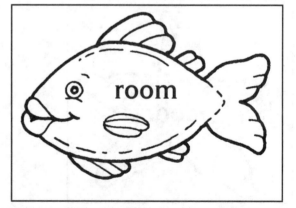

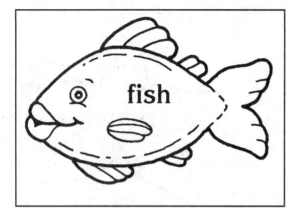

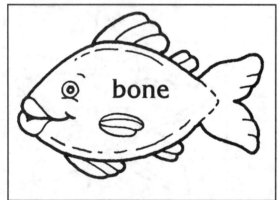

Fish Cards *(cont.)*

 stick

 house

 bell

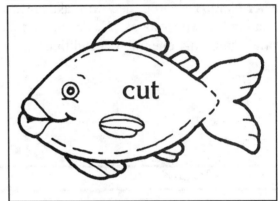 cut

 bag

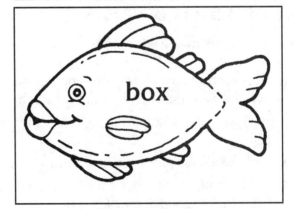 box

 bow

 boat

Stations 5 and 6—Art

Make a Rainbow Fish

Materials:

- wiggle eyes
- scissors
- aluminum foil
- brushes
- glue
- crayons
- pencils

- 9" x 12" (22.8 x 30.4 cm) light blue construction paper
- 12" x 15" (30.4 x 38.1 cm) construction paper for matting
- fish pattern (page 315)
- yellow construction paper
- paint (shades of blue, purple, fuschia, pink, and green)
- paper plates for paint

Teacher Note: This art project will take up two session times so the students will need to stay at this station for two rotations. However, the first group at station #6 will have to save their materials after only one rotation and finish their projects when they finally rotate to station #5.

Stations 5 and 6—Art *(cont.)*

Make a Rainbow Fish *(cont.)*

1. Give each student a piece of light blue construction paper. Ask the students to draw the ocean floor on their papers and color it brown.
2. Pass out fish patterns from page 315 and tell them to trace the patterns in the center of their papers.
3. Make available paper plates with various colors of paint.
4. Let the children dip their thumbs into the paint colors and make thumbprint scales on their fish. Make sure that they leave the fish faces empty.
5. Help the children glue one foil scale to each fish. Tell them to paint or color the fins in rainbow stripes.
6. Next, have them cut out bright yellow, heart-shaped mouths and glue these in place.
7. Add a wiggle eye to each fish with glue.

At this point, they may add seaweed and other plant life with shades of green paint or crayons. Let the pictures dry and then frame them with purple, dark blue, or fuschia construction paper.

Art Fish Pattern

Station 7 Activity Card—Literature

Materials:

- *Whales, the Gentle Giants* (or another nonfiction book about whales)
- chalkboard or butcher paper for Venn diagrams
- chalk or a marker

To Be Done in Advance: Draw two large intersecting circles (an empty Venn diagram) on a chalkboard or a piece of butcher paper. Label one circle "Baleen Whales" and the other circle "Toothed Whales." Label the intersecting section "Both."

Make a second Venn diagram with the labels "Mammals," "Fish," and "Both."

Directions:

1. Read *Whales, the Gentle Giants* or any other nonfiction book about whales.
2. Using a Venn diagram, compare and contrast baleen and toothed whales.
3. Using a Venn diagram, discuss how mammals differ from fish.

Station 8 Activity Card—Math

Materials:

- octopus activity sheet (page 317)
- crayons
- pencils

Directions:

1. Give each child a copy of the activity sheet on page 317. Explain that the octopus has eight legs and in this activity they will be looking for equations which have the sum of eight.

2. Do the first problem with the group. Ask the students to color some of the legs blue and then ask them to color the remaining legs red. Tell them to count the blue legs and then the red to find out the equation that equals eight. Instruct them to write the equation below the octopus.

3. If the older students finish early, practice doing their 8 times table with them.

Octopus Math

In each box, find a different equation with a sum of eight.

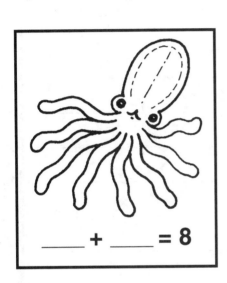

____ + ____ = 8

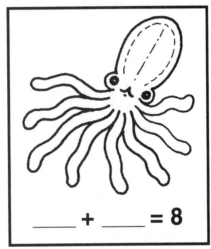

____ + ____ = 8

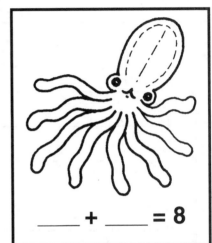

____ + ____ = 8

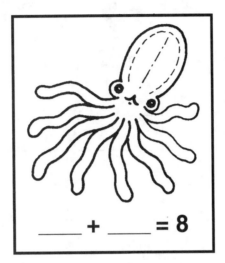

____ + ____ = 8

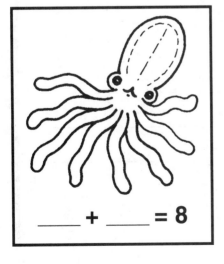

____ + ____ = 8

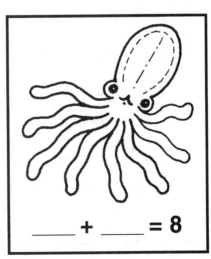

____ + ____ = 8

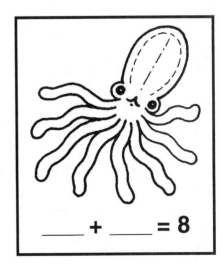

____ + ____ = 8

Stationery

Incentives

Use the following cards for positive reinforcement during your rotations. When a student successfully demonstrates positive behavior and completion of his or her tasks, cut out a fish square and paste it onto his or her ocean card. If you do not have time to cut and paste, a star sticker or stamp would work well. Distribute awards/name tags and bookmarks where appropriate.

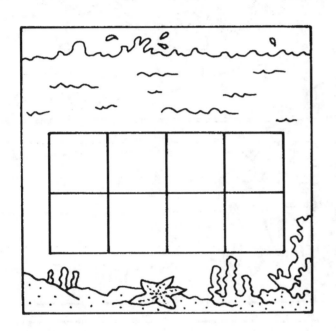

Fill the ocean with fish!

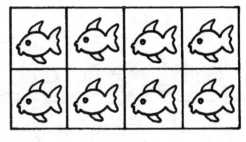

Award/Name Tag

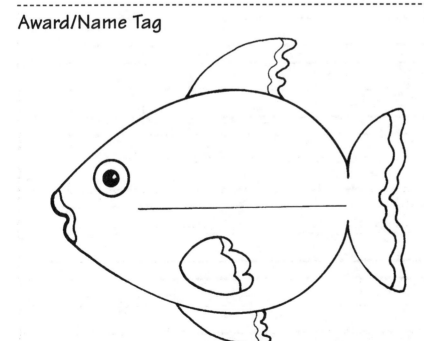

Bookmark

Vehicles

Teacher Note: Use this page as an introduction to the Vehicles theme. Have your students color the picture. Lines are provided for writing activities of your choice.

Unit Materials

Bibliography

Jeunesse, Gallimard. *Airplanes.* Scholastic, 1992.

Piper, Watty. *The Little Engine That Could.* Putnam, 1978.

Scarry, Richard. *Busy Town.* Western Publishing Company, 1994.

Uggla, Goran. *The Car Book.* Chronicle Books, 1993.

Van Allsburg, Chris. *The Polar Express.* Houghton Mifflin, 1985.

Materials Checklist

Station 1—Literature
_____ books by Richard Scarry, such as *Busy Town*
_____ graph on a piece of butcher paper
_____ markers
_____ activity card

Station 2—Reading/Writing: Airplanes
_____ *Airplanes* or another book about airplanes
_____ pencils
_____ shape books
_____ crayons
_____ activity card

Station 3—Reading/Writing: Trains
_____ *The Polar Express, The Little Engine That Could,* or another book about trains
_____ pencils
_____ shape books
_____ crayons
_____ activity card

Station 4—Model Trains, Puzzles
_____ word search puzzles
_____ pencils
_____ several train sets
_____ activity card

Station 5—Cooking
_____ graham crackers
_____ icing in tubes
_____ small round candies
_____ vanilla wafer cookies
_____ activity card

Station 6—Writing
_____ shape books
_____ pencils
_____ crayons
_____ activity card

Station 7—Math
_____ word problems
_____ pencils
_____ scratch paper
_____ manipulatives
_____ scissors
_____ crayons
_____ activity card

Station 8—Art
_____ *The Car Book* or another book about cars
_____ easel paper (or large construction paper)
_____ paint
_____ paintbrushes
_____ newspaper
_____ black markers
_____ tape
_____ activity card

Alternate Activities:
1. Writing
_____ shape books
_____ pencils
_____ crayons
_____ activity card

2. Vehicle Categorization
_____ category game cards
_____ crayons
_____ scissors
_____ activity card

Station 1 Activity Card—Literature

Materials:

- books by Richard Scarry, such as *Busy Town*
- graph on a piece of butcher paper
- markers

To Be Done in Advance: On a piece of butcher paper, prepare a graph which has five or six columns. At the top of each column, write one common color for a car.

Directions:

1. Read and discuss with the children one of Richard Scarry's books about transportation. These books illustrate a variety of cars and other vehicles.
2. Ask the children what their favorite car colors are.
3. Let each child write his or her name on the butcher paper graph in the correct color column.
4. Discuss the results of the graph.

What Is Your Favorite Car Color?					
white	purple	red	blue	silver	green

Station 2 Activity Card—Reading/Writing: Airplanes

Materials:

- *Airplanes* or another book about airplanes
- pencils
- shape books
- crayons

Directions:

1. Read *Airplanes*, or any other children's book about airplanes, to the children.
2. Discuss air travel with the group.
3. Prepare shape books (see page 323) as described on previous book shape activity cards. Give each child a plane-shaped book. Ask them to imagine that they are airplane pilots. Tell them to create stories about where they would fly. On each page of their books have them write about a different place, for example . . .

    I flew over a _____.

    Then, I flew over the _____.

    Next, I flew over _____.

4. Ask the children to illustrate their stories.

Shape Book Pattern

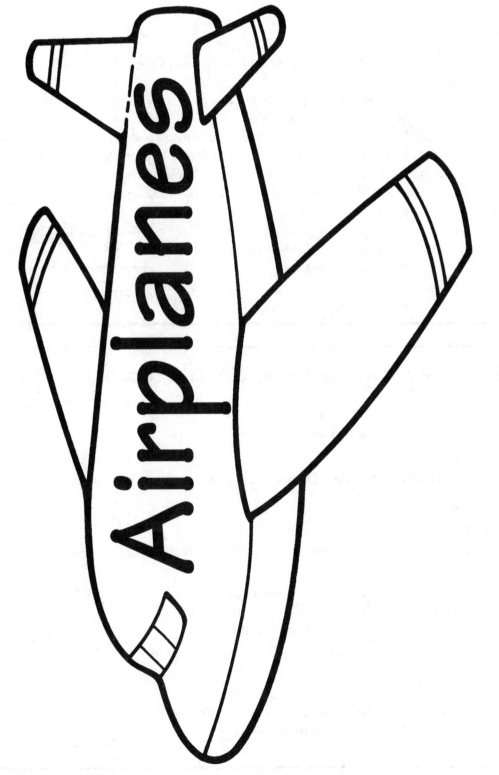

Station 3 Activity Card—Reading/Writing: Trains

Materials:

- *The Polar Express, The Little Engine That Could,* or another book about trains
- pencils
- shape books
- crayons

Directions:

1. Read *The Polar Express, The Little Engine That Could,* or any other book about trains, to the children.
2. Prepare shape books (see pattern on page 325) as described on previous shape book activity cards. Give each child a shape book.
3. Ask the children to write the following sentences, one per page, in their shape books. (You can just dictate the sentences for older children, but for younger children you might want to write them on a chalkboard or in the shape books ahead of time. If you do choose to write the sentences in the books in advance, ask the children to trace your letters.)

> *The train went up the hill.*
> *The train went down the hill.*
> *The train went over the bridge.*
> *The train went through the tunnel.*
> *The train went around the lake.*
> *The train stopped at _____ .*

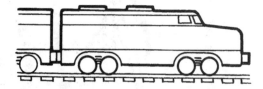

Station 4 Activity Card—Model Trains, Puzzles

Materials:

- word search puzzles (page 326)
- pencils
- several train sets (**Note:** Do not use expensive collector train sets for this activity.)

Directions:

1. Discuss different types of vehicles with the students. Ask the students to list as many vehicles as they can.
2. Give each child a copy of the word search puzzle on page 326. Allow the children some time to work on their puzzles together or individually.
3. If some of the students should finish early, let them play with the train sets.
4. During the last five minutes of this rotation, take the students to the restrooms to wash their hands in preparation for the next activity, cooking.

Shape Book Pattern

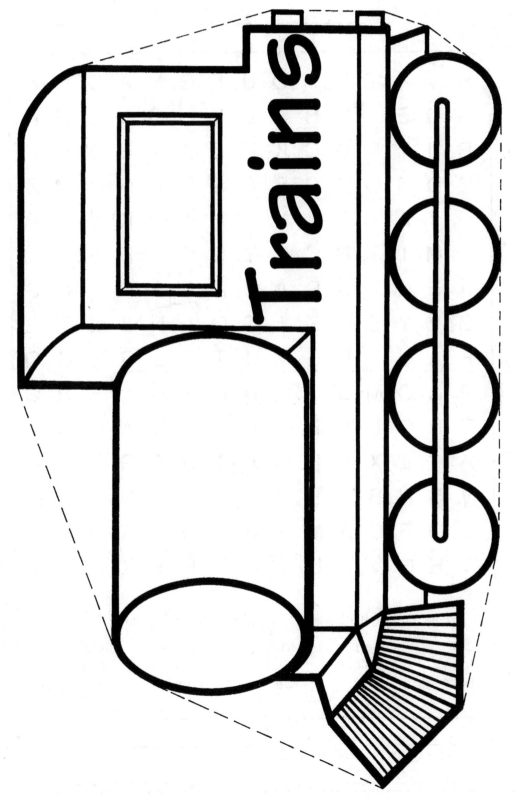

Vehicles Word Search

```
B V R T E I O U F G Y A D N H
A D E L C B A L L O O N O H N
R U T R U C K P Z K I R W C I
G D R O J C S F S E K H B M Z
E J A I T J X S H I P K Y Q P
Z M I T R C T Y U D L E S J M
J P N L A D A B N C A R A E S
B V Y E M Z I Q O A N J L T R
E A U X D E M J T C E R H B Q
P N O M O T O R C Y C L E R G
T R O L L E Y B F K X W B Q A
A I L X V B O A T U W G L L W
V S N B W F H P G M B N I R Z
I O F C A M P E R Q G A M J P
T H G V A U O C K F Y X P I V
```

Find the following words going across and down in the puzzle:

car	plane	truck	camper	trolley
train	balloon	ship	jet	barge
boat	blimp	van	tram	motorcycle

Station 5 Activity Card—Cooking

Edible Trucks

Materials:

- graham crackers
- icing in tubes
- small round candies
- vanilla wafer cookies

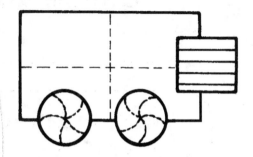

Directions:

1. Give each child an unbroken graham cracker (this will be the body of the truck) and two vanilla wafer cookies (for the wheels).

2. Break a graham cracker into quarters and then into eighths. Give each child one of these small, square pieces (it will be the cab of the truck).

3. Help the children use the icing to "glue" their cabs and wheels onto the bodies of their trucks.

4. Give each child two small round candies to "glue" on as hubcaps.

5. Allow the children to use the icing to decorate their trucks.

6. Be sure to leave enough time for the children to eat their creations!

Station 6 Activity Card—Writing

Materials:

- shape books
- pencils
- crayons

Directions: On pages 328–330 there are covers for three different types of shape books. Either choose one type of book or make available all three types. (Prepare shape books as described on previous shape book activity cards.) Then assign one of the following activities.

1. **Vehicle:** Ask the students to write about a different vehicle or mode of transportation on each page and then to illustrate the pages.

2. **Boat:** Ask the students to write about different types of boats and then to illustrate them.

3. **Truck:** Ask the students to write about different jobs that trucks perform and then to illustrate the pages.

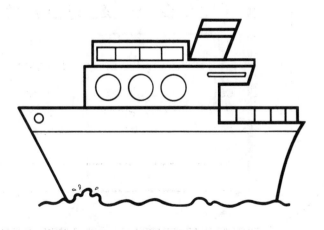

Shape Book Patterns

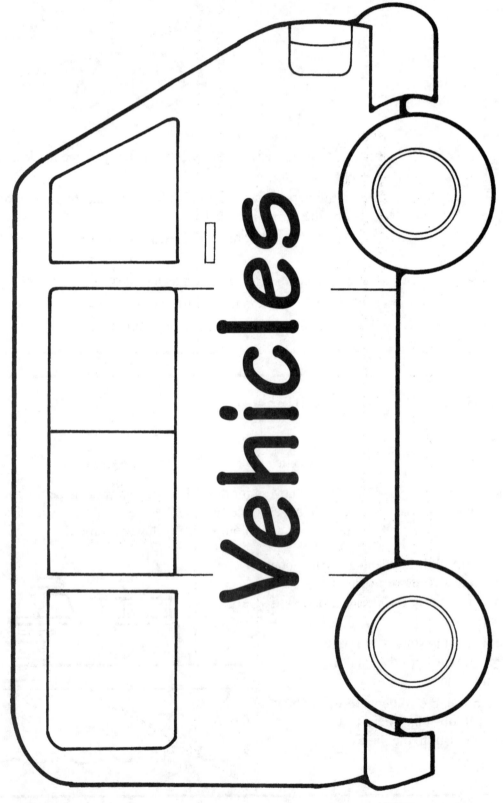

Shape Book Patterns (cont.)

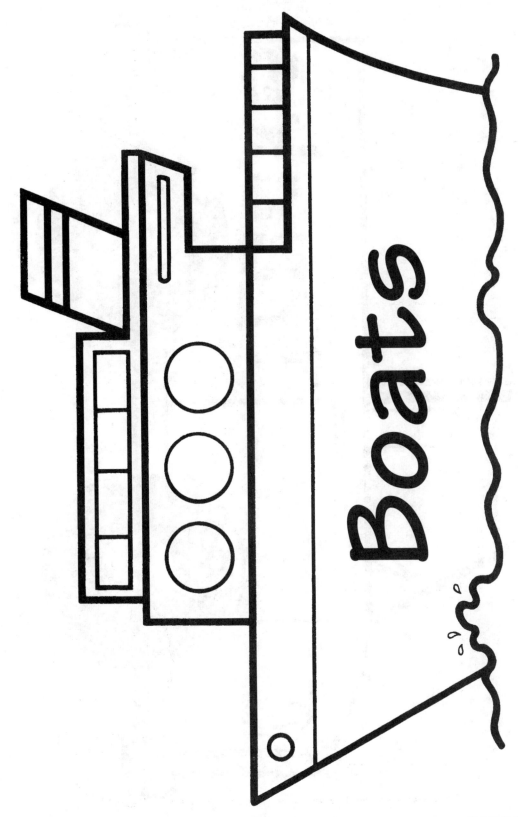

Shape Book Patterns (cont.)

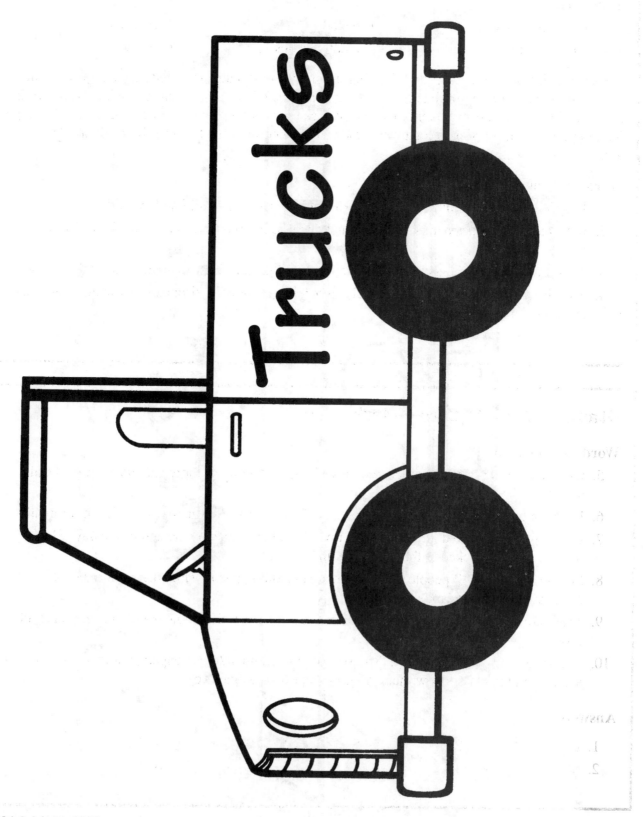

Station 7 Activity Card—Math

Materials:

- word problems
- scratch paper
- pencils
- manipulatives
- crayons
- scissors

Directions: Before presenting the following problems to the students, decide which ones are the most age- and ability-appropriate for the group. You may wish to write each problem on a card in advance. Have students use manipulatives, such as toy cars, to solve each word problem. On page 332, there is also a set of manipulatives which can be cut out, used to solve the math problems, and, if there is extra time, colored.

Word Problems

1. Jerry had 13 cars on his used car lot. He sold 5. How many did he have left?
2. If Mike, the car salesman, sold 6 cars and made $100.00 on each car he sold, how much money did he earn?
3. Amy and 5 of her friends went on a bicycle trip together. How many tires were there in all?
4. The airport has 12 hangars on the field. Each hangar holds 2 airplanes. How many airplanes are stored at the airport in all?

Station 7 Activity Card—Math *(cont.)*

Word Problems *(cont.)*

5. One train has 18 cars. Another train has 13 cars. How many more cars does the first train have than the second?
6. If a train has 10 cars and it stops to pick up 7 more cars, how many cars will it have in all?
7. Eight boats are docked at the marina. Five more boats dock by the end of the day. How many boats are docked at the marina in all?
8. My boat can hold 12 people. Mark's boat can hold 8 people. How many more people will my boat carry than Mark's?
9. There are 3 trucks in the parking lot. If each truck has 6 tires, how many tires are there all together?
10. A class is going on a field trip. The school bus can hold 24 passengers, but there are only 19 students in the class. How many adults can also go on the trip?

Answers:

1. 8	3. 12	5. 5	7. 13	9. 18
2. $600.00	4. 24	6. 17	8. 4	10. 5

Vehicle Manipulatives

Station 8 Activity Card—Art

Materials:

- paint
- paintbrushes
- newspaper
- tape
- *The Car Book* or another book about cars
- easel paper or 12" x 18" (30.4 cm x 45.7 cm) construction paper
- black markers

Directions:

1. Read *The Car Book* or any other children's book about cars to the group. Discuss the children's dream cars.
2. Give each child a piece of easel paper or construction paper.
3. In a newspaper covered area, ask the students to paint their dream cars.
4. At the bottom of each painting, write: This is _____'s car.
5. Allow the paint to dry.
6. Tape the paintings together as shown to make a class or group car book.

Alternate Activities

1. **Writing**

   Materials: shape books, pencils, and crayons

   Directions: Prepare shape books (see page 334 for pattern) as described on previous shape book activity cards. Give each child a balloon shape book (see page 334). Ask them to write about different types of air travel. If there is extra time, encourage them to illustrate their books.

2. **Vehicle Categorization**

   Materials: category cards (pages 335 and 336), crayons, and scissors

   To Be Done in Advance: *For younger students,* make single copies of pages 335 and 336. Color the vehicles, cut them out, and then laminate them. Do this activity as a group. *For older students,* make enough copies so that each student will have his or her own set to color, cut out, and categorize.

   Directions: Lead the group in a discussion about the many types of vehicles that exist. Show them the category cards. Challenge the students to place the cards into the categories you name. For example, you may ask the group to put the cards in categories according to how they travel, by land, sea, or air.

Shape Book Pattern

Hot Air Balloon

Vehicle Category Cards

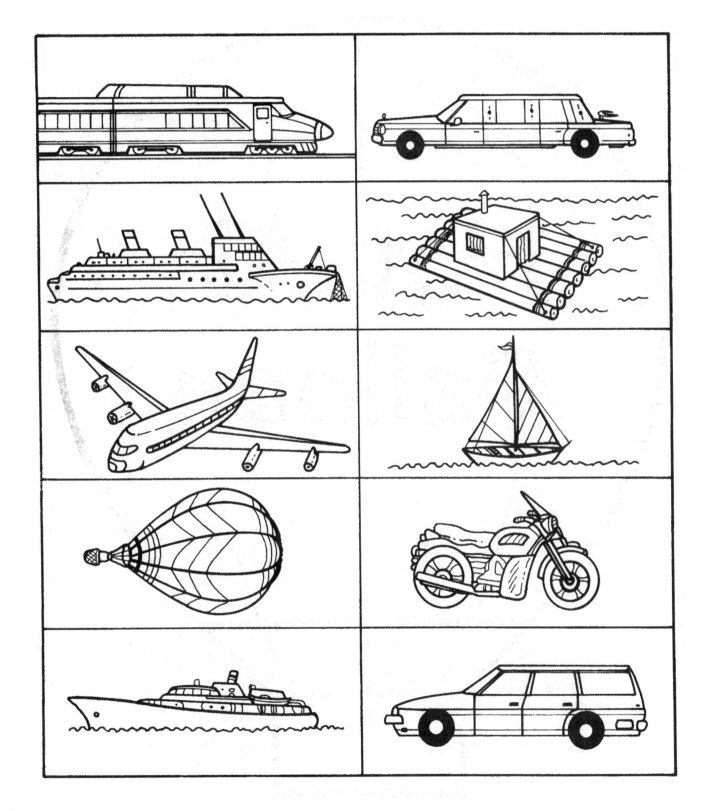

Vehicle Category Cards *(cont.)*

Stationery

Incentives

Use the following cards for positive reinforcement during your rotations. When a student successfully demonstrates positive behavior and completion of his or her tasks, cut out a car square and paste it onto his or her parking lot card. If you do not have time to cut and paste, a star sticker or stamp would work well. Distibute awards/name tags and bookmarks where appropriate.

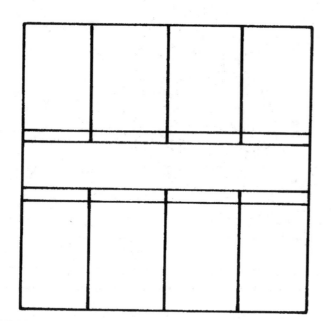

Park the cars in the parking lot!

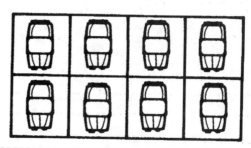

Award/Name Tag

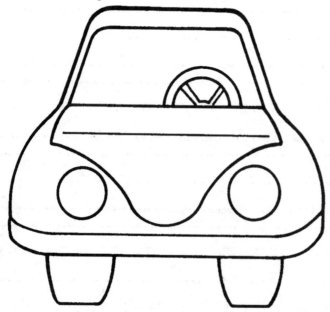

Bookmark

All Aboard the Reading Express!

Weather

Teacher Note: Use this page as an introduction to the Weather theme. Have your students color the picture. Lines are provided for writing activities of your choice.

Unit Materials

Bibliography

Aardema, Verna. *Bringing the Rain to Kapiti Plain.* Dial Books for Young Readers, 1981.

Barrett, Judi. *Cloudy with a Chance of Meatballs.* Atheneum Children's Books, 1978.

Branley, Frank M. *Flash, Crash, Rumble, Roar.* HarperCollins Children's Books, 1987.

dePaola, Tomie. *The Cloud Book.* Holiday House, 1975.

Rico, Ulde. *The Rainbow Goblins.* Thames and Hudson, 1994.

Shaw, Charles. *It Looked Like Spilt Milk.* HarperCollins, 1947.

Simon, Seymour. *Storms.* Mulberry Books, 1989.

You may also choose any appropriate nonfiction books about the weather or clouds.

Materials Checklist

Station 1—Literature

_____ *Bringing the Rain to Kapiti Plain* (book or video)
_____ *Flash, Crash, Rumble, Roar,* or *Storms,* or any other book about weather
_____ television
_____ VCR
_____ activity card

Station 2—Writing

_____ *Cloudy with a Chance of Meatballs*
_____ shape books
_____ pencils
_____ crayons
_____ activity card

Station 3—Rainbow Painting

_____ paints in containers or crayons (yellow, dark blue, black, red, green, purple, orange, medium blue, brown)
_____ easel paper
_____ newspaper
_____ paintbrushes
_____ pencils
_____ activity card

Station 4—Cooking

_____ *The Rainbow Goblins*
_____ paper plates
_____ napkins
_____ sugar cookies
_____ milk
_____ cups
_____ icing in tubes (red, orange, yellow, green, blue, purple)
_____ activity card

Stations 5 and 6—Mosaic Rainbows

_____ rainbow pattern, copied onto construction paper or other heavy paper
_____ glue
_____ construction paper (red, orange, yellow, green, blue, purple) or seven different types of beans and seeds
_____ activity card

Station 7—Estimations

_____ eye droppers
_____ containers of water
_____ pennies, nickels, dimes, and quarters
_____ estimation charts
_____ pencils
_____ paper towels
_____ activity card

Station 8—Writing

_____ *It Looked Like Spilt Milk* or *The Cloud Book*
_____ royal blue construction paper
_____ white paint in a container
_____ paintbrushes
_____ pencils
_____ newspapers
_____ sentence strips
_____ colored construction paper (for matting)
_____ activity card

Alternate Activities:

_____ shape books
_____ pencils
_____ crayons
_____ activity card

Station 1 Activity Card—Literature

Materials:

- television
- VCR
- *Bringing the Rain to Kapiti Plain* (book or video)
- *Flash, Crash, Rumble, Roar,* or *Storms,* or any other book about weather

Directions: If you have obtained a copy of the *Bringing the Rain to Kapiti Plain* video read the first set of direction; otherwise, continue on to the second set.

1. *Bringing the Rain to Kapiti Plain* (video)

   Show the *Reading Rainbow* video of *Bringing the Rain to Kapiti Plain* to the children. The video is about 25–0 minutes long, and the story is read by James Earl Jones. Stop it after the story is read or continue watching it until the rotation time is up. Rewind the tape for the next group. When searching for this video, check your local library.

2. *Storms, Bringing the Rain to Kapiti Plain,* or *Flash, Crash, Rumble, Roar* (or any other book about weather)

   Read *Bringing the Rain to Kapiti Plain* to the group. The children will want to read it over and over. Allow them to join in as much as they can. Then read and discuss another weather-related book.

Station 2 Activity Card—Writing

Materials:

- *Cloudy with a Chance of Meatballs*
- shape books
- pencils
- crayons

Directions:

1. Read *Cloudy with a Chance of Meatballs* to the children.
2. Prepare shape books (see page 342 for pattern) as described on previous shape book activity cards. Give each student a cloud shape book (page 342).
3. Ask them to write at the bottom of each page, "It rained _____." Then, ask them to go back and fill in the blank on each page. Encourage them to get a little silly, for example, "It rained pillows," "It rained spaghetti," and "It rained cats and dogs."
4. Leave enough time for the children to illustrate their books.

Shape Book Pattern

Weather

Station 3 Activity Card—Rainbow Painting

Materials:

- paints in containers or crayons (yellow, dark blue, black, red, green, purple, orange, medium blue, brown)
- easel paper
- newspaper
- paintbrushes
- pencils

Directions:

1. Ask the children to paint or color scenes with rainbows. If the children are painting, protect the work area with newspapers.
2. With any extra time take the children to the restrooms to wash their hands in preparation for the next activity, cooking.
3. After the paintings have dried, compile a class book and call it "Somewhere Over the Rainbow."

Station 4 Activity Card—Cooking

Rainbow Cookies

Materials:

- *The Rainbow Goblins*
- napkins
- milk
- paper plates
- sugar cookies
- cups
- icing in tubes (red, orange, yellow, green, blue, purple; if you cannot find all of the colors, just use as many as you can)

To Be Done in Advance: Bake enough sugar cookies in advance so that each child may have one. Cookies from a bakery will also work well.

Directions:

1. Give each child a sugar cookie. Let the children use the colored icing to paint rainbows onto their cookies.
2. Serve the cookies with milk.
3. If you finish early, read and discuss any good literature selection about rain, rainbows, and/or weather. *The Rainbow Goblins* is a wonderful example.

Stations 5 and 6—Mosaic Rainbows

Materials:

- rainbow pattern (page 345), copied onto construction paper or other heavy paper
- glue
- colored paper (for each color in the rainbow) or seven different types of beans and seeds

Directions: This card describes two ways of doing this activity. Option 1 uses paper to make the mosaic while Option 2 uses beans and seeds. This art project will take up two session times so the students will need to stay at this station for two rotations. However, the first group at station #6 will have to save their materials after only one rotation and finish their projects when they finally rotate to station #5.

Option 1: For this version, you will need paper scraps in the following colors: red, orange, yellow, green, blue, indigo (deep violet blue), and violet. Give each child a copy of the rainbow on page 345. Tell the students to tear small pieces of construction paper and glue these onto the pattern to form a rainbow.

Option 2: For the second version, you will need seven different types of seeds or beans.
(**Note:** Try to get as many different colors as possible.) Give each child a copy of the pattern on page 345. Tell the children to glue the different beans or seeds onto the pattern to form rainbows.

Station 7 Activity Card—Estimations

Materials: eye droppers, one per student; containers of water; pennies, nickels, dimes, and quarters; estimation charts, page 346; pencils; and paper towels

Directions:

1. Provide each student with an eye dropper, a container of water, a pencil, a penny, and one estimation chart (make your copies two at a time from page 346).
2. Ask the students how many drops of water they think will stay on a penny before the water flows over its edges.
3. Have them write their guesses on their estimation charts.
4. Demonstrate how to find the answer: Draw water up into the eye dropper. Then carefully drop water, drop by drop, onto the penny. (They should practice controlling the amount of water in the drops on paper towels before trying it on pennies.) Count the drops as you go until the water finally runs over the edges. Finally, write how many drops it actually took in the "Answer" column of the estimation chart.
5. Tell the students to now try doing the same steps with nickels, dimes, and quarters on their own. Remind them to continue filling out their estimation charts as they go.
6. Discuss the results of the charts. Did their estimations get any better towards the end of the activity?

(**Note:** This activity may also be done in pairs.)

Mosaic Rainbow Pattern

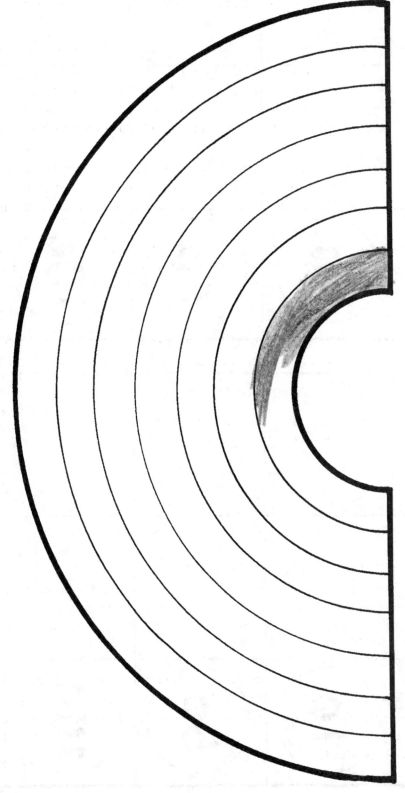

Estimation Charts

	Estimate	Answer
1¢		
5¢		
10¢		
25¢		

	Estimate	Answer
1¢		
5¢		
10¢		
25¢		

Station 8 Activity Card—Writing

Materials:

- paintbrushes
- pencils
- newspapers
- 2" x 11" (5 x 27.9 cm) sentence strips
- 12" x 18" (30.4 x 45.7) colored construction paper, for matting
- *It Looked Like Spilt Milk* or *The Cloud Book*
- 9" x 12" (22.8 x 30.4 cm) royal blue construction paper
- white paint in a container

To Be Done in Advance: Write " _____'s cloud looks like a _____." on a sentence strip for each student. You may wish to have older students do this themselves.

Directions:

1. Read *It Looked Like Spilt Milk* or *The Cloud Book* to the children.
2. Give each child a sheet of royal blue construction paper. Tell children to fold the paper in half and then unfold. Cover the work area with newspapers. Let the children drip white paint over one half of their blue papers.
3. Ask the children to again fold their papers and this time to squish the sides together firmly. Tell them to gently open up their papers and then ask, "What does your blob look like?" Have them fill out the sentence strips. For example, "Kevin's cloud looks like a book."
4. After the paintings have dried, glue each one onto a large sheet of colored construction paper as a matting. Glue each sentence strip to the bottom border.
5. Compile the pages to make a class book about clouds.

Alternate Activities

Materials:

- shape books
- pencils
- crayons

Directions: Prepare shape books (see pages 348 and 349 for patterns) as described on previous book shape activity cards. Give each child a shape book in the shape of either a raindrop (page 348) or a rainbow (page 349) and then assign one of the following activities:

Raindrop:

1. Ask the students to write a different weather word on each page of their shape books. Have them then illustrate the pages.
2. Tell the students to write and illustrate a word that starts with the letter "w" on each page. You may want to ask older students to write sentences using some "w" words instead.

Rainbow:

Have the students write about the colors of the rainbow, describing one color on each page of the books.

Shape Book Patterns

Weather

Shape Book Patterns *(cont.)*

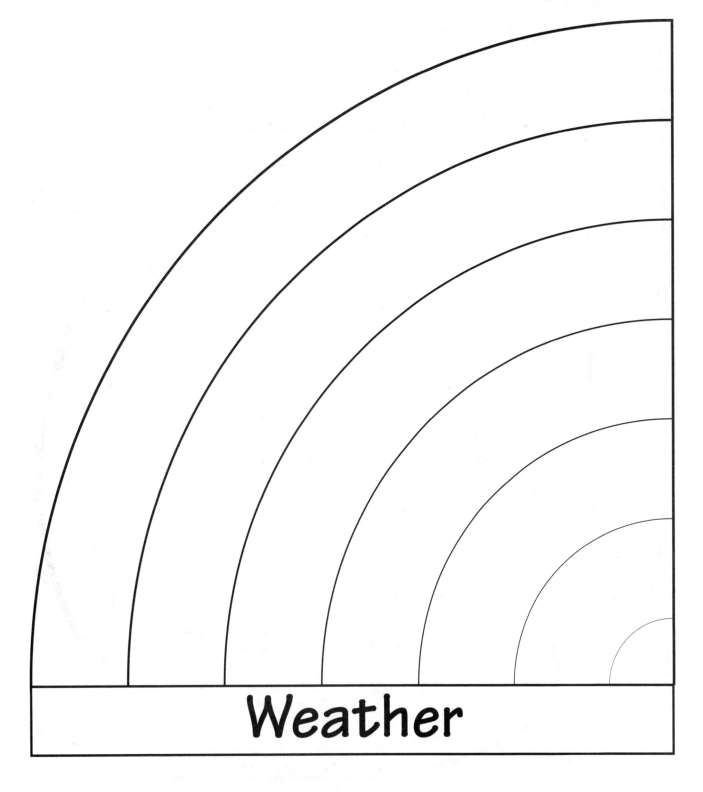

Weather

Stationery

Incentives

Use the following cards for positive reinforcement during your rotations. When a student successfully demonstrates positive behavior and completion of his or her tasks, cut out a snowflake square and paste it onto his or her cloud card. If you do not have time to cut and paste, a star sticker or stamp would work well. Distribute awards/name tags and bookmarks where appropriate.

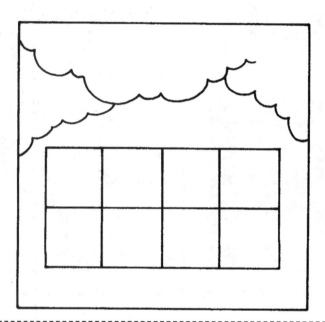

Let it snow!

Award/Name Tag

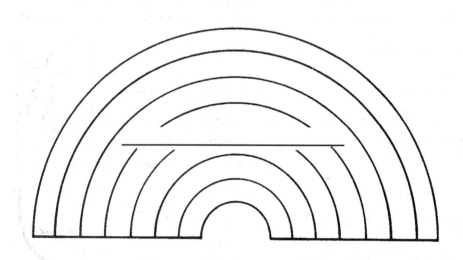

Bookmark

**Curl Up
with a
Good Book . . .
Rain
or Shine!**

X-rays and Bones/Foxes and Boxes

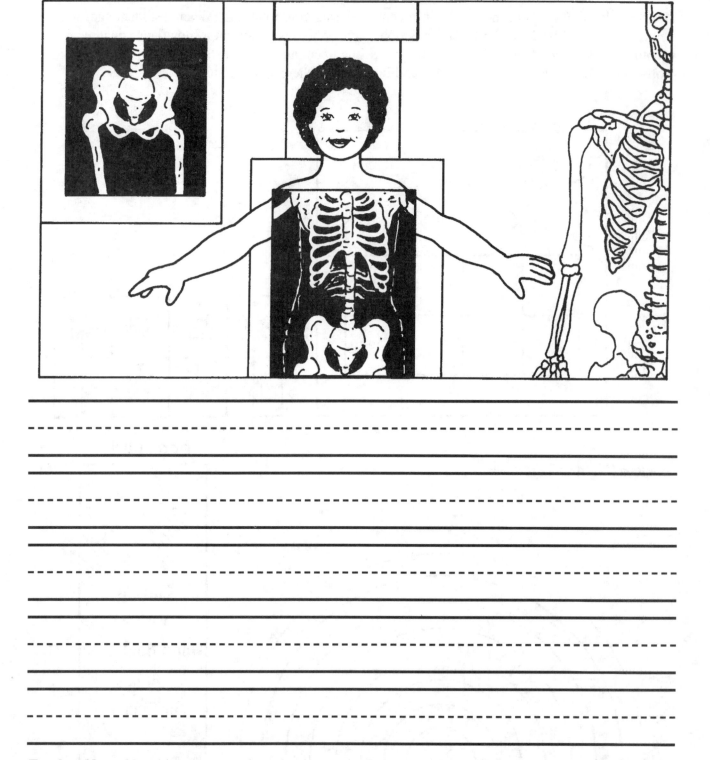

Teacher Note: Use this page as an introduction to the X-rays and Bones/Foxes and Boxes theme. Have your students color the picture. Lines are provided for writing activities of your choice.

Unit Materials

Bibliography

Cole, Joanna. *The Magic School Bus® Inside the Human Body.* Scholastic, 1993.

Grimm, Jakob and Wilhelm. *The Gingerbread Boy.* (any version)

McKissack, Patricia. *Flossie and the Fox.* Dial Books for Young Readers, 1986.

Seuss, Dr. *Fox in Socks.* Random House, 1965.

Provide several nonfiction books about bones.

Materials Checklist

Station 1—Literature

_____ *The Magic School Bus® Inside the Human Body*

_____ x-rays or pictures of x-rays

_____ activity card

Stations 2 and 3—Science

_____ butcher paper

_____ pencils

_____ black markers

_____ skeleton information sheets

_____ rubber bands

_____ activity card

Station 4—Literature

_____ *The Gingerbread Boy*

_____ lunch-sized paper bags

_____ puppet patterns

_____ scissors

_____ crayons

_____ construction paper

_____ glue

_____ activity card

Station 5—Estimating Dog Biscuits

_____ a box of large dog biscuits

_____ a box of small dog biscuits

_____ paper

_____ pencils

_____ activity card

Station 6—Art

_____ large, medium, and small dog biscuits

_____ paper towels

_____ scissors

_____ wiggle eyes

_____ glue

_____ brown and red construction paper

_____ tiny, black, fuzzy pompons

_____ activity card

Station 7—Writing

_____ *Fox in Socks*

_____ chalk

_____ chalkboard

_____ shape books

_____ pencils

_____ crayons

_____ activity card

Station 8—Matching Game

_____ envelopes

_____ scissors

_____ crayons

_____ pencils

_____ word and picture cards

_____ activity card

Alternate Activities:

1. Scrimshaw—Art

   _____ foam meat trays

   _____ black ballpoint pens

   _____ scissors

   _____ yarn

   _____ activity card

2. *The Gingerbread Boy*—Writing

   _____ coloring page

   _____ writing paper

   _____ pencils

   _____ crayons

   _____ activity card

Station 1 Activity Card—Literature

Materials:

- *The Magic School Bus® Inside the Human Body*
- x-rays or pictures of x-rays

Directions:

1. Read *The Magic School Bus® Inside the Human Body* to the group.

2. Stop to point out body parts on each other as you read about them.

3. Look at x-rays or pictures of x-rays. What do they show?

4. Ask the children to feel their own ribs and the bones in their hands, arms, legs, and feet. Ask them what is different about their noses and earlobes? (These flexible structures are made out of cartilage, not bone.)

5. Finish with a discussion about bones. Ask such questions as What do bones do for us? What happens if you break a bone? etc.

Stations 2 and 3—Science

Materials: butcher paper, pencils, black markers, skeleton information sheets (page 355), and rubber bands

Directions: This project will take two session times so the students will need to stay at this station for two rotations. However, the first group at station #3 will have to save their materials after only one rotation and finish their projects when they finally rotate to station #2. (**Note:** This activity will work best if you keep the students all together while drawing the bones.)

1. Give each child a copy of page 355 and a sheet of butcher paper long enough for him or her to lie on.

2. Pair the students. Tell the partners to outline each others' bodies in pencil onto the paper. (You may need to help younger children.)

3. Using the skeleton outline as a guide, tell the students to draw and label bones inside the body outlines. Suggest that they begin by drawing the pelvis and the skull first to use as reference points. Then they should draw the neck, spine, and ribs. (**Note:** The foot and hand bones will be difficult to replicate because they are so intricate. Accept any reasonable effort.)

4. If there is any extra time or if you would like to offer more of a challenge to older children, let the children research more detailed diagrams of skeletons and include more labels.

5. Remind the students to write their names on their papers and then roll up the drawings for storage.

The Human Skeleton

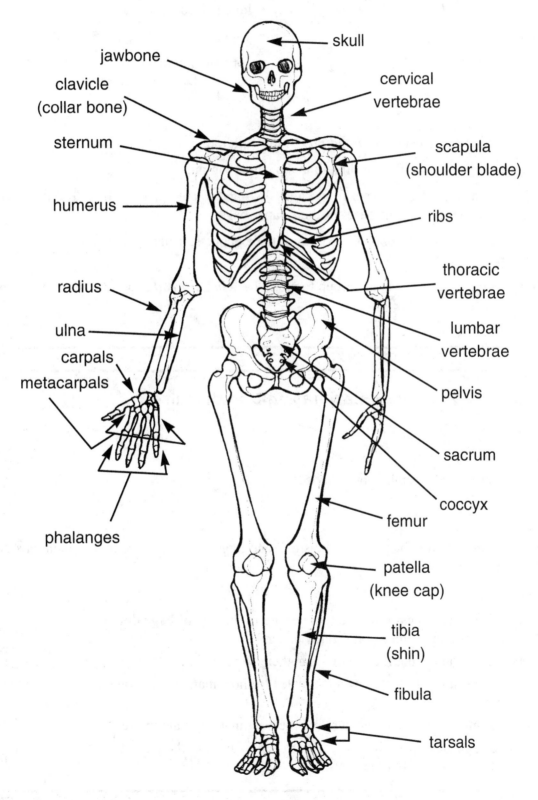

jawbone

clavicle
(collar bone)

sternum

humerus

radius

ulna

carpals

metacarpals

phalanges

skull

cervical
vertebrae

scapula
(shoulder blade)

ribs

thoracic
vertebrae

lumbar
vertebrae

pelvis

sacrum

coccyx

femur

patella
(knee cap)

tibia
(shin)

fibula

tarsals

Station 4 Activity Card—Literature

Materials:

- *The Gingerbread Boy*
- scissors
- crayons
- glue
- lunch-sized paper bags
- puppet patterns (pages 357–360)
- construction paper

Directions:

1. Read a version of *The Gingerbread Boy* to the children.

2. Allow enough time for the children to make paper bag puppets.

    a. Give each child a character from pages 357–360 to color and cut out. Tell the children to glue the faces to the bases of their paper bags.

    b. Let the students decorate the bodies of their puppets, using crayons and construction paper.

3. If there is enough time, ask the group to retell *The Gingerbread Boy* story with the puppets.

Station 5 Activity Card—Estimating Dog Biscuits

Materials:

- a box of large dog biscuits (bone shaped)
- a box of small dog biscuits (bone shaped)
- paper
- pencils

(**Note:** Even though the dog biscuits will be small and large, try to buy products which have boxes of about equal size.)

Directions:

1. Ask the children to guess how many bones are in the box of large dog biscuits. Have each child write down an estimate on scratch paper.

2. Empty the box and count the biscuits together. Who was the closest?

3. Now, have the students write down estimates for how many small dog biscuits are in the second box.

4. Count the small dog bones together. Did their estimates get any closer?

5. Have students make up math problems for each other. Let them use the dog biscuits as manipulatives to figure out the answers.

Puppet Patterns

Old Lady

Old Man

Puppet Patterns *(cont.)*

Gingerbread Boy

Farmer

Puppet Patterns *(cont.)*

Cow

Horse

Puppet Patterns *(cont.)*

Boy

Fox

Station 6 Activity Card—Art

The Dog Bone Family

Materials:

- paper towels
- scissors
- glue
- tiny, black, fuzzy pompons
- dog biscuits
- wiggle eyes
- brown and red construction paper

Directions:

1. Give each child a large bone-shaped dog biscuit on a paper towel.

2. Ask the children to each cut out two dog ears from the brown construction paper. Help them glue the ears to the biscuits as shown.

3. Next, tell them to cut out tongues from the red construction paper and then glue these onto the biscuits.

4. Let the students glue on wiggle eyes and fuzzy noses.

5. Now, repeat these instructions for the medium and small dog bones to make dog families.

Station 7 Activity Card—Writing

Materials: *Fox in Socks*, chalk, chalkboard, shape books, pencils, and crayons

Directions:

1. Read *Fox in Socks* to the group.

2. On the chalkboard write the words "fox" and "socks." Point out to the students that the endings on these two words sound similar (-x and -cks) even though they are spelled differently. Brainstorm with the students a list of other words with these endings, for example:

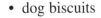

fox		socks	
fix	ax	rocks	locks
tax	box	blocks	ducks
wax	mix	clocks	packs
Max	six	docks	sacks

3. Prepare shape books (see page 362 for pattern) as described on previous shape book activity cards. Give each child a shape book. Have them write a word with the letter "x" in it on each page. Then ask them to illustrate the pages. Besides the words in the first list above, here is a small list of words which might be useful:

x-ray	mixer	flex	tyrannosaurus rex
xylophone	textbook	Mexico	

Shape Book Pattern

Station 8 Activity Card—Matching Game

Materials:

- envelopes
- crayons
- word and picture cards (pages 364 and 365)
- scissors
- pencils

To Be Done in Advance: Color, cut out, and laminate the cards on pages 364 and 365. Spread out the cards, face down, on a table.

Directions: This game can be played like a memory game.

1. Ask the first player to choose two cards and look at them. If they are an illustration and a word that happen to match, he or she will get to keep them. If the cards do not match, he or she should show them to the other players and then place them back where they were found.

2. Continue playing until all of the cards have been matched. The player with the most matches will be considered the winner.

3. When the game is finished, store the cards in an envelope.

(**Note:** This activity may be done in partners. If so, give each pair of students a set of cards to color, cut out, and play with. They will also need envelopes for storing their games.)

Alternate Activities—Art

1. **Scrimshaw**

   Materials: foam meat trays, black ballpoint pens, scissors, and yarn

   Directions:

   a. Explain to the students that scrimshaw is an art form in which the artists carve pictures and designs into animal bones. Sometimes the scrimshaw has been used to make jewelry.

   b. Show the children how to draw small designs onto the foam trays (the trays are meant to represent the bone), using black ballpoint pens.

   c. After they have completed their designs and drawings, help the children cut out the bone beads.

   d. String the beads onto yarn to make scrimshaw necklaces or bracelets.

2. *The Gingerbread Boy*—**Writing**

   Materials: coloring page (page 366), writing paper, pencils, and crayons

   Directions: Ask the students to rewrite the story of *The Gingerbread Boy* in their own words or with a new twist. Give each child a copy of the coloring picture on page 366. The colored pictures may be used as the covers to their stories.

"X" Word Cards

Use these cards with Activity 8 on page 363.

x-ray	**fix**
six	**fox**
box	**xylophone**
mixer	**tyrannosaurus rex**
flex	**Mexico**

"X" Picture Cards

Use these cards with Activity 8 on page 363.

Gingerbread Boy Coloring Page

Stationery

Stationery *(cont.)*

fox

Incentives

Use the following cards for positive reinforcement during your rotations. When a student successfully demonstrates positive behavior and completion of his or her tasks, cut out a bone square and paste it onto his or her box card. If you do not have time to cut and paste, a star sticker or stamp would work well. Distribute awards/name tags and bookmarks where appropriate.

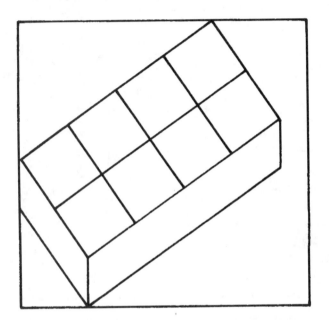

Fill the box with bones!

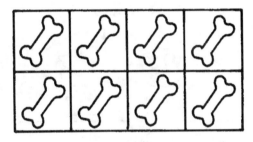

Bookmark

Extra! Extra! Read All About It!

Award/Name Tag

Yellow

Teacher Note: Use this page as an introduction to the Yellow theme. Have your students color the picture. Lines are provided for writing activities of your choice.

Unit Materials

Bibliography

Cole, Joanna. The Magic School Bus®—any book in this series. Scholastic.

O'Neill, Mary. *Hailstones and Halibut Bones.* Doubleday, 1990.

Materials Checklist

Station 1—Literature
- _____ any book from The Magic School Bus® series
- _____ lined writing paper
- _____ drawing paper
- _____ yellow construction paper
- _____ crayons
- _____ pencils
- _____ glue
- _____ activity card

Station 2—Writing
- _____ shape books
- _____ pencils
- _____ crayons
- _____ activity card

Station 3—Sunflower Art
- _____ thick brown yarn
- _____ scissors
- _____ glue
- _____ construction paper (orange, black, and yellow)
- _____ black markers
- _____ sunflower seeds
- _____ patterns
- _____ pencils
- _____ activity card

Station 4—Math
- _____ measuring tapes
- _____ tape
- _____ paper
- _____ scissors
- _____ pencils
- _____ activity card

Station 5—Finger Painting
- _____ yellow finger paint
- _____ easel paper
- _____ construction paper (royal blue, brown, black, and/or green)
- _____ newspapers
- _____ yellow painting patterns
- _____ scissors
- _____ glue
- _____ activity card

Station 6—Cooking
- _____ lemonade
- _____ lemon gelatin mix
- _____ pineapple slices
- _____ bananas
- _____ yellow apples
- _____ sunflower seeds (without shells)
- _____ non-dairy whipped topping

- _____ cups
- _____ paper plates
- _____ mixing bowls
- _____ tablespoon
- _____ paring knife
- _____ plastic knives and forks
- _____ activity card

Station 7—Poetry
- _____ *Hailstones and Halibut Bones*
- _____ pencils
- _____ paper
- _____ glue
- _____ crayons
- _____ yellow construction paper
- _____ activity card

Station 8—Art
- _____ construction paper (yellow, green, white, orange, and brown)
- _____ flower patterns
- _____ black markers
- _____ crayons
- _____ scissors
- _____ glue
- _____ pencils
- _____ activity card

Station 1 Activity Card—Literature

Materials:

- lined writing paper
- drawing paper
- crayons
- glue
- any book from The Magic School Bus® series
- 12" x 18" (30.4 x 45.7 cm) yellow construction paper
- pencils

Directions:

1. Read a Magic School Bus® book to the group.

2. Give each student a sheet of lined writing paper.

3. Ask the children to write about "If we had a magic school bus, I would like to go to _____. I think I would see _____."

4. If there is any extra time, let the students illustrate their stories.

5. Later, glue the stories and illustrations onto sheets of construction paper.

6. Combine the papers to make a class book.

Station 2 Activity Card—Writing

Materials:

- shape books
- pencils
- crayons

Directions: Choose one of the shape book patterns on pages 373 and 374. Prepare shape books as described on previous shape book activity cards. Give each child a shape book. Then assign one of the following activities.

1. Yellow School Bus

a. Ask the students to write and illustrate a word that is related to the color yellow on each page of their books, for example, school bus, banana, sun.

b. Discuss with the children some safety rules for riding on a school bus. Tell the children to write and illustrate a rule on each page of their books.

2. Yield Sign

a. Ask the children to write and illustrate a word beginning with the letter "Y" on each page of their shape books. ·

b. Explain to the students what a yield sign means. Discuss other signs. Tell the children to draw and label a sign on each page of their shape books.

Shape Book Patterns

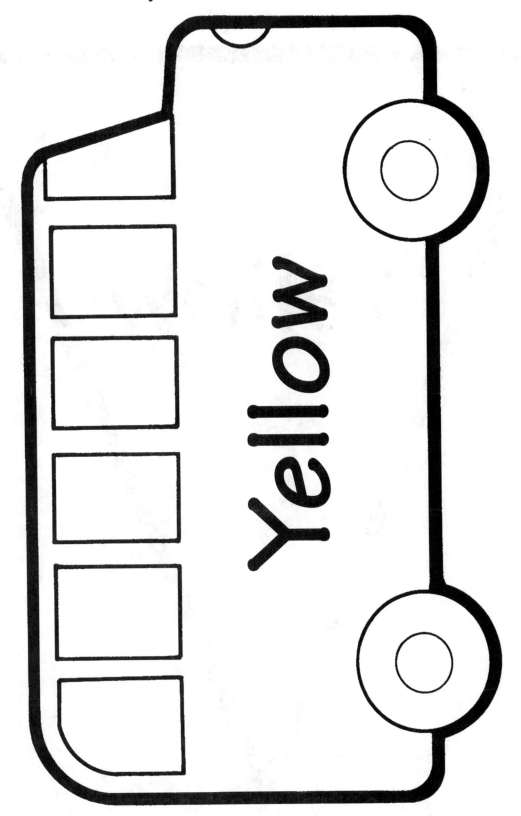

Shape Book Patterns *(cont.)*

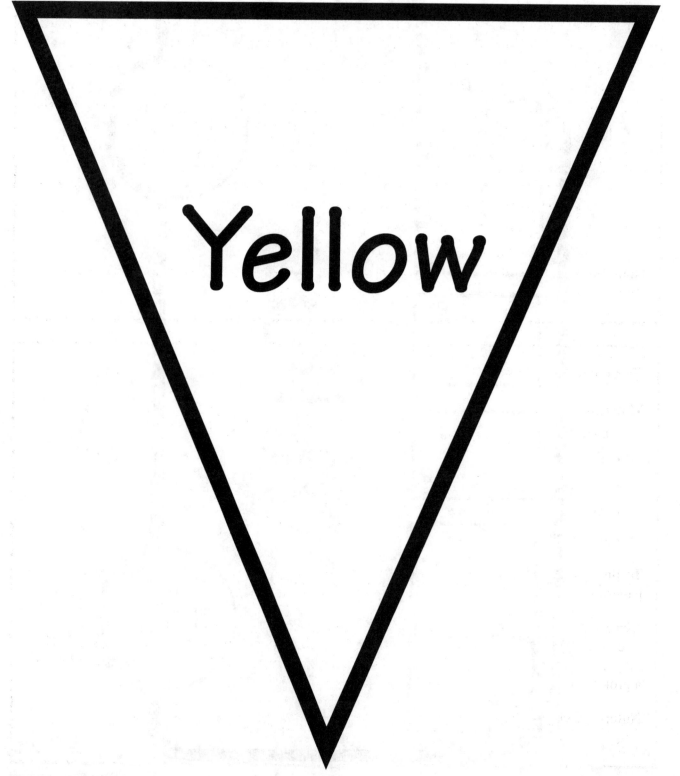

Yellow

Station 3 Activity Card—Sunflower Art

Materials: thick brown yarn, scissors, glue, construction paper (orange, black, and yellow), black markers, pencils, sunflower seeds, and patterns (page 376)

Directions:

1. Give each student a piece of 9" x 12" (22.8 cm x 30.4 cm) orange construction paper. Have them write their names on the backs of their papers with black markers.

2. Tell the children to each use a circle pattern (page 376) to draw a circle in the middle of the paper in pencil. This circle will be used as a guide.

3. Next, tell them to use the petal pattern to draw eight to ten petals each on yellow construction paper. Help the students cut out the petals and glue them around the flower circles, just overlapping the circles' edges.

4. Let the children use the circle pattern again to trace and cut out circles from black construction paper (one per child). Each student will then need to glue the black circle at the center of the petals (over the original drawn circle).

5. Help the students outline the black circle by gluing on thick, brown yarn.

6. Glue several sunflower seeds inside the black circles.

Note: For younger children, you may need to help them cut out the flower pieces or even have them prepared in advance.

Station 4 Activity Card—Math

Materials:

- measuring tapes
- tape
- scissors
- paper
- pencils

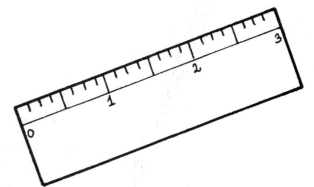

To Be Done in Advance: If you do not have enough measuring tapes for one group, use the pattern on page 183 (or page 184 for metrics) to make measuring tapes.

Directions: As a group, individually, or in pairs, let the children go on a measuring safari. Encourage them to especially seek out yellow items to measure, such as pencils, paper, etc. Ask them to write down what they measured and the measurements they found. Discuss the results as a group.

Note: You may wish to take the students outside for further exploring.

Sunflower Patterns

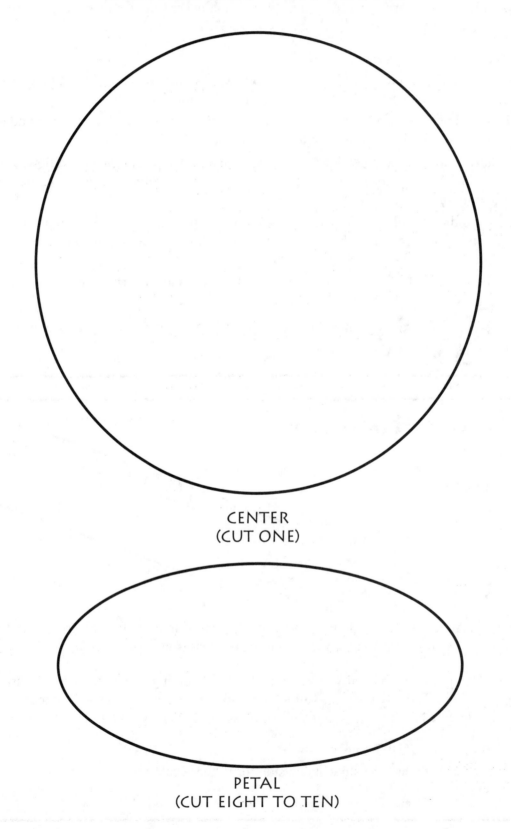

CENTER
(CUT ONE)

PETAL
(CUT EIGHT TO TEN)

Station 5 Activity Card—Finger Painting

Materials:

- yellow finger paint
- easel paper
- newspapers
- pencils
- scissors
- glue
- 12" x 18" (30.4 x 45.7 cm) construction paper in royal blue, brown, black, and/or green
- yellow painting patterns (pages 378–380)

Directions:

1. Give each child a piece of easel paper and have him or her write his or her name on the back.
2. Let the children freely finger paint with yellow paint in an area protected by newspapers. They do not need to make any particular designs or pictures.
3. Let the children choose one of the three patterns on pages 378–380.
4. Give each child a piece of construction paper folded in half. Help the children place their patterns along the fold lines and cut out their shapes (one per child).
5. Write the children's names on the construction paper pieces and save them.
6. After the paint has dried, lay the construction paper pieces over the finger paintings so that the yellow shape shows in the center. Glue the construction paper in place.

Station 6 Activity Card—Cooking

Fruit Suns

Materials:

- lemonade
- bananas
- cups
- mixing bowls
- sunflower seeds (without shells)
- lemon gelatin mix
- yellow apples
- paper plates
- tablespoon
- pineapple slices (rings)
- plastic knives and forks
- nondairy whipped topping
- paring knife

Directions:

1. Have students wash their hands before starting this cooking activity. Place a pineapple slice in the center of each paper plate.
2. Give each child a third of a banana. Have them slice the bananas with plastic knives and put the slices in the centers of their pineapple slices.
3. Cut and core yellow apples into thin slices, keeping the skin intact. Place the apple slices around the outside of the pineapple slices to represent the sun's rays, leaving the skin intact. Leave the peels on. Give each child five slices.
4. Let the students mix the lemon gelatin mix with the non-dairy whipped topping. Spoon a heaping tablespoon onto each fruit sun.
5. Sprinkle with sunflower seeds. Serve with lemonade and enjoy!

Finger Painting Patterns

Sun

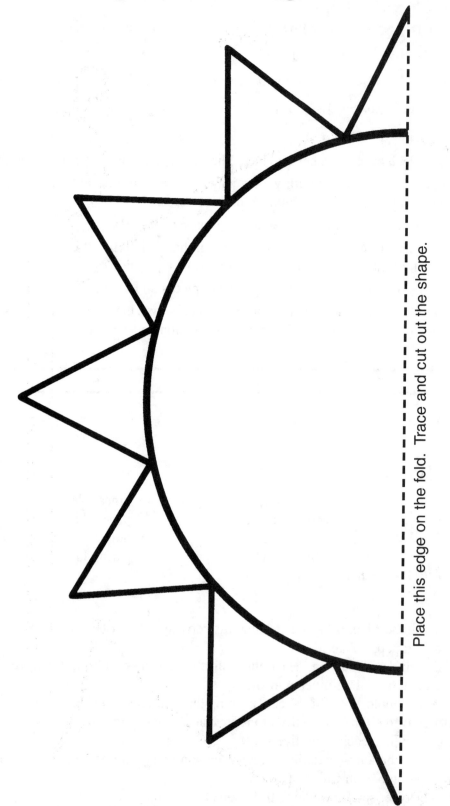

Place this edge on the fold. Trace and cut out the shape.

Finger Painting Patterns *(cont.)*

Butterfly

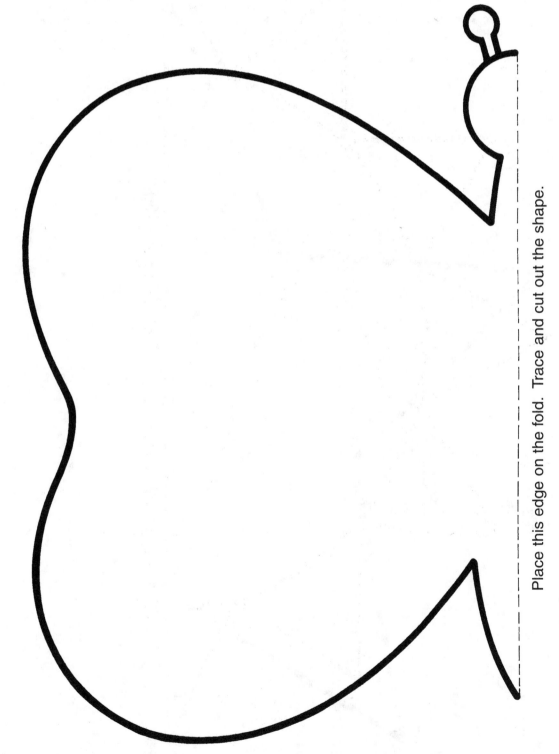

Place this edge on the fold. Trace and cut out the shape.

Finger Painting Patterns *(cont.)*

Star

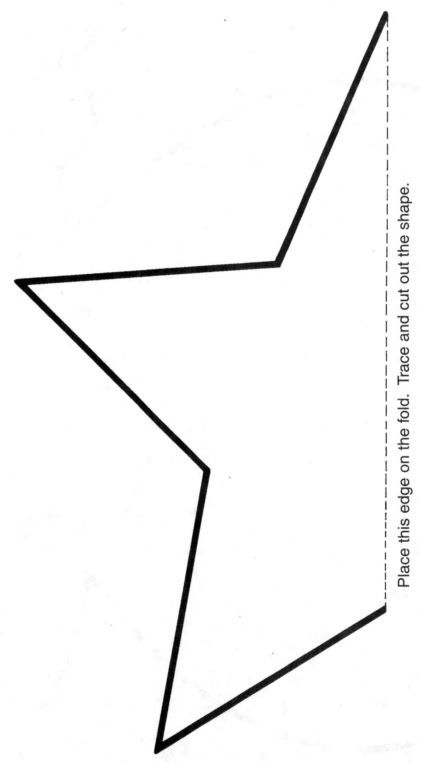

Place this edge on the fold. Trace and cut out the shape.

Stationery

Incentives

Use the following cards for positive reinforcement during your rotations. When a student successfully demonstrates positive behavior and completion of his or her tasks, cut out a flower square and paste it onto his or her garden card. If you do not have time to cut and paste, a flower sticker or stamp would work well. Distribute awards/name tags and bookmarks where appropriate.

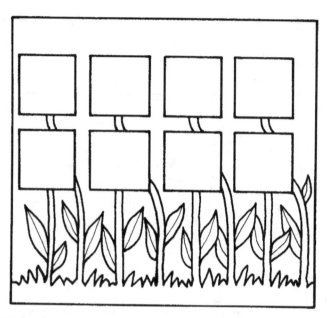

Fill the garden with flowers!

Award/Name Tag

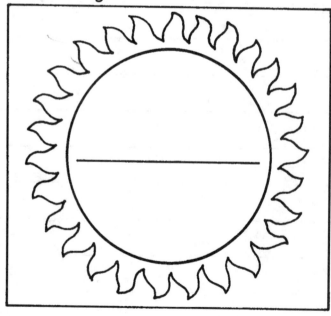

Bookmark

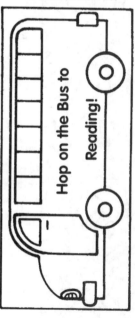

Zoos

Teacher Note: Use this page as an introduction to the Zoos theme. Have your students color the picture. Lines are provided for writing activities of your choice.

Unit Materials

Bibliography

Gibbons, Gail. *The Zoo.* HarperCollins, 1987.

Loomans, Diane. *The Lovables.* H.J. Kramer, 1994.

Madwick, Wendy. *Animaze!* Knopf, 1992.

Provide nonfiction zoo animal books, such as Zoobooks.

Materials Checklist

Station 1—Literature
_____ any zoo animal literature selection
_____ blackboard or chart paper
_____ chalk or marker
_____ activity card

Station 2—Writing
_____ shape books
_____ pencils
_____ crayons
_____ activity card

Station 3—Giraffe Art
_____ giraffe patterns
_____ crayons
_____ glue
_____ wiggle eyes
_____ red or yellow rickrack
_____ orange or brown yarn
_____ cloves
_____ scissors
_____ construction paper
_____ activity card

Station 4—Clay Animals
_____ clay
_____ activity card

Stations 5 and 6—Cooking
_____ measuring spoons
_____ measuring cups
_____ grater
_____ mixer
_____ 2 medium bowls
_____ toaster oven or school oven
_____ baking cups
_____ mixing spoons
_____ paper towels

Ingredients (*per one dozen muffins*):
_____ 1 cup grated zucchini
_____ $\frac{1}{2}$ cup sugar
_____ 1 egg
_____ $\frac{3}{4}$ cups milk
_____ $\frac{1}{2}$ cup vegetable oil
_____ 2 cups flour
_____ 2 teaspoons baking powder
_____ 1 teaspoon salt
_____ 1 teaspoon cinnamon
_____ $\frac{1}{2}$ teaspoon nutmeg
_____ chopped nuts
_____ activity card

Stations 7 and 8—Zoo Mural
_____ butcher paper
_____ crayons
_____ markers
_____ animal and people patterns
_____ pencils
_____ construction paper
_____ scissors
_____ glue
_____ rulers
_____ activity card

Alternate Activities:
1. Stamp Stories
_____ animal stamps
_____ paper
_____ pencils
_____ activity card

2. Math
_____ plastic zoo animals
_____ pencils
_____ scratch paper
_____ activity card

Station 1 Activity Card—Literature

Materials:
- any zoo animal literature selection
- blackboard or chart paper
- chalk or marker

Directions:
1. Read *The Zoo, The Lovables, Animaze!*, any of the Zoobooks series, or any other book about the zoo, to the children.
2. On a chalkboard or chart paper, brainstorm with the group a list of the many types of animals at the zoo.
3. Help the students think of a sound and/or a motion for each animal, for example:

    monkeys—oo oo oo (while scratching head)

    snakes—ss ss ss (put your arms together and slither from side to side)

    elephant—ah oooo guh (use one arm as a trunk and raise it high in the air)
4. Now sing "Old MacDonald Had a Zoo" to the tune of "Old MacDonald Had a Farm." Instead of farm animals, sing about zoo animals. If you cannot think of a sound for a particular animal, just use a motion instead.

Station 2 Activity Card—Writing

Materials:
- shape books
- pencils
- crayons

Directions: Choose one of the two shapes on pages 388 and 389. Prepare shape books as described on previous book shape activity cards Give each child a shape book. Then assign one of the following activities.

1. Zoo Ticket
   a. Ask the children to write about zoo animals. Have them draw one animal on each page and write a sentence about it. (You may want to ask younger students to simply label the animals and not write full sentences.)
   b. Help the children think of words that have the letters "oo" in them as in the word "zoo." Have them write one word on each page of their books and then illustrate the words. (**Note:** Not all of the words have to rhyme with "zoo," as with the word "book.")

2. Zebra

   Ask the children to write and illustrate books about "Z" words. These words may start with "Z" or just have "Z" in them.

Shape Book Patterns

Welcome to the

Zoo

Admit One

Shape Book Patterns *(cont.)*

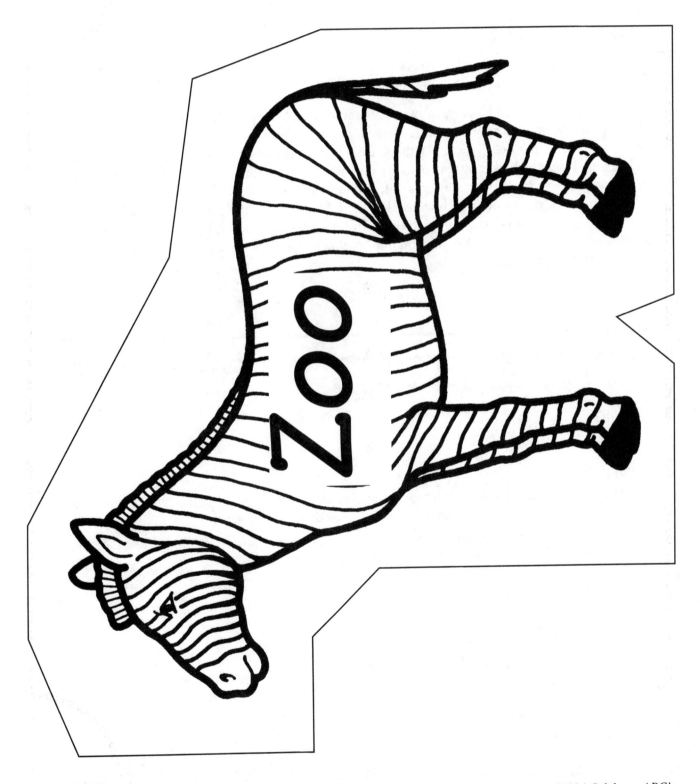

Station 3 Activity Card—Giraffe Art

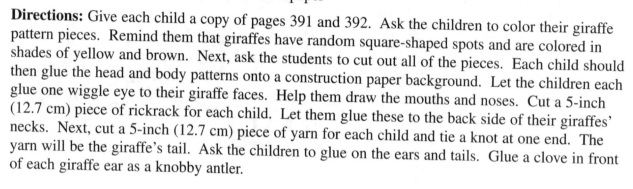

Materials:

- crayons
- wiggle eyes
- red or yellow rickrack
- orange or brown yarn
- 9" x 12" (22.8 x 30.4 cm) construction paper
- giraffe patterns (pages 391 and 392)
- glue
- cloves
- scissors

Directions: Give each child a copy of pages 391 and 392. Ask the children to color their giraffe pattern pieces. Remind them that giraffes have random square-shaped spots and are colored in shades of yellow and brown. Next, ask the students to cut out all of the pieces. Each child should then glue the head and body patterns onto a construction paper background. Let the children each glue one wiggle eye to their giraffe faces. Help them draw the mouths and noses. Cut a 5-inch (12.7 cm) piece of rickrack for each child. Let them glue these to the back side of their giraffes' necks. Next, cut a 5-inch (12.7 cm) piece of yarn for each child and tie a knot at one end. The yarn will be the giraffe's tail. Ask the children to glue on the ears and tails. Glue a clove in front of each giraffe ear as a knobby antler.

Station 4 Activity Card—Clay Animals

Materials:

- clay

Directions:

1. Allow the students to make animals, using clay or dough. If you use the type of clay that dries hard, you may wish to paint these at a later date.
2. Leave enough extra time so that the students can clean up the activity area. Take the children to the restrooms to prepare for the next activity, cooking.

390

Giraffe Patterns

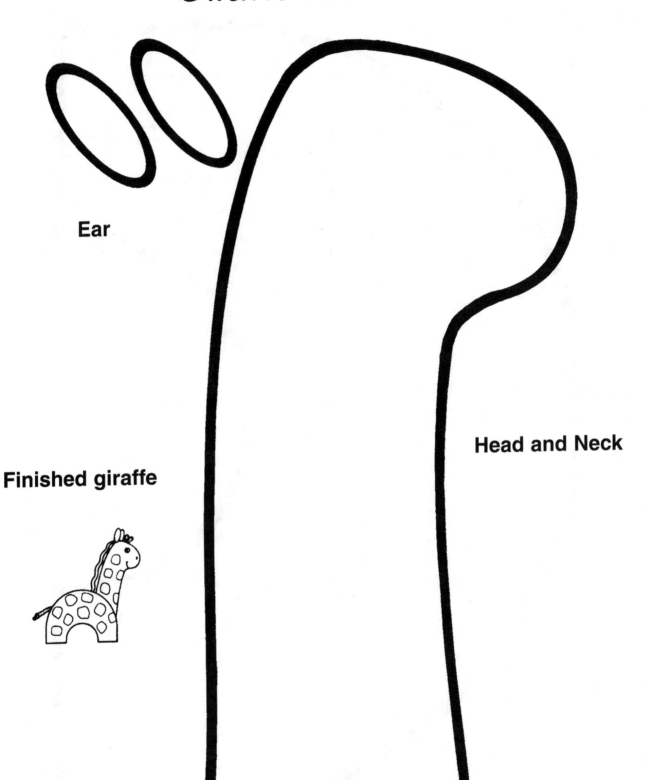

Ear

Head and Neck

Finished giraffe

Giraffe Patterns (cont.)

Body

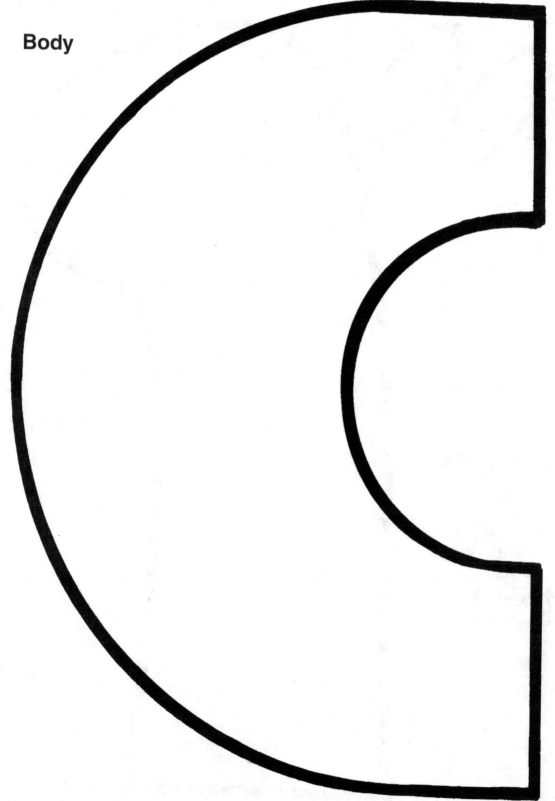

Stations 5 and 6 Activity Card—Cooking

Zoo-kini Muffins

Materials:

- measuring spoons
- measuring cups
- grater
- mixer
- 2 medium bowls
- toaster oven or school oven
- baking cups
- mixing spoons
- paper towels

Ingredients *(per one dozen muffins)*:

- 1 cup grated zucchini
- ¹/₂ (125 mL) cup sugar
- 1 egg
- ³/₄ (188 mL) cup milk
- ¹/₂ (125 mL) cups vegetable oil
- 2 cups (500 mL) flour
- 2 teaspoons (10 mL) baking powder
- 1 teaspoon (5 mL) salt
- 1 teaspoon (5 mL) cinnamon
- ¹/₂ (2.5 mL) teaspoon nutmeg
- chopped nuts

To Be Done in Advance: Make a dozen muffins in advance so that the first group to visit the station will have some ready to eat. The muffins that the first group prepares will then be eaten by the second group, the muffins the second group prepares will be eaten by the third group, and so on. Send leftover muffins home with the children.

Stations 5 and 6 Activity Card—Cooking *(cont)*

Directions:

1. Let a student beat one egg in a bowl. Ask another student to pour in one cup (250 mL) of grated zucchini.
2. Have two other children pour in the milk and the oil. Stir these ingredients.
3. Help the children add the rest of the ingredients and then mix the batter until moistened (the batter will be lumpy).
4. Carefully fill the baking cups ¹/₂ to ²/₃ full. Bake the muffins at 400 degrees Fahrenheit (204 degrees Celsius) for 15–20 minutes.

Note: In baked goods, applesauce can be substituted for oil in equal amounts. Also, it is important to check beforehand on student allergies to eggs, various dairy products, and nuts. Make substitutions where possible.

Stations 7 and 8—Zoo Mural

Materials:

- butcher paper
- pencils
- glue
- crayons
- scissors
- rulers
- markers
- construction paper
- animal and people patterns (pages 395–398)

Directions:

1. Give each group (there will be two groups at this station at a time) a 6-ft. (1.8 m) piece of butcher paper. Explain that they will be working within their groups to make zoo murals. Each student will need to choose one or two animals to add to the mural.

2. Ask the children to draw the mural background, using crayons, during the first session time. Offer rulers to the students to help draw straight edges for such things as cages and fences. They will also need to add trees, bushes, flowers, and water sources.

3. During the second session time, tell the students to create the animals at the zoo and the people visiting the zoo. Using patterns on pages 395–398, help the students trace and cut out their animals and people. Tell them to draw details with crayons. They will then glue the characters onto the mural.

4. Hang the finished project in the hall or school cafeteria for all to see.

(**Note:** The first group to visit station #8 will have to put their materials aside when it is time to rotate. They will be able to finish their mural when they finally rotate back to station #7.)

Alternate Activities

1. **Stamp Stories**

   Materials:

   - animal stamps
   - paper
   - pencils

   Directions: Give each child several sheets of paper. Tell the children to write stories about the zoo, using animal stamps and words.

2. **Math**

   Materials:

   - plastic zoo animals
   - pencils
   - scratch paper

   Directions: Ask the students to make up simple word problems for each other about the zoo. Let them use plastic animals as manipulatives. Solve the problems. Give them an example to follow, such as, If the zoo has two boa constrictors and three rattlesnakes, how many snakes are there in all?

Animal and People Patterns

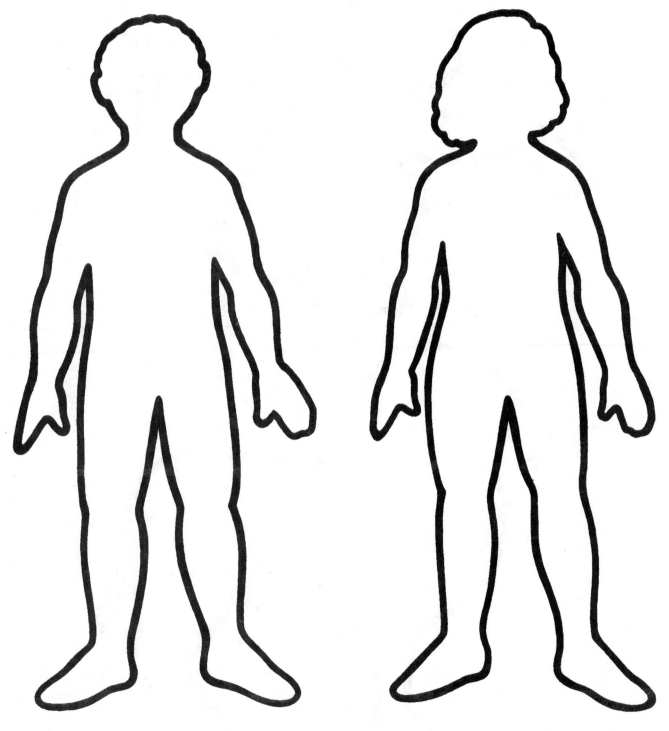

Boy

Girl

Animal and People Patterns *(cont.)*

Monkey

Lion

Animal and People Patterns *(cont.)*

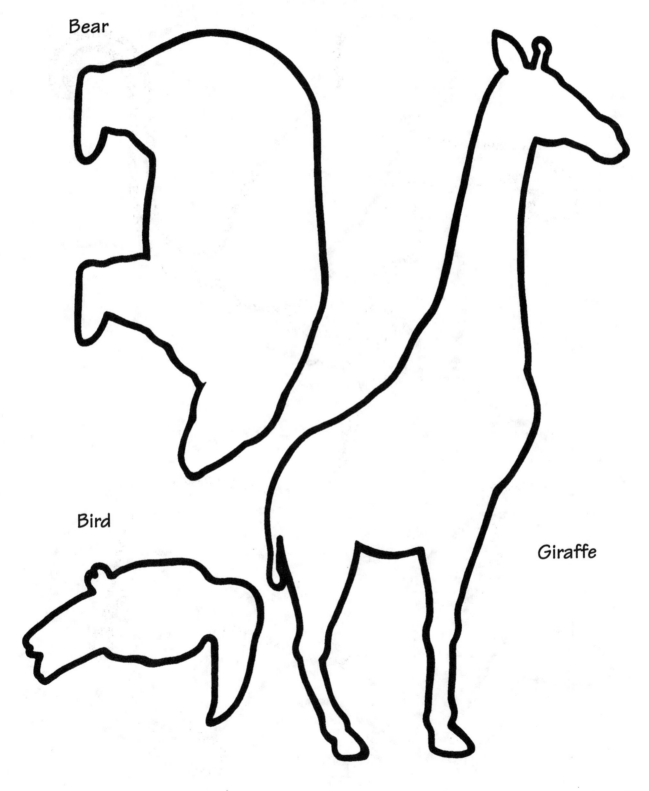

Bear

Bird

Giraffe

Animal and People Patterns *(cont.)*

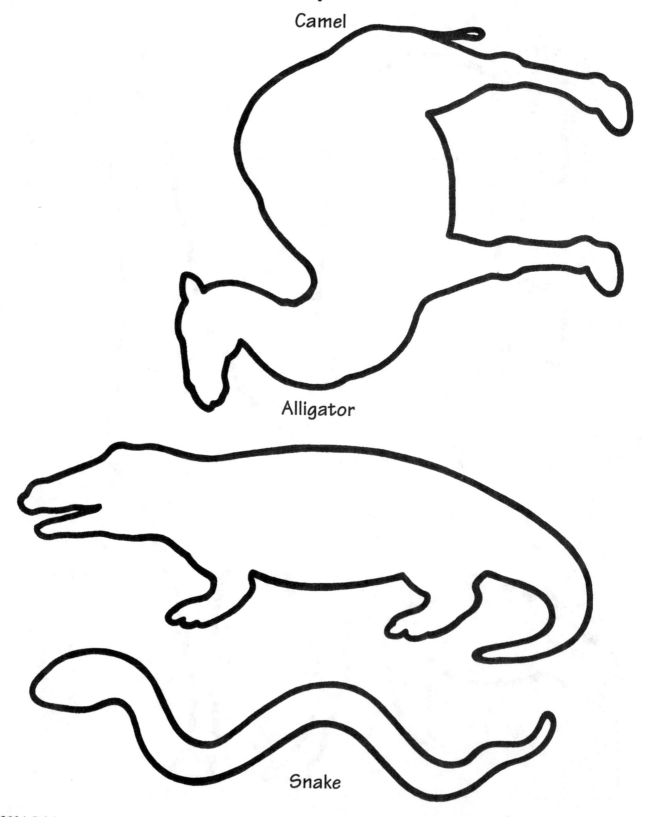

Camel

Alligator

Snake

Stationery

Incentives

Use the following cards for positive reinforcement during your rotations. When a student successfully demonstrates positive behavior and completion of his or her tasks, cut out a banana square and paste it onto his or her monkey card. If you do not have time to cut and paste, a star sticker or stamp would work well. Distribute awards/name tags and bookmarks where appropriate.

Feed the bunch of bananas to the monkey!

Award/Name Tag

Bookmark

REACH
HIGH . . .
READ!